Alan M. Kent

Ordinalia

The Cornish Mystery Play Cycle
A Verse Translation

Introduction by Brian Murdoch

First published by Francis Boutle Publishers
272 Alexandra Park Road
London N22 7BG
Tel/Fax: +44 (0)20 8889 7744
Email: admin@francisboutle.co.uk
www.francisboutle.co.uk

ISBN 1 903427 27 4

Printed by Progress Press, Malta

Contents

From the Creation Window of St Neot's church, Cornwall, 16th Century. Noah's Ark, detail of the Dove and Raven. © Sonia Halliday Photographs

Introduction

The three surviving medieval plays known as the *Ordinalia* are the high point of medieval Cornish literature and one of the peaks of medieval literature in Britain overall. This is where Cornish merges most fully into the literature of medieval Europe, and it is difficult to stress enough the European dimension. They are biblical dramas, mystery plays, and as such were perhaps felt thematically to be more important in general terms than the other surviving Cornish dramas – the two days performance dealing with the Breton Saint Mereadoc, *Beunans Meriasek*, the Life of St Meriasek, or the recently discovered (and not yet fully evaluated) *Beaunans Ke*, the Life of St Kea, another saint with Breton connections, found in 2000 together with a play containing secular Arthurian material. Beside these, all that we have is a fragment of dialogue, perhaps from a play (the so-called *Charter Fragment*), and a later and rather different (though there are some overlaps) play of the Creation and Passion of which we have one day only, taking us down to the Flood.

Although the Cornish plays, and the *Ordinalia* in particular are often linked more or less exclusively with the English dramas contemporary with them, no medieval drama existed in a vacuum. Drama – people acting out stories – is used throughout the middle ages to put over the story of the Creation and the Redemption, the two poles of the divine economy of history, to an audience largely unable to read the Bible. When the language used is not Latin, the language of the Church, but one of the European vernaculars, the implied audience is a broad one. The task of such drama, then, is to present key elements of the Old and New Testaments in a clear and vivid, and above all *understandable* form, so that the implications of the narrative are absolutely clear. But we have to remember that we are in a period well before close textual criticism of the Bible, and even the Lutheran idea of the 'well-versed layman' is a long way off. The plays are presenting a story, it is true, but they are doing so in a specifically theological manner, making clear the way in which the Old Testament prepares the way for the Redemption by allegory, as well as being causally linked with it. And again, a story is a story. Medieval methods of reading the Bible included what was called the *sensus historicus*, the literal interpretation, which added things which are not mentioned but which are assumed to have happened. Of course, the Bible omits a great number of things which might well be felt to be important, especially for the visual media, including drama. Did the serpent in paradise have legs? (It is condemned to crawl afterwards, so presumably it walked beforehand: and anyway, what did id look like and how did it talk?) Who killed Cain? (Someone must have done, or was he perhaps drowned in the Flood? And whom did he marry?) Medieval religious drama, like much medieval biblical writing, embellishes and adds to the bare bones of the Bible stories (not usually autonomously, but by drawing on theological writings, hagiography, legends and the like), and it supplies new emphases and links.

The existing Cornish trilogy known collectively as the *Ordinalia*, and consisting of – effectively – three plays, one each on the Creation, the Passion and the Resurrection (there is no surviving Nativity), differs from the English cycles in several respects other than the language, and in fact matches more closely some of the continental biblical plays. The Cornish cycle is less fragmented than the English cycles and displays a clearer unity, depending very unusually on the apocryphal legends of the Cross and its origins, which provides a material link between Adam and Christ and underlines the link (made by St Paul in Romans 5: 12) between the first Adam, who sinned, and the second Adam, who saved.

There are other incidents depicted in the Cornish trilogy which are not in the English plays but which have continental parallels, though these are usually found also in the great and equally fragmented work, the fifteenth-century French *Mistère du vieil Testament* (such as the story of David with Bathsheba or the death of Pilate). The *Ordinalia* can be compared not only with the English mystery plays but with works like Arnoul Greban's fifteenth-century *Mystère de la Passion*, which has a relatively brief Old Testament section, but does have a Nativity, or with the Protestant plays – the Reformation was not an immediate cultural divide, and literary periodisation is always debatable – of sixteenth-century German-language writers like Valten Voith (whose play about the Fall and Redemption, written in the 1530s, is barely known to the modern world) or the Swiss Jakob Ruf, who 'staged' a major spectacle from the Creation to the Flood in front of the Cathedral in Zurich in 1550. Close, too, is a Breton mystery-cycle, which is incomplete, and survives in a far later transcript, but which – like the *Ordinalia* – makes use of apocryphal legends, extra-biblical legend material, that is, not to be confused with the deutero-canonical books referred to as 'Apocrypha' in the Protestant Bible tradition.

There is a principal manuscript of the *Ordinalia* and some later copies. The former, now in Oxford as Bodleian MS 791, was written in the fifteenth century, but the plays were more likely to have been composed in the late fourteenth century (after a Cornish poem on the Passion which was known to the dramatist, since parts of it are used in the second play). They seem to have been written somewhere near Penryn, where there was, at Glasney, a substantial and well-endowed college of secular canons established in the thirteenth century by the Bishop of Exeter. Places like this were major centres of what we might call theological literature throughout Europe. Though Glasney was not the only secular college in Cornwall, there are strong links with the major works of Cornish literature, not just the *Ordinalia* and the Passion-poem, but also a later and rather different Creation play which cites a few passages from the first part of the *Ordinalia*. The college was dissolved in 1545.

A major difference between the Cornish plays and the medieval English dramas is that the former were produced in open-air amphitheatres called rounds or playing-places (*plen-an-gwary*), of which one of those surviving, at St Just-in-Penwith, had links with Glasney, and may be where the plays were first put on. They seem to have had earth banks for spectators, openings, a central area and a pit (possibly for entrances or for concealment). The nature of the arena would have determined the structuring of the play to an extent, and also permitted very easily the shift of action from one part of the round to another without scene-change, and indeed allowed for things to happen at the same time. Religious drama in the middle ages is typified in any case by what is known in German as the *Simultanbühne*, 'simultaneous staging', highlighting the coexistence of events on earth with things going on in heaven or indeed in hell. The surviving rounds are about 40 metres in diameter, and from early sketches in manuscripts, there seem to have been platforms (later on covered booths) around the edge of the circle, from which characters descended into the main area when necessary. The Cornish plays have full stage directions (in Latin) with indication of action and props, and they have been performed in the round in modern times. The *Ordinalia* clearly lasted several days, and performances must have had considerable social significance. Possibly the (summertime) liturgical feast of Corpus Christi, which became popular in the fourteenth century, was when they were put on.

The *Ordinalia* plays were around three thousand lines in length, and show us the Creation, the Passion of Christ and the Resurrection, but each contains a range of other stories – the first play covering Old Testament characters, and the last including what looks from the heading like a separate play on the death of Pilate, before the work finishes with the Ascension. Latin headings separate off the Pilate story, but it is very dangerous to talk about 'separate plays' within the three major divisions in this context, since there is a coherent wholeness about the plays underpinned by thematic links, most specifically and unusually in the way in which the legend of the Holy Rood joins the old Adam – everybody's ancestor – with Christ as the new Adam, everybody's Redeemer. Criticism has often pointed to the apparent variety of episodes in these works, but medieval connections have to be recognised, and once they are, it is the unity which is clearest.

The legend of how the tree used for the Cross grew from seeds from paradise buried with Adam is indeed a distinctive feature of the *Ordinalia*, but it does appear in some continental dramas and drama-cycles as well, even if it is not found elsewhere in Britain. The (largely) twelfth-century legends which tell the story of the Holy Rood – the Cross – from Adam to Christ (and sometimes beyond, to its discovery later by St Helena) appear in prose and verse in a very wide variety of European vernacular languages indeed (including Icelandic!) as well as Latin. It may have disappeared after the Reformation, but in the medieval period it is very well-known indeed. The Holy Rood legends themselves build upon an earlier set of Adam and Eve legends, in which Seth returns to paradise when Adam is dying and receives not the Oil of Mercy (the purpose of his quest) but seeds, which, placed in the dead Adam's mouth, grow into a tree which will become the Cross and thus *represent* the Oil of Mercy, the promise of an ultimate Redemption. The Holy Rood stories also begin with Adam and the quest of Seth, who receives the seeds, but the history of the tree that grows from the grave of Adam is then traced through Moses and David to Solomon, who places (and tries to incorporate it) into his Temple.

We do not know the exact source for the Cornish plays, but it cannot be stressed enough how well-known these legends were. The Cornish dramatist probably knew the story in English (it was particularly well-known in England, the Netherlands and Germany), because he often uses English terms from the story. For the same reasons we may judge that he knew in English, too, the separate legend of the death of Pontius Pilate. Other, different, legends crop up (unusually and not always with a recognisable source, although many come from much-used compilations, like the so-called *Golden Legend*) in the work, including Adam's bargaining with God over the land he is allowed to take, details of the Harrowing of Hell, and stories like that of the smith who refuses to make nails for the Crucifixion.

The first play of the trilogy sets the tone of the whole by showing us first the Fall and the sinfulness of man, but then the story of the Cross (which of course incorporates the idea of Redemption). In the Fall story, the serpent-devil assures Eve that he comes from heaven, and indeed she refers to him afterwards as an angel. Of course, in a sense, he is one (at least, he was), and it is interesting that the *Ordinalia* does not contain (as most medieval plays of this kind do) a separate presentation of the fall of Lucifer. The serpent-devil tricks Eve and also calls her a fool, then tells her she can put the blame upon him. Usually Eve gets the devil to bend the branch towards her, she eats the fruit – here called, as usual, an apple (it is not named in the Bible), and she in her turn tricks Adam into eating by telling him how an angel began to sing to her on the tree. In the English cycles, too, the serpent is described by Eve to Adam as a 'ffayr Aungell', and later as a 'werm with an Aungelys face'. But here Adam refuses to eat, so that Eve has to threaten him with the withdrawal of her love until he eats as well, realising immediately that what he has done is wrong. Even from this brief summary it is clear the details elaborate the biblical account, which does not tell us how Eve persuaded Adam to eat, for example. But medieval writers speculate a great deal on these things and the literal interpretation of the Bible is very varied, so that most of the added ideas were familiar ones, either from one of the legend-collections or from the numerous commentaries on the biblical text. The punishment by God closely follows the Bible, but there is an interesting visual solution of one of the problems: while God is cursing the serpent (as in the Bible – there is no sign of the devil anywhere in Genesis, even in the Adam and Eve story), the devil is nevertheless present, because a stage direction tells us so. The devil himself now tells the story of his own fall, which is out of jealousy of the newly created couple, again a common medieval idea.

Expelled from paradise, Adam asks for the Oil of Mercy, the first indication of the legend of the Rood, and Redemption is promised. In fact in many English and continental vernacular treatments of the Fall a promise is given to Adam that things will be resolved in the fullness of time, this being linked usually with the familiar interpretation of Genesis 3: 15, that the serpent's head will be crushed, as a promise that Christ will one day crush the devil. The verse is sometimes called 'protovangelical', or 'pre-Gospel'. When Adam tries to dig, however, the earth cries out and will not allow him to cut into the soil until God commands it to do so, and then Adam haggles with God over how much land he can have. As indicated, many of the – to modern eyes – strange motifs are very familiar in the middle ages, but these last points are in fact most unusual, and it is not clear where the dramatist got them. But looking for originality in a work of this kind is not appropriate, and indeed, originality in a biblical narrative is for the medieval mind not a recommendation. Biblical, however, and very much stressed in middle ages, is the question of tithing and sacrifice, and this leads to Cain (who tries to cheat God out of a sacrifice) and to the tale of Noah, who sacrifices after the Flood. Cain is not keen on the idea of sacrifice at all, and God accepts only Abel's tithe, so that the jealous Cain kills Abel by striking him on the jaw (rather than *with* a jawbone), and Abel is taken to hell by Lucifer and his associates, the first appearance of the devils. These figure at various points in the plays, and are also a common feature of medieval European drama as a whole. Even the Swiss Protestant Jakob Ruf has (against the Bible) a whole range of devils, including even 'little devils', presumably played (appropriately enough) by small boys, and these are likely to have been the source for much stage business. When God looks for Cain, it is interesting that in Cornish (it is another unusual motif) the blood of Abel actually does cry out – *vox clamat* says the stage direction.

With the birth of Seth and then the death of Adam we move to the important Holy Rood story proper, and the most strikingly individual feature of the whole trilogy. For a comparison, we need to look at works like the play known (not very usefully, since it goes on to the birth of the Virgin) as 'The Fall' by the Low German writer Arnold Immessen, who also uses the story to similar effect. In the *Ordinalia* (it is slightly but significantly different in the later Cornish Creation-play, in fact) Seth is sent to Paradise, and sees a tree that is dry in the upper part, with roots reaching to hell and a serpent in it, but he sees a child in the tree, which he hears is the Son of God, who is also the Oil of Mercy, after which he is given three seeds to place under the tongue of the dead Adam, which will grow into the Cross. In fact, three rods grow, and intertwine to make a single tree only later. After a brief retelling of the story of Noah (the animals taken on board are notably domestic ones!) contrasting greatly with some of the English cycles and with Jakob Ruff's spectacular version, an altar is set up, not as in the Bible, but very unusually at Calvary, which takes us back to the Rood cycle. In medieval legend, though, Adam's grave is on Golgotha, 'the place of the skull', with the implication that the skull concerned is Adam's. Medieval paintings often have a skull underneath the Cross, and this is taken to be the skull of Adam; in one case, blood from Christ's feet (as a symbol of the Eucharist) runs down into the mouth of the skull, thus very graphically giving Adam the sacrament. The Cornish play also includes, as do most medieval dramas, the sacrifice of Isaac, and here as ever it is because it is a typological parallel to the Crucifixion. In the English Chester plays, for example, an Expositor comes on at the end of the Abraham and Isaac section and explains 'This deed you se done in this place/In example of Ihesu done yt was/that for to wyn mankinde grace/was sacrifsed on the rode.' So Isaac's near-sacrifice prefigures the New Testament sacrifice of Christ.

The Holy Rood legend is resumed properly with Moses, who finds the three rods. Before he dies, Moses re-plants them on Mount Tabor, the location of the Transfiguration. The next to find them is David, but the Cornish play shows first a comic scene between David and his butler, and then David dreaming of how the rods will eventually assist at the Redemption, which leads him to find them. He uses them at once to heal the sick, and places a silver ring around them. The soteriology (in the proper sense of the healing of man by Christ) is therefore underlined. David himself is an ancestor of and a prefiguration of Christ, and here he is using something which will be directly associated with Christ in material terms. The dramatist adds additional material here too, however, most notably the story of David and Bathsheba, and this requires special comment as it is rare in any medieval drama cycle, probably because of staging difficulties. Nevertheless, it provides a good story, and it is a testament to the skill of the dramatist that he chose to include it. It is more often present in non-dramatic works, and certainly provides a theme for later paintings, but only the French *Mistère* has a full version, with a slightly shorter one by Valten Voith and a much later independent English play by George Peele.

Of course, the story is adapted. Bathsheba is seen washing clothes rather than herself because nakedness could not easily be shown, and the biblical Joab and more importantly the critical Nathan are left out, the latter's role being taken over by Gabriel. Bathsheba mourns her husband in the Bible only after his death, but here she is hypocritical, made into a wicked hussy with a great economy of dramatisation (she has very few speeches). How does this tie in with the Holy Rood story? Prose versions of the legend usually have a simple and unspecific reference to David's sinfulness, without any reference to Bathsheba. But David sits in contrition beneath the Rood-Tree (not by the way, the Tree of

Knowledge, which is an error from an early edition), and composes the Psalms, as he does in the Holy Rood legends, after which he embarks upon the task of building the great Temple (rewarding the builders with land-grants of manors near Penryn and linked with Glasney). The play, still following the Holy Rood legends, has God indicate that Solomon will complete the Temple (and in the play he, too, rewards the masons with Cornish land), but when the Holy Rood is cut as a timber for the Temple, it will fit nowhere and changes its dimensions, and so is simply placed inside. The play ends with one of the oddest parts of the Holy Rood story. A lady called Maximilla enters the temple, sits on the wood and her clothes burst into flames. When she invokes Christ (somewhat anachronistically, since He hasn't been born yet, unless we are thinking *sub specie aetnitatis*) she is promptly martyred as a blasphemer. The nineteenth-century Breton scholar Hersart de la Villemarqué, incidentally, in a bout of excessive patriotism, saw Maximilla as a thinly disguised but (to him, at least) obvious representation of Joan of Arc, but one has to say that this view has not been widely accepted. Maximilla is the proto-martyr, however, and a prefiguration of Christ, dying in association with the Cross. The torturers – here as in the scenes with Christ – are sadistically realistic, and very much a feature of these and other Cornish plays. The wood which will make the Cross, and which has caused all the trouble, is removed and thrown into a pool at Bethsaida.

It is important not to underestimate the significance of the use of the Holy Rood material as a structuring feature. Even the great French mystery cycle, the *Mistère du vieil Testament* (which has some of the Holy Rood episodes), does not develop it in detail, and other dramas merely hint at the story. Although the use of the legend by Arnold Immessen in his Low German play and rather later (in two plays) by the Spanish dramatist Calderón is more extensive, there is no use of it at all in English or Welsh drama, although it is present in prose and verse in both languages. In a European context, then, the Cornish material is of considerable importance for using the Holy Rood material throughout to underline the typological link between Adam and Christ so firmly, and stressing at the same time the importance of the Trinity as the eternity of its existence. Getting across the theological message that the whole of the New Testament is present in the Old Testament – the basis of medieval Christian thought – is a difficult problem, especially in a popular and visual medium like a play, and the solution adopted by the Cornish dramatist is an excellent one.

The second play of the original trilogy follows the Bible more closely, although there is again additional material, such as the miracle of the nails, mentioned already, as well as another medieval story, again very well known – the story of Longinus (Longius in the *Ordinalia*), the soldier at the Crucifixion. In the *Passio* we start with Christ in the desert. In fact, the temptation scene is not very dramatic, the disciples have to be added in here, so that Christ has an audience, and even the devil knows that he cannot tempt Christ. Palm Sunday and the cleansing of the Temple, Simon the Leper, the Magdalene and the ointment, the thirty pieces of silver, the Last Supper, Peter and the swords, and the betrayal by Judas follow in the biblical pattern. The torturers once again have a large part, tormenting and mocking Christ. One interesting further addition, though, which is also in the Cornish Passion-poem, is the idea that Judas's soul cannot leave through the mouth which had kissed Christ (Satan himself points this out), and Judas is taken to hell in despair, that ultimate medieval sin, the failure to acknowledge the possibility of Redemption.

Of greater interest is the development of the figure of Pilate, the subject of a series of extra-biblical legends, and the element which provides a link between the last two plays of the trilogy, pivoting on the Passion, just as the tale of the Rood did for the first. Always ambiguous in medieval writings, Pilate is already presented negatively when he puts Christ into prison, and this approach to Pilate is developed to link this play with the final work, the Resurrection, in which Pilate's own plight after death will provide a ghastly counterpoint to the Resurrection. In spite of his wife's dream that the killing of Christ will lead to trouble (a dream sent by devils who are trying to avoid the Harrowing of Hell), the torturers are again given much scope for sadism (and we might wonder about the nature of this aspect of the dramatisation as visual theatre). Pilate is reluctant to kill Christ (afraid of what his wife has said, not for any moral reasons of his own), but when the people cry out for crucifixion he washes his hands, as in the Gospels. Pilate will return as a link in the final play, but it is at this point that the connection with the first play is restored through the legends of the Holy Rood. The oddly-shaped beam from the Temple is recalled, and retrieved to be made into a cross for Christ. When a smith is commissioned to make the nails, however, his hands appear diseased as by a miracle, but in fact his wife organises their manufacture. This legend (not unknown, though fairly rare in drama) is located in Cornwall in the play, but the fact that the smithy is in Market Jew is not really a genuine localisation, but comes about because the Cornish name, *Marghes Yow,* is a handy rhyme for *kentrow*, meaning 'nails' (and in spite of the fact the Cornish means 'Thursday Market' and we are on Good Friday). The Crucifixion is graphically done with much stress on the sufferings of Christ, and the Virgin, who has already uttered a poignant lament, a *planctus*, on seeing Christ with the Cross, utters a second lament now, with a third after the deposition. The play also includes the legend of Longinus or Longeus, the blind soldier who pierces Christ's side, and whose sight is restored by the blood. The symbolism of 'opening the eyes' is straightforward here as he acknowledges Christ. This is an episode that is very frequent in medieval drama, but it is significant that the dramatist has recognised its importance for drama, which is much concerned with the juxtaposition and integration of seeing and believing. Interestingly, we are also given a scene in hell, where the devils are raising the barricades in fear of the coming of Christ. Nicodemus takes and embalms the body of Christ and pronounces a final blessing.

The three main sections (Resurrection, Pilate, Ascension) of the last play are all linked, both to each other and to events of the Passion-play. The Harrowing of Hell and the release of the imprisoned souls is matched by a miraculous release from prison of Joseph and Nicodemus; the emperor Tiberius is cured by the sight of St Veronica's kerchief, which mopped the brow of Christ; and Pilate, who refuses to believe what he has actually seen, is imprisoned, kills himself, but cannot be buried, a contrast with the triumphant resurrection of Christ, who rises from, rather than being expelled from, the grave. Seeing, believing, and the contrast are the main themes here, magnificently appropriate in a dramatic presentation. Pilate is shown refusing stubbornly to believe in Christ at all, even though he is protected for a while by Christ's robe; Mary Magdalene and the Marys at the tomb believe, and so eventually does the doubting Thomas, after he has been convinced by the risen Christ. The assumption is that the audience will also believe what they have seen represented.

Although the first part of the play – the Resurrection, Nicodemus, the Marys and the tale of Thomas, all showing the power of Christ – seems fairly distinct from the rest of the work, the Pilate story does relate closely, as indicated, with the themes of seeing and believing, shown especially with the doubts of Thomas. The Pilate legend is again unusual in drama (it is not present in the English cycles and rare elsewhere), and is one of the high points of the Cornish plays. There are various Latin versions of these legends, but the Cornish dramatist again used an English version (as is evident from one of the names). In the precise legend upon which the play is based, an ailing Tiberius sends a messenger to find Christ so that He can heal him, and Pilate has to conceal the Crucifixion. However, the messenger encounters Veronica with her cloth and the image of Christ imprinted upon it. Tiberius is healed and Pilate is put on trial. However, Pilate wears Christ's seamless robe, which protects him. When it is removed, Pilate commits suicide in despair, just like Judas. When they try to bury him, however, his body is rejected by the river and the earth. In the Latin legends (which were widely translated) his body is eventually thrown into a well, which remains haunted, but here it is sent out to sea, while Pilate's soul goes to hell. The parallels with those who do believe and are saved are very clear, as is the contrast with Christ himself. The earth could not keep Christ, but it actively refuses Pilate (and again we may wonder at the staging of this). The Pilate section is the pivot between the Resurrection of Christ, which it parodies, and the final, triumphant scene of the Ascension, in which Christ himself recapitulates the story of the Passion, as the angels stress the kinship of Christ.

The way in which motifs are linked in the three plays is striking, and the return after the three days – of the play, just as of the Passion and the Resurrection themselves – to the idea of the way man has been redeemed is, in dramatic terms, extremely impressive. Some of the additional episodes have been seen as technically unskilled, as 'medieval padding'. Of course, they are no such thing. There is great dramatic variety, which keeps the audience interested, but the constant strand that runs through all is the theme of Redemption for those who see (the play) and believe (the content). Positive and negative examples are provided to which thc audience must relate.

It should be clear from this sketch that the existing trilogy is a tightly-knit presentation of the theme of man's fall from grace and its restoration in triumph, and as such is a masterpiece which may stand beside – and indeed may be compared very favourably with – parallel dramatic treatments of this central medieval (and hardly just medieval) theme right across Europe. This indeed is the context in which it should be viewed. Religious drama in the form of the mystery play reached its height in the fourteenth and fifteenth centuries, and it is appropriate to compare the Cornish work with the English cycles, of course, but just as much with the French Passion and mystery plays, with the High and Low German Easter plays, later on with the continuing tradition in the Catholic south in Spain and Italy, as well as with late survivals, such as the Breton Creation-play.

We need too, however, to consider the importance of the *Ordinalia* specifically in terms of its Celtic background, of its importance to the Cornish people. The point is an interesting one, but it is a difficult one as well, and it needs to be expressed carefully, because in a sense, the historical presentation just given stresses a rather *different* point. The *Ordinalia* is important because it is a particularly good example of a *European* phenomenon, the popular presentation of a universal theme, which simply happens to be in Cornish. In those terms, the form transcends nationality, just as the theme transcends time, all in an objectively impressive manner, so that there is no question of regarding the plays 'merely' as part of a relatively slightly represented literature in what is often seen as a minor Celtic language. The language, however, is of course, the main point. The plays are Cornish because they are in Cornish, and that is what provides their importance in the Celtic context. It is not even very important that some local place-names occur. The figures represented are not Cornish any more than they are French or German or English in other 'national' dramatic traditions.

The verse form used – strophic, with a variety of different stanza forms, many with distinctively short lines (seven syllables), and the use of a limited number of repeated rhymes within the strophes – is also to an extent specific to Cornish, but in this case only to an extent, and this is not by any means such a specific marker as the language itself. The most common line has seven syllables – measurement is syllabic – with an irregular rhythm. Four-syllable lines also occur, arranged in a variety of strophic forms, ranging from couplets to the relatively common strophe of six seven-syllable lines rhyming *aabaab* or *aabccb*, although longer strophes can have ten or twelve lines, often in combinations of length. The texture of any work can be affected by such variations, or by the use of rhetorical devices, and there is a range of linguistic registers. Rhymes do tend to be repetitive, something which is difficult to imitate in English, but it has to be said that very similar strophic patterns occur in medieval French, in Breton, and indeed in some of the English plays, although seven-syllable lines are uncommon and the rhythmically regular octosyllabic lines are more usual in English.

The Cornish language used, incidentally, contains both verbal borrowings and whole lines in English, the extent of the English being used, however, without pattern. It is a nice idea, but quite untrue, for example, that the 'bad' characters use more English and the 'good' characters a Cornish which is somehow purer. In fact the three Marys at the tomb, for example, sing a song in English. Variety in register within the language is a different matter entirely.

So how 'Celtic' is the work? Summing up, it is in Cornish, and of a kind, which represents, we may assume, the literary standard of the period, as far as that can be ascertained. It uses verse-forms that are found in other medieval Cornish works and are fairly distinctive. The trilogy is designed too for the typically Cornish production of medieval drama in a playing-place. All these features should suffice – if they are needed at all – to establish the work as a Celtic masterpiece as well as (and this is important) a medieval European one. As indicated, features such as the choice of a Cornish location for the smith depends more on rhyme than on local patriotism, and certainly not upon sense, and other features might apply anywhere in the middle ages – the choice of animals for the ark, for example. The work is, we might say, 'set in Cornish', but it is not 'set in Cornwall' as such. The fact that Galilee, Rome and the Tiber are all present as well as Marazion really underlines the universality of the message – after all, the Gospel story takes place in those lands – and the use of local names simply make clear that the story being presented is applicable to all men and women, including those Cornish people watching and understanding this dramatisation. There is no need to seek for elements that are somehow uniquely Cornish or even uniquely Celtic: the language and style do that for us. That it can be compared, and compared favourably, with the Coventry Corpus Christi play, with the great French *Mistère*, with the Creation and Redemption play of the Saxon Arnold Immessen, or with Jakob Ruf's spectacle of Adam and Eve put on in 1550 for the citizens of Zurich in front of the cathedral is just as important.

Studies of the *Ordinalia* focused in the early stages, as might be expected, on the text, establishing what the plays actually are, and translating them for working purposes. For a long time the edition of Edwin Norris, first published in 1859 was the standard version, and indeed in many ways it still is, although there are now modern prose translations and an edition with translation in Unified Cornish, one of the various modern forms of the revived language. Several individual episodes of the *Ordinalia* were published separately (the Holy Rood material was even collected), and while this was doubtless useful for language reasons, it did tend to detract from the fact that the *Ordinalia* is large-scale but coherent work, with the parts interdependent, the whole offering an overview of the divine economy. Critical studies of the plays were relatively limited for a long time, and were often restricted to local publication. However, from the 1970s, full-scale studies began to appear, implicitly acknowledging the value of these plays to students of the medieval world and of medieval drama in particular. Jane Bakere and Robert Longsworth produced full-length studies. There were also works like Allardyce Nicoll's much reprinted *British Drama* (London, Harrap, 4th edition 1947) which had dismissed the 'set of [sic] of five [sic] plays in the Cornish tongue' in a single line. The Pelican *Drama in Performance* by the Cambridge critic and drama specialist Raymond Williams, which first appeared in 1954, dealt in the context of world literature with the three Marys in the *Ordinalia*. Later still, I was delighted to be asked to contribute a chapter on the Cornish plays in the *Cambridge Companion to Medieval English Theatre* – English in the sense of 'theatre in England', of course; this seemed like an important acknowledgement of the significance of the new plays, and I have tried since then to include details of the plays in comparative studies, to stress not their importance in the Celtic world and in Britain, but in their European context. Neville Denny commented in an article in 1973 that the open-air amphitheatrical matrix of Cornish medieval drama was one in which 'a form of native European staging reached a pitch of maturity from any consolidation and evolutionary development of which it was deflected only by the mesmerising false promises of the Renaissance'. Of course, there is more to be done to integrate the dramas with the European medieval traditions; Sandro Sticca's interesting study of the *Planctus Mariae in the Dramatic Tradition of the Middle Ages* (Athens, Georgia, University of Georgia Press 1988) does not mention the Cornish plays, for example, though it might well have done so in view of the effective use of the lament of the Virgin. Much has been written on the idea of performance in the round in medieval drama, and here of course Cornwall and the *plen-an-gwary* plays a major part. Critical works run from Richard Southern's earlier study down to the more recent and interesting work of Sydney Higgins. It is appropriate to mention here, too, Alan M. Kent's own impressive study of the literature of Cornwall, locating *Ordinalia* into the wider continuum of writing from the territory, and well as his *Reader* (with Tim Saunders) in Cornish Literature, which has done much to make Cornish medieval drama accessible to a wider readership. Kent has also used the plays as a starting-point for literature of another kind in his own extended poem *Out of the Ordinalia*, published in 1995.

What follows in this volume then is not simply a translation into English of a medieval Cornish work, but an altogether bolder venture, an adaptation that is at the same time designed to convey an impression of the original, even though it is in another language. It aims, then, to retain more than just the sense: it wants to put across something of the essence of the original language and to convey some idea of Cornishness. Translators are aware that there are special problems with translating any work, and that those special problems are different with every original. Moving beyond the very basic notions either of a word-for-word gloss (which would probably not be understandable at all), or of plain prose (as exemplified by that celebrate series *Kelly's Keys to the Classics*, much used in the days when the classics were still taught), the basic aim in offering a translation is the presentation of a work in a form that allows a new audience to forget that it is a translation, while still retaining as much as possible of the original. Translators are often vilified as traitors, but like it or not, they perform a necessary task, or how else would works become known across languages? The difficulty lies in that notion of 'retaining as much as possible of the original'. The content may have elements specific to the original language, and the style of the original has to be imitated as well. With a work that is in verse, moreover, a decision has to be made whether and how far the form can be imitated in the new language at all, and poetry of course makes greater demands than just translating the words. With the *Ordinalia* we are at a certain advantage because the plays have been translated several times, and studies of the plays have sorted out minor, but significant linguistic problems; a century or so of scholarship has helped the raw understanding of the text. Even so, translating the work to give an idea of the poetry and the verse form will always require some fine judgement about freedom of translation, and sometimes poetic essence will take precedence over lexical exactitude.

What, however, of the Cornishness? How does one – indeed, *can* one – convey, when the topic is not local but universal, and where the distinctive verse forms are not recognisable as Cornish, that this is a work originally in Cornish and not, say, French or Breton or German? Those Cornish writers over the years who have stressed the otherness of Cornish may this time find themselves served, rather than disadvantaged, by the fact that Cornwall is and has long been part of an English-speaking land. As such, we are able to draw to some extent (the reader will see that it is not excessive) at least on a particularly Cornish form of English, the modern dialect, a dialect with a long and interesting history and literary tradition of it own. Of course, great judgement has to be exercised, and various new problems arise if the decision is made – as Alan M. Kent has – to convey the Cornishness by the occasional use of Cornu-English. There is a danger too, that some dialect words themselves may be incomprehensible to an outside audience, so that attention has to be paid to the contextualisation of such words. An ear must be kept open at all times, too, for variety in register, which the augmented use of dialect might itself imply. Adopting such an approach needs to be handled carefully, but as the reader will see, we are in capable hands. Kent has completed a breathtaking verse translation for the modern theatre, which has considered all the issues outlined above, not only in terms of the play's universality but also its specifically Cornish dimension.

So finally, what are we meant to see in the *Ordinalia*? The audience sees something which they have to believe in a way different from the normal theatrical suspension of disbelief. The point is not just that they have to accept that a local player 'is' God, or Pilate, or Christ. The point is that they have to believe the essence of the story they have seen, in the way that Pilate and the torturers (who have also seen the events) do not. Seeing and believing are the twin points of *Ordinalia* in its time and our time:

> Good people around, all your friends tell
> how you saw Christ's resurrection from the tomb
> and how He broke down the gates of Hell...

That was what the audience was supposed to see, not just a play.

Professor Brian Murdoch,
University of Stirling

Ordinalia

From the Creation Window of St Neot's church, Cornwall, 16th Century. The Temptation. © Sonia Halliday Photographs

Origo Mundi

The Beginning of the World

Cast in order of Appearance

+ after the character indicates a role in Passio Christi
 # after the character indicates a role in Resurrexio Domini

GOD THE FATHER+ #
LUCIFER/DEVIL + #
ADAM #
EVE #
CHERUB
CAIN
ABEL
SATAN+ #
BEELZEBUB + #
SERAPH
SETH
NOAH
NOAH'S WIFE
SHEM
HAM
JAPHET
SHEM'S WIFE
HAM'S WIFE
JAPHET'S WIFE
ABRAHAM
ISAAC
GABRIEL
MOSES
KING PHARAOH
AARON
1ST MESSENGER
PHARAOH'S COUNSELLOR
CALEB
JOSHUA
1ST SOLDIER
2ND SOLDIER
SQUIRE
KING DAVID
BUTLER
KING'S COUNSELLOR/SOLOMON'S
BISHOP
KING DAVID'S 1ST MESSENGER
MINSTRELS
BLIND MAN
LAME MAN
DEAF MAN
KING DAVID'S 2ND MESSENGER
BATHSHEBA
URIAH
1ST MASON
2ND MASON
KING SOLOMON
1ST CARPENTER
2ND CARPENTER
MAXIMILLA
CROZIER-BEARER
1ST EXECUTIONER
2ND EXECUTIONER
3RD EXECUTIONER
4TH EXECUTIONER
GEBAL
AMALEK
3RD MESSENGER

Here beginneth the Script of the Beginning of the World.

GOD THE FATHER

I am the Father of Heaven,
Creator of all that shall be made.
One and Three together woven –
into Father, Son and Spirit's braid;
By grace I desire today
to begin the making of the world.
So let Heaven and Earth – I say
from my mind, be fully unfurled.

Now that Heaven is made for us
and is filled with wondrous angels bright
we will create the world thus.
The Three and One, here and now unite –
Father, Son and Spirit – we three
all rightly confident and certain
that in our creativity
these fine things are nobly begotten.

On the second day I will make
more Heaven, a cloudy, starry sky;
for all I made on day one's take
appears fine and proper to my eye.
Let the sky be wrapped round the sphere
covering all I have created,
allowing rain on high to appear
and fall below to its earthly bed.

On the third day I will divide
the lands, separating the sea's flow,
and upon the land I'll provide
healthy trees and plants which there will grow.
Let every tree grow each upright,
producing full fruit and leaves – these both,
and at the summer-time's twilight
let them form seeds for shelter and growth.

On the fourth day, let there be made
for all the world, bright lights so fine;
Name those who'll make the light and shade

the sun and the moon and the starshine.
Above the trees I will have yet
the sun by day and the moon by night
in the middle of the sky set,
for they may give out brilliant light.

On the fifth day it is my wish
that there be created by my might
all manner of beasts, birds and fish,
to fill the land and the sea finite.
And soon a time shall come to pass
when one beast shall rise above the band.
But for now though, to nature's mass –
long live and increase, I here command.

Here GOD *comes down from the upper stage, and says (Here* LUCIFER *plays from Heaven):*

In truth, today is the sixth day
since I began this creation work,
making Heaven, sea, land, to stay,
trees, beasts, fish, light, from the former murk.
These things are respectful of me,
they'll be obedient from this day.
And next, in my creation spree,
I'll make mankind from perfect clay.

Here let him make ADAM, *and* GOD *says, in the Damascene Field:*

As we are One and Three this day –
Father and Son in Trinity –
we make you, a man, from the clay
moulding your face to look like me.
Into your body we give breath
of the spirit, so that you will live;
and when you lose that life for death
back to earth, your body shall give.

Adam, arise, and know your worth.
Turn, and into flesh and blood transform.
Know that I've made you from the earth,
head to foot modelled upon my form.
Hereon, assume complete control

over all that lives on sea and land.
Raising children shall be your goal,
and you'll live until you're grey and grand.

Adam, as I'm a gracious God,
you'll have guardianship for all this –
Paradise's flora, fauna and sod,
but listen well for your future bliss.
O'er every fruit, plant and seed
that lives and grows here from edge to edge;
one fruit alone must not be freed –
that fruit grows on the Tree of Knowledge.

If you eat this fruit you now know
which here is named the Tree of Knowledge
out from Paradise you must go,
and from that day you'll take death's pledge.

ADAM

O Father, Son, and Holy Ghost,
To You I'll always offer worship.
Of creation, You've made the most,
shaped from Your old block, a fine chip.
I'm not one to complain or bleat.
Everything here is harmony.
But it would be nice and complete
if, please, I might have company.

GOD *and* ADAM *shall go to Paradise.*

GOD THE FATHER

Yes, I can understand his moan,
that he should not be left alone
without a 'friend' or a partner.
Go, lie you down right on the ground
and sleep and do not make a sound
until I've made this new creature.

And ADAM *shall sleep. Here* GOD *makes* EVE, *and shall lead her to* ADAM, *and he shall receive her at his hand: and* GOD THE FATHER *says:*

Adam, from one of your own ribs
I've made you an equal – no fibs.
Then promise to help each other.
Adam, see how she's wonderful.

Give her a name and be thankful
for her – now you have a partner.

EVE

Dear Father, Lord of Heaven's space,
even though You are full of grace
I will worship You forever.
You have done much for me – 'tis true,
creating me like unto You.
One God, three persons – some clever.

EVE *waits in the same place.*

ADAM

Father, You took from me a bone –
to give me a mate of my own.
As a friend, she is truly fit.
The name Virago – her I'll call,
and I will worship God through all
who made her for my benefit.

GOD THE FATHER *and* ADAM *pass from Paradise.*

GOD THE FATHER

Adam, see all the fishes fair,
the beasts, and birds up in the air,
both from the land and from the sea.
Give them all their names one by one.
They'll come – each and everyone,
but do not oppress them I plea.

ADAM

I name cow and bull as a pair
and horse, a beast without compare
for helping people in their work.
Forget not goats, the stag and deer;
nor the woolly sheep standing near –
she's not a beast her tasks to shirk.

The goose and hen I name in glee,
birds which I consider to be
perfect food for people on earth;
the swan, buzzard, crows and great eagle,
duck, dove, peacock, partridge – birds regal
named by me as being of worth.

I will give names to all the fish,
past porpoise, salmon, eel I'll swish.
They'll be obedient to me:
even the playful cod and ling.
All fish will come under my wing
if I worship God completely.

GOD THE FATHER

Because it is both fair and good
all creation, in six days fully,
will be as blessed as it should;
the seventh day is therefore holy.
That will be called the day of rest
for every person whom we'll save.
Recognising that this is best
now, we will rest in this enclave.

GOD THE FATHER *shall go to Heaven; and afterwards the* DEVIL, *like a serpent, speaks to* EVE *in the Tree of Knowledge, and he says wickedly to her:*

DEVIL

Eve maid, why dun't 'ee come near
an' speak with me all s'pure?
I do knaw somethin' – 'tis clear
it would delight 'ee for sure.
If you knew 'un, you'd laugh loud
full a' deep mirth I contend;
'zactly like a goddess proud,
and up to Heaven, you'd ascend.

EVE

Tell me straight – who makes this row?
Whose can that curious voice be?

DEVIL

Eve, I can't say that right now,
for I fear you would denounce me.

EVE

Because I am a woman
you can declare it to me.
And as I'm truly human
I wun't be denouncing 'ee.

DEVIL

I'm from heaven – as a treat
– for a better life, my beaut:
Dun't you hesitate to eat
the Tree of Knowledge's fruit.

EVE

Get away from me you brute.
Say nothing more untoward:
I dun't want to eat the fruit
'gainst the wishes of my Lord.

DEVIL

Woman, how stupid you be.
You don't believe what I say!
If you do eat from the tree,
you and your husband, this day
would – I say with no worry –
be like gods standing on high.
Eat the apple and hurry.
I 'ent telling 'ee no lie.

EVE

But God – who did make us both
He has forbid us, you see,
to eat the apple's growth,
or to go near to the tree.

DEVIL

I knaw the reason my beaut:
'Tis a virtue tree, of kind.
He who eats of the fruit
will knaw what's in Father's mind.
There won't be a thing 'round here
that the Father'll keep secret.
He's foolish, to me 'tis clear,
when fruit's left there like a banquet.

EVE

I'm so distraught, full of fear.
What will soon become of me
by plucking the apple near?
I'm scared of your trickery.

DEVIL

Well look – pluck it on my risk.
Quick, without hesitation.
To Adam the apple whisk
for his joy and digestation.

EVE

Help me to bend down the tree,
so the apples I may reach.

DEVIL

Careful – do it quietly.
Now be on your way, my peach.

The DEVIL *withdraws and let him walk in the plain. Let* ADAM *go to Paradise. Then* EVE *shall take the apple and carry it to* ADAM, *and* EVE *says:*

EVE

Sweet Adam, give me your hand:
and take this apple from me.
Do it without noise husband;
eat it immediately.

ADAM

Tell me Eve, my dearest love,
where did you pick this fine fruit?
I hope it's not from above –
from Father's tree, an offshoot.

EVE

While I was strolling along,
truly I heard beside me
an angel singing his song
up above me on the tree.
And here is what he told me:
that if the fruit I did pluck,
greater than God we would be,
our lives filled with joy and luck.

ADAM

Oh, you'm daft, you wisht woman.
Why fall under its dark wing?
'Twas a bird of bad omen
that you heard so sweetly sing.
This'll bring brave misery
unless we refrain right now.
Think of future's drudgery
that could result from this row.

EVE

Listen – so preached the angel
of God's virtue and the tree.
Whosoe'er the fruit sample
would be a God, strong and free.

ADAM

Eve, I do not believe you,
nor the feigning words you say.
God's service is what we do.
To that, I ask you to pray.
For He Who made us from clay
prohibits us here, you see,

says we shouldn't – any day –
eat the fine fruit of that tree.

EVE
Since you will not believe me,
my love, you will forthwith lose.
As long as you live and see
me, you'll nevermore misuse.

ADAM
Rather than you be angry,
Sweetest Eve, I'll do this task.
Give me the fruit of the tree
and I will eat as you ask.

And then ADAM *eats of the apple and sees that he is naked and says with a groan:*

Oh no! No! I am sinful,
and I have broken God's word.
Over my eyes, you pulled wool,
you and your deceitful bird.
Our bodies are now naked.
Here, clothe yourself with a leaf!
Certainly for what you did,
God will be mad, full of grief.

ADAM *hides himself in Paradise. Then* GOD THE FATHER *shall come to* ADAM, *and He says to him in Paradise. Let the* CHERUB *come with Him:*

GOD THE FATHER
O Adam, what are you doing?
Why don't you come out to welcome me?

ADAM
I'm naked – not fit for viewing.
Lord, I've no clothes, so I hid from 'Ee.

GOD THE FATHER
What revelation made you think
you were naked, head, arm and toe?
At my own tree you did not shrink
from eating the fruit that does grow.

ADAM
Father, You gave me a wife.
She picked the apple chaste
and is to blame for this strife,
bringing it to me to taste.

GOD THE FATHER

This mess Adam, you have made worse
ignoring my wish for your home.
Know that this world I will now curse
and all your works in times to come:
In your sweat and labour to eat
right to the end, I'll not forgive.
Sharp thorns and briars shall you meet
always in misery you'll live.

GOD THE FATHER *speaks to* EVE*:*

Come now, why did you do this Eve,
deceive him, and Paradise split,
by taking the fruit you now grieve,
after I had forbidden you it?
Wilfully you broke this rule,
and brought him to great misery.
You made him eat, made him a fool,
tasting fruit from the hallowed tree.

Here let the DEVIL *be present.*

EVE

Beloved God in Your Glory,
I was deceived by the serpent.
I believed all its false story.
I wish my greed had been absent.
Were one to eat it – this He said,
one would become a mighty Lord.
If 'tis to evil I've been led,
slash it down with Your sturdy sword.

GOD THE FATHER

Since you listened to the Serpent
and deceived your faithful spouse Adam,
you must be more obedient,
so I will make this new addendum:
Her sorrow shall not be mild,
for her breach of my commandment
she will never have a child
but that grievous labour be spent.

GOD THE FATHER *speaks to the* SERPENT.

Now devil, answer me in truth.
Why did you deceive her without cause
with an apple to tempt her tooth?
It is my virtuous fruit, not yours.

DEVIL

I'll tell 'Ee how it happened then.
While I was burning in my den,
they were full of such wondrous joy.
Thus, in short, I tempted these two,
so 'Alas' might be their song too,
as much theirs as 'tis mine t'enjoy.

GOD THE FATHER

Then you shall be accursed to go
beyond all the beasts, high and low
that walk upon the earth's surface.
There'll always be hostility
'twixt your evil society
and all those of the female grace.

GOD THE FATHER *speaks to* ADAM *and* EVE. *The* DEVIL *goes home.*

You won't be living here no more.
Get out of here. I tell you: Shoo!
You'll lose all the joy I did pour
into Paradise for you two.
'Tis no use shuffling on your feet.
Your wife plucked the fruit I banned.
Because you heeded her so sweet
future thousands will be damned.

ADAM

O Father God, in Your glory true,
give to your handiwork, I beg you,
some of the Oil of Mercy please.

GOD THE FATHER

Well, come the end of the world you see,
I'll grant Oil of Mercy to 'Ee
and to Eve, your wife, for her own ease.

And then GOD *ascends to Heaven and says to the* CHERUB:

Cherub, here, take a sharp sword
and head over towards Paradise.
A pair you'll find as your reward.

Drive them out with this keen device.
They shall be filled with great concern
and all those not yet created.
And for my laws, they will yearn
cursing the God, they violated.

CHERUB

To Paradise I'll repair,
to achieve all that you say.
If I find some people there,
I will drive them out this day.

Here the CHERUB *goes down.*

Adam, it's time to leave these lands.
In some other spot you must live,
a place to mould with your own hands.
There, your wife Eve, you may forgive.
See, you've angered the Father fair,
and full repentance is the score.
Your path now lies way over there.
You'll not live here a moment more.

The CHERUB *remains in Paradise. Here* ADAM *and* EVE *depart from Paradise.*

ADAM

I understand this reprimand.
Alas that I betrayed my Lord;
when I disobeyed His command
my legacy went by the board.
I don't know where I now shall go.
I have no lodging, shelter, house.
My heart is pierced with such sorrow,
the pain of which I'll never douse.

From all my happiness and joy
ruination now's a stronghold.
Lack of shelter will us destroy
and we shall surely die of cold.
Wretchedness will pursue our track
living out in field and wood.
My small stomach – an empty sack,
famished and starved for lack of food.

Eve, take the distaff for spinning.

Round it, wool for clothes shall be wound,
and I will go and start digging
with all my might into the ground.

And ADAM *shall dig, and the earth cries: and again he shall dig, and the earth cries.*

Why on earth can't I dig it so?
The soil won't break, blows it does balk.
All this work has brought me so low
that now I can scarce move or walk.
Although for Paradise not fit,
please give this land your leave I cry.
Allow me to seek food from it
for we two – rather than to die.

Here GOD THE FATHER *comes down.*

GOD THE FATHER
From this you shall not be banned,
so use your spade's full length – dig true.
O mighty earth, I do command,
allow Adam to open you.

ADAM
Perfect Lord. Some soil make fit.
Our small wishes you can meet.
One day, all that grows in it.
my wife Eve and I will eat.

GOD THE FATHER
Well then, take two lengths of the earth
to provide for you and your wife neat.

ADAM
But Lord, 'tis too small by my worth
if there be patter of tiny feet.

GOD THE FATHER
A'right then Adam, take some more.
You can have three lengths of your spade;
three times the tool's width on the floor,
but don't you cheat this rule I've made.

ADAM
Lord, sorry to cause you more strife –
but if I had three lengths of earth –
'twudn be enough to support wife,
myself and a child's future birth.
If more d'come, they'll get nothun':

chield-upon-chield will faint for hunger.
And such sorrow I'll have begun,
though Lord, I don't wish to scaremonger.

GOD THE FATHER
Right boy – take everything you need,
and have the whole world all around.
It will be useful to your creed
wherever you and they are bound.

ADAM
Father, thanks for this addition.
Forever Lord, we'll know Your worth.
Eve, I now have God's permission
to rule o'er all this lovely earth.

EVE
Oh, I'm so happy with our lot,
that permission from God is got.
Wondrous Father will allow us
to dig the earth and cultivate.
My distaff I will activate
and soon spin splendid garments thus.

GOD THE FATHER
I am sorry to have made man
as a mirror of my own face.
By listening to a woman
he has fully lost that fine place
which I had made with my right hand.
If only he had kept his grace.
But when he took what I had banned
he angered me to my heart's base.

Adam, when you finish this harvest
leave a tenth for me. This I request
as payment for my counsel wise,
and ungrudgingly, in your labour
take it to the top of Mount Tabor.
Burn it in my honour I advise.

ADAM
Lord, I will do this for sure,
though you're welcome to have more.
There, this harvest will be burnt
to fulfil Your will and worth.
You've no equal on this earth.
You're full of grace I have learnt.

Here GOD THE FATHER *shall pass on to Heaven.*

Cain and Abel, go pay our price
at once, and make this sacrifice
to our God, on that mountain high.
And sons, make sure you are not blithe.
Take care to offer the true tithe.
Of His command do not be shy.

CAIN

Dear father, I'll do as You ask
and Lord of Heaven, in each task
grant us to do all that's good.
Abel, to the mountain toward
to honour there the wondrous Lord,
just as father said we should.

CAIN *retires.*

ABEL

Brother Cain, gladly will I come so,
and climb with you, high up the mountain,
but my dear father, before I go,
give me your full blessing, clear and plain,
for I would have hope of appeal
that mercy, I'll readily obtain.
Your blessing would please a great deal,
and mother's blessing I'd like to gain.

ADAM

Abel, my blessing you'll always know,
between night and day, there to and fro,
and may all that's on this earth be yours.

EVE

And Abel, know my blessing this day.
Likewise for you, I will always pray,
and so I say Amen to your cause.

ABEL

Blessings on the two of you
for granting me my request.
I'm so fortunate, 'tis true,
that I am indeed so blest.

Then with those four ceremonies let CAIN *go to the altar, walking into the plain; and he says:*

CAIN Abel, hurry up for the climb.
You oughtn't waste our precious time
in going to the sacrifice.

ABEL I only stopped for a moment,
for the blessings of each parent.
Twudn' nothun' more to be precise.

CAIN 'Tis mad, the object we defeat
to burn something people can eat.
We must be cakey in the head.
What true honour for God alone
that tithe be burnt upon the stone,
and turned to black ashes instead.

ABEL Cain, this moment think of your soul
and love Father of Heaven whole.
It is best to obey His command.
Do not feel such selfish anguish,
since it is surely His own wish.
Burning the tithe I understand.

CAIN Abel, you must follow this sham,
but I've had enough of His ways.
I have come up with a good scam
to save my tithe for better days.

ABEL You're certainly mad and foolish.
Cain, if you do not act as I say,
torment you'll suffer right hellish,
and down below will lie your way.

Assuredly, to live here so fine
God's given us parts one to nine
in His true mercy and His full grace;
'Tis proper then that He should claim true
this small tithe (without a grudge) as due,
and burn it properly at this place.

Here ALL *shall come into the plain. And then let* CAIN *offer a part of the tithes, that he may keep another part of the tithes; and he says:*

CAIN Now between we two, I'm telling 'ee –

I 'ent giving all my tithe for free.
He can have some of the tithe though.
O Father God – so full of pity,
here's my offering entirely.
Lord, take it and receive it so.

GOD *does not accept it.*

Look here God! See my off'ring.
Come and receive my tithe then.
If You'm busy gathering,
I will take 'un home again.

ABEL

Father God, sublime Lord and true,
with all my strength I worship You.
I give this fully from my heart,
and offer You – cut with my scythe,
the full amount of my true tithe,
burnt in honour of who thou art.

GOD THE FATHER

Abel had the right tithe in his hand,
and he shall be given in the end
untold joy in future on my land.
To well-earned rest, I will him send.

CAIN

What?! God gives me no respect at all.
All I grow, back into the earth will fall.
Now all my crops and plants will not thrive;
and whilst Abel's splendid cattle
do much better, I move to battle.
Abel'll pay for this – as I'm alive.

ABEL

My dear brother, let's go home.
I am feeling much oppressed.
Something in my heart does roam.
What is it here in my breast?
May the Father Who made me
show thanks for my offering.
When I from this earth do flee,
may I fall beneath His wing.

CAIN

Abel my bird, do not fret.
All will turn out fine and well

with the help of God's sweet sweat,
Who up in Heaven does so dwell.
In the name of God alive,
go before me as you tread.
So that you will never thrive,
take this scat upon your head!

Then CAIN *shall strike him on the head, and* ABEL *shall die; and* LUCIFER *says:*

LUCIFER

Beelzebub and Satan I plead,
go right now with every speed.
Show your love for me is endless;
and fetch the fellow Abel home here,
so he may sing 'Alas' in fear,
forever in this dense darkness.

SATAN

Gladly to you Lord Lucifer,
we'll ably bring this bounder.
We'll capture him who would go in,
seeking penance for old Adam,
and as it's our corrupt custom,
he'll see no light, for we shall win.

The DEVILS *shall go to* ABEL.

BEELZEBUB

Oh Abel, we'm on a mission,
to place you in perdition.
You'll be a fine tormentor's toy.
To this dark dwelling you are due,
in spite of giving the tithe true.
You'll live in blackness with no joy.

SATAN

Let's head home, where we may gloat
and give Lucifer some glee:
I will sing the counternote
whilst you descant to me.

BEELZEBUB

In us pair be a proud believer.
Lucifer, to you I give
the son of Adam the deceiver,
and here with us he shall live.

LUCIFER

Abel, for your precious offering

you shall dwell here evermore;
with devils at you grinning
poking, prodding at your core.

Then GOD THE FATHER *shall come to the earth; He speaks with* CAIN *and* GOD THE FATHER *says:*

GOD THE FATHER

Cain, your brother have you observed
Who always faithfully me served?
Why is Abel not with you at all?

CAIN

Go ask those who You gave him to keep.
Go ask the devil, that foolish creep.
I'm not his keeper as I recall.

A voice calls.

GOD THE FATHER

Behold the voice of Abel's death –
your brother's last calls of breath
come up to me from out the ground.
Forever you will be accursed
and for all that you did and said,
now curses on your land are bound.

May it never bear good fruit,
nor leaves until this world shall end.
It is your curse and made to suit.
My angels' also curses send.

CAIN

Your voice Lord, I do hear,
and so great is my fear
Your face I cannot see.
Alas true creator:
that my sin is greater
than my own God's mercy.
Now feeble, I begin to cry.
The world will soon see what I have done.
There is no earthly reason why
I'll not be a target for everyone.

GOD THE FATHER

Cain, I promise that will not be so;
if a man would kill you with a blow,
he shall have seven times your torment

and his earthly pain will surely show,
if you are harmed and your life is spent.

For I will provide protection
that no one will ever kill you.
Man'll have joy and affection
if good deeds of him I shall view.

Here GOD *ascends to Heaven. Then* CAIN *shall come to* ADAM, *his father; and* ADAM *says:*

ADAM — Cain, son, where did your brother go?
Why didn't he come home your way?

CAIN — If worry for him you do show,
ask his keeper is what I say!

ADAM — Ah! Your deed is truly hurtful;
by my faith, I know you killed him,
and to think, he loved me so full.
May curses fall on you, my son grim.
It's so sad that I have lost him –
sweet Abel was my dearest son.
Oh the pain of creation's trim,
made to suffer the evil one,
that this boy Cain was ever born.
What awful problems there have been,
with me so snared by woman's thorn.
On Eve, I shudn' have been s'keen,
yet there is a dear God living.
Each day – this I rediscover,
but I will no more be sleeping
with this maid Eve, as my lover.

EVE — The shame for all my listening
to the devil and his word.
Now so much evil's happening
both night and day I have heard.
This causes me to weep and bawl.
Tears of blood will surely flow.
Woe's me that I'm alive at all
with all the sorrow I d'know.

GOD THE FATHER

Go to Adam, my seraph sweet.
Use your power, but be discreet,
and tell him, from Me, to sleep
again with Eve his dear wife.
They will produce a new life –
a fine and good son to keep.

SERAPH

Sweet Lord, I will do what You ask.
It is my place to help any plan,
I will straightaway do this task,
and go to earth to advise this man.

And then the SERAPH *shall go to* ADAM, *and he says to him:*

My message comes from God the great.
You must sleep again with your wife,
so you and her can procreate
and bring a new child to your life.

ADAM

Since the sweet Father wants it done,
'Tis best that we get on with it.
He wills that a child be won.
Time to throw off this outfit.

Come dear Eve, my wife and soulmate,
let's to bed for a good old while.
God's decree we will follow straight.
May our loving give Him some smile.

So now this, it's been a long, long time –
at least two hundred years dear wife,
since I have touched your skin sublime
or had any dealings in your life.

EVE

As this is what God does require,
to His Will we shall now aspire,
obeying whatever is His wish.
Through the grace the Lord does wield,
we will have a loving chield,
to serve us and not be selfish.

ADAM

In God the Father's name and way
so may we have a 'andsome mite.

To the Father God we do pray
that His grace will meet our sight.

And then let ADAM *go away a little while from* EVE.

And again ADAM *shall come to* EVE.

EVE

I knew the mite'd come in the end.
Oh Adam, I have given birth.
To this little boy, come and tend,
born by our Father's Will and worth.
It was truly a blessèd ploy
when sweet God's demand for Him came.
What shall we call the little boy?
Adam, tell me what is his name.

ADAM

Seth! That, I shall name him proper,
and may our beloved Father
grant him the grace to serve Him well.
I must go and dig the ground
and begin to grow crops sound.
I need to labour for a spell.

Here ADAM *shall go to his work. Here, let him take a breath, saying:*

My dear life – some weary I feel.
Could I but finish this ordeal
I would be a happy man.
So strong are these vurze in the dirt
that my arms do sting and hurt
from working at each tough span.

Seth my son, this message precise
take to the tall gates of Paradise.
The guardian Cherub find you there.
Ask if the Oil o' Mercy he'll give
to end this life that I now live,
from gracious Father God's share.

SETH

Dearest father, at your command,
right away I'll do the task,
but I'm not sure of my errand
and as to what I should ask.

ADAM Tell 'un I'm wearied of my life.
I pray to him to end my strife
and at last, the truth to fashion
concerning the Oil of Mercy
which was always promised to me
by dear God in His compassion;
when the angels drove us away
for committing such a foolish crime
and we were driven out that day
from Paradise's wondrous clime.

Along the track that I did go,
check where prints of my feet still show,
where no grass nor flower does grow.
That is where together we stood –
your mother, and I, her mate.
You will see the signs I state.
Though you'll see radiance great
do not be scared, for it is good.

SETH I'll gladly this accomplish
and fulfil your errand's wish.
Father, your heart I d'know
I will no longer delay.
I will go upon my way.
Please bless me before I go.

ADAM Go on your journey dear son
and my blessing on you take.
Complete this errand you've begun
before your return you make.

SETH Father, have no fear,
I'm off, on my way.
To God's mercy dear,
for His help I'll pray.

And then SETH *shall go to Paradise; and the* CHERUB *says:*

CHERUB How can I be of assistance
after you have come this distance?
Seth – tell me at once your mission.

SETH
Oh sweet angel, I will tell 'ee.
See, my father's old and weary
and he dun' care much more to live;
and through me his son, he prays for you
to give here and now the truth, and say
'bout the Oil of Mercy you knew
promised to him on that last day.

CHERUB
Then put your head in at the gate,
but no more than that, by your fate,
even though you'll surely be tempted.
Seth, give it a good look, long and sound.
Examine everything around.
See it all, but know it's exempted.

SETH
I'll be happy to do what you ask
and I'm thankful for your permission.
In the view beyond the gates I'll bask,
and then tell father its condition.

And SETH *looks, and he turns round, saying:*

Oh God, this is a wonderful sight!
Much woe to him who lost these fine lands,
but look, it's given me a fair fright
to see the tree dry, parched as it stands.
The state, I suppose, it's in
was caused by the gravest sin
made by my foolish father and mother.
Just like their footsteps and trail,
the tree is dried, its leaves frail.
Oh that the fruit eaten was another.

CHERUB
So Seth, you've come back I see.
Tell me what gave you most glee
to observe in Paradise.

SETH
No man's tongue on this whole earth
can ever tell all the worth
and beauty, to be precise.
It was filled with fine fruit and flowers,
music and sweet song from the bowers.
Silver bright splashed there a fountain

and from it, ran four great streams.
'Twas 'andsome, a place of dreams.
I long to stay there, staring at 'un.

Past all of this, there is a tall tree
with many branches as I did see,
but they are bare and stripped of leaves
and from the tips to the trunk
the bark was here torn and shrunk,
as if ripped away by thieves.

When to the bottom, my eyes fell
its roots I could then clearly see
thrusting down through soil to Hell,
into evil's cavity.
Yet its branches grew so high
up to Heaven lofty and bright,
despite the bark stripped and dry,
and boughs appearing full of blight.

CHERUB — Well, go and look again inside.
Make sure that everything's been eyed,
before you come back here to me.

SETH — Well, I'll gladly act as his envoy.
I'll go back, another gake enjoy,
and see what else is in the tree.

SETH *goes, looks in and returns.*

CHERUB — Did you see anything this instant?
Was there anything to make you quake?

SETH — Yes, in the tree, there is a serpent –
a foul, fearsome beast and no mistake.

CHERUB — Go again, see what you may glean.
At the tree, take another look.
There, consider what may be seen
at each worn branch, and each root's nook.

Again SETH *goes up.*

SETH Cherub, God's angel, I swear I saw
in that same tree, something to adore.
High on a branch a tiny mite,
a little baby, newly-born.
and all the boughs he did adorn,
in swaddling clothes, wrapped warm and tight.

CHERUB It was the Son of God that you saw
– as a baby – whom those branches bore.
Adam your father, He will redeem
with His pure flesh and blood, so I tell,
saving your mother, others as well,
when the world is ready for His scheme.

He will be the Oil of Mercy
which was promised to your father:
and by His death most verily,
the world will be saved forever.

SETH Blessèd is this in its accord!
What utter happiness I know,
now the whole truth has been assured.
Ah Cherub, from you I must go.

CHERUB Before you go, take these three pips
which your father Adam did eat.
When he dies, place them on his lips
where his tongue and teeth do meet.
From his cold lips you'll swiftly see
three trees spring up, quickly take root.
Of days to go, he has but three,
so promptly homewards you must shoot.

SETH Cherub, blessèd are you in this.
To meet you has been my fortune.
My father will be full of bliss,
to pass from the world so soon.

And then SETH *shall come to his father* ADAM, *and he says to him:*

Dear father, I saw for certain
in Paradise, a bright fountain,
and over its flowing, a tree.

Many branches did its form house,
and in the middle of its boughs
a swaddled child I then did see.

He is the Oil of Mercy,
which that day was promised to 'ee
by the Father of Heaven whole.
An angel, so wise in his ways
told me that you, in three full days
will finally give up your soul.

ADAM

Praise to You Lord, for doing Your stuff,
for truly my life's been long enough.
Please God take unto You my soul.
I'm happy that I've conquered now
this world's trouble, toil, and row,
and that God's will I made my goal.

Dearest son, it is pointless to hide
that which will never be hidden.
I'm brave n' weak, death comes like the tide
and my life is surely riven.
May The Father God above
bring me, Adam, to rest and peace.
Let all pray for the Lord's love
as my body and soul now cease.

And then ADAM *shall die, and* SETH *says:*

SETH

I've never felt such fear and dread
now that Adam, my father's dead.
He begat me as his line,
and tried to be a man of worth.
I'll dig a hole down in the earth.
There, he will have a cover fine,

SETH *makes a grave and* ADAM *is buried. Here* SETH *shall place three pips of the apple in* ADAM*'s mouth and* SETH *says:*

and I'll shape it long and deep.
Oh, it makes me truly weep
to bury my father this fast!

Here SETH *shall put the pips in* ADAM*'s mouth.*

But for sure, on his lips
I will put these three pips
as the good angel did forecast.

All of this is the Lord God's will.
When his grave, my father does fill
'tis necessary, with some skill
to place them in his open jaw.
The Father of Heaven, being astute
an image of Himself, did execute,
and when this Adam, picked that fateful fruit,
anger on him, the Lord did pour.

LUCIFER

Ah, Beelzebub and gents,
here's a fine turn of events.
Now gather yourselves 'round.
In spite of Adam's importance, 'tis clear
that in a moment, we will fetch him here,
and to Hell, he'll be bound.

SATAN

I'll fetch the man right now,
so he will soon learn how
to lie with us in darkness.
Beelzebub boy, give me a hand
to help this wretch join our lovely band.
You'll do us a good service.

Here the DEVILS *go down.*

BEELZEBUB

As a swift fox upon a sweet lamb,
I'll help, and Adam, into Hell ram.
The dear of 'un'll like the heat.
In spite of the bragging he has shown,
he'll sit with us upon our throne,
and some misery he will meet.

Here let SATAN *receive the soul, and he shall carry it to Hell.*

SATAN

Adam, you were proud and nice
when you were up in Paradise,
lording it up like a king

and for all those fine, happy times,
we're carrying you off for your crimes,
to where torture is the thing!

BEELZEBUB — Hail Lord, see who we've brought back –
Adam's body we did ransack.
O'er his sad soul we're dominant.
He thought he'd never end with us,
but this is it – his terminus!
Soon he'll become subservient

LUCIFER — For this, all of you I bless.
How well you do my business
anytime and anywhere.
Put he, who refuses to submit
with Abel, and then make the pair sit
in hellfire's flame and flare.

Here beginneth the story of NOAH *and the Ark, and* GOD *says:*

GOD THE FATHER — I am sorry that I made man
like me, in my ambitious plan.
For listening to a woman,
he's completely lost his place
at my right hand, to be precise.
But when the fruit did him entice
out of this joyful Paradise
the cherub quickly made him pace.

O my spirit will never live
or flourish in human physique,
and for this, the reason I give
is that their flesh is far too weak.

Faithfully, truly, I believe
there are no humans who serve me
better in this world, I perceive
than Noah and his family.

Then GOD THE FATHER *shall come to* NOAH, *and He says:*

GOD THE FATHER — Stand up Noah, my servant true.
Come, and talk with me for a bit.

I have some secrets to tell you,
some private matters to transmit.

NOAH

O my Father on high, my Lord God dear,
always blessèd are Your words and Your face.
Speak of the secrets You want me to hear
for I am willing to walk in Your grace.

GOD THE FATHER

Noah, the world is so full
now of wickedness and evil fun,
that I must stop it once and for all
and put an end to everyone.
They stink with sin so ripely
that I can't refrain any more
from a punishment shortly
on all, save you and those you bore.

Therefore, go and construct a ship.
Of wooden planks, make an ark,
with rooms stretching from bow to tip
and dwellings 'neath the seamark.
Inside and out, to stop the sea
daub thick black pitch to make it strong.
In full size the vessel shall be
a good three hundred cubits long.

It will be fifty cubits wide
and for space, make it thirty high.
Over these dimensions preside
for they will keep you warm and dry.
In a section of the aft,
make a narrow entrance door.
Here, put strong beams in the craft
that water through the hull won't pour.

NOAH

Lord, I will do as You say
and certainly, I'll make the ship.
But what is the need, I pray
to labour so, the ark equip,
when clearly You wish to kill
the whole of the human race
'cept my family, by Your will.
Why preserve us with Your grace?

GOD THE FATHER

Noah, because of your good heart
you will always have my favour.
Put your wife, and all your sons smart
and their wives on this lifesaver.
From the land, take every creature
and bring two of them with you.
Also, every bird should feature
so find two for your ark's queue.

I will bring a great flood forth
which will cover the earth's sphere.
Humans all, from south and north
for their sin, will drown in fear.
The floodwater shall not abate,
while one thread of life may survive.
Noah, from this don't deviate,
and when 'tis done, then I'll arrive.

Of each and every species,
there'll be a male and female.
Then put each creature at their ease
and inside place each snout and tail.
Stock up on every sort of food
there is, that's fit and good to eat.
Both men and beasts will be your brood.
On your fine ship there, they will meet.

NOAH

Lord, I respect Your command,
and will do all as you say.
This ark, I do understand.
I'll set to it, this very day.

Here let GOD *pass over to Heaven. Then* NOAH *shall go to his* WIFE, *and says to her:*

NOAH

Quick, hand me my axe to chop,
my auger and my hammer!
We have got to work non-stop,
so to each task, give clamour.

NOAH'S WIFE

Of course Noah! Here they are!
Dear Lord indispensable
may all the work here go far
to make us acceptable.

Then NOAH *shall go to build his ship, and he says:*

NOAH

Dear Lord, with tiredness I ache
from cutting down timbers of oak.
I'll never have a rest or break.
My limbs hurt with every stroke.
When You tell me the job is done,
that will be a marvellous day,
and though the risk of wrath I run,
Have mercy on me, Lord, I pray.

And then GOD THE FATHER *shall come to* NOAH, *and He says to him:*

GOD THE FATHER

Noah, it's time to climb aboard.
With all your kinsfolk quickly stow.
Since you have fully served your Lord,
my peace, you shall forever know.
Take a male and a female
of every animal on earth,
and of the birdies, do not fail
to take a couple in each berth,

so later they may reproduce.
Then just a week or so past this,
for forty days I will induce
rain to fall, the earth to kiss.
Every person on the land
and every other living thing
will drown beneath the watery band
except your own, and your shipping.

NOAH

O Father, blessèd as you be,
Your wishes here, I will obey.
I shall go home immediately
to tell my children what You say.

NOAH *says to his* WIFE*:*

O wife, sons, each and every daughter,
be pleased that the ark we did equip.
By the will of the loving Father
we've been provided with this strong ship.
Let us run quick before things worsen,

for the flooding of the earth is set;
and every single hapless person
even beast, bird and fowl shall drown in wet.

WIFE

Ah dear Noah, I will do
everything that you would wish.
Quick – to the ship that we view
We shouldn't swim like some poor fish!

SHEM

This to us, our dear God told,
that beasts and birds in their brood
shall be lead in, to the hold,
and Ham, bring over their food.

HAM

I've got their fodder 'ere on my back:
Let Japhet carry another load.
In the Father's name, let's onwards crack,
for I'm fearful as to how things bode.

JAPHET

I've a brave bit o'food here
a lovely mix of corn and hay –
enough food for twelve months or near,
for all these beasts who'll with us stay.

Then let all go in, men and cattle, and NOAH *says:*

NOAH

In the Father's name, Lord of all,
let's get inside the vessel's hold,
for soon the rain will start to fall
and flood the world as we've been told.
At once, the horse and cattle herd,
for the pigs and the sheep search,
but each and every blessèd bird,
they can fly up and find a perch.
Father, as we are Your work,
created from the soup and slime
help us, this task not to shirk.
To You, we pray over time.

SHEM

The very top of the ark
I'll cover with tarpaulin.
Such work and louster I mark
will stop the rain from enterin'.

HAM

In the name of the Father
we'm goin' to have a drop o' rain.
'Eave 'un over good brother.
Our ark's dryness we'n maintain.

JAPHET

Boys, see how 'tis enting down with rain.
Can anyone weather it for long?
Tidn' slowering up across the plain –
great streams of it do sheet down strong.

NOAH

By our graceful Father's decree,
we'll overcome it, despite its strength.
See how our ship floats on this sea!
May the Lord on high, preserve its length.

GOD THE FATHER

Now that everything is dead
wherein was the breath of life.
May the last droplet be shed,
and rain stop its drowning strife.
Let the floodwaters withdraw.
I command the rain, this instant.
Somewhere else, now let it pour.
Let the ark find earth emergent.

NOAH

The heavy rain's gone clean away.
The waters, they will soon abate.
We'll send a raven o'er the spray
to see if land, it can locate.

SHEM

I'll send it out across the sea,
but it well might not come back.
If it finds carrion on its spree
then it will stay, and eat its whack.

And then SHEM *shall send out a raven which returned no more.*

NOAH

To your words son, I must retreat
for the raven has not returned,
from feeding upon carrion meat.
Our hopes of finding land are spurned.
Send out the pretty, grey-eyed dove.
I can't think of a loyaller bird.

Now, by our dearest Father's love,
if there's land, it will bring word.

SHEM Father, I will release the dove.
If it returns 'twill be most grand –
transversing space, below, above.
If it's there, he will find land.

And then SHEM *shall send out the dove which shall immediately return to the ship, and be taken in.*

HAM Then I will send one out
in the dear Father's name.
Go, seek some sign of drought.
Find us some land to claim.

Here the dove comes, bringing a branch of olive in her mouth.

JAPHET It's back and carrying in its beak
a twig of olive green and new.
That I may have a closer peak,
I'll take it back inside to view.

NOAH Dear Father God, so truly great.
we're in his debt until we die.
The floodwaters, it seems abate
for top parts of the trees are dry.
Sons, from where you both do stand
another grey-eyed dove let out:
and if it finds new dry land,
it won't fly back or turnabout.

JAPHET Father, your wish I'll satisfy,
and I'll follow your command.
Sweet grey-eyed dove, now go and fly
off to some new discovered land.
And if you find a nice dry spot,
in truth and no word of a lie,
first, you take care of your own lot
and seek your food where'er you pry.

SHEM I hear not its 'coo' sound
nor see it in the air.

I'm certain it has found
dry, solid ground somewhere.

NOAH — In glorious God's good name I cry,
let us open up the hatches,
and offer thanks to God on high,
that heaven's showing sunny patches!

And let them uncover the ship, and NOAH *says:*

Worshipful Lord, You've salved our gloom.
The world has seen the waters leave.
No others have survived their doom,
excepting us, so I believe.

WIFE — Let dearest God His will make straight,
whatever 'tis in His mind's worth,
for verily His power is great
both in Heaven and here on earth.

Then GOD THE FATHER *shall come to* NOAH, *and standing in the plain says:*

GOD THE FATHER — Noah, leave the ark this instant,
and with you take your children, wife,
the birds and beasts must make it vacant.
All things that creep and have a life,
they must go forth and multiply,
yes, each and every living thing,
and think about your food supply.
Teal the land and start ploughing.

NOAH — Lord, I'll do just as You say,
and your wishes soon complete.
From the ark, we'll step away
and dry land once again meet.
May our dear God be given praise.
First, let us a fine altar make
and then a sacrifice we'll raise
to honourable God for His sake.

HAM — To make amendment for our sin,
an altar, it would be ideal.

Then, if we could some livestock win
'twould make the sacrifice some real.

JAPHET

A finer altar in the land
Ham boy, you'll never ever see,
as this one 'ere beneath my hand,
except p'haps that one at Calvary.

Here an altar is made ready, and let GOD THE FATHER *stand near it.*

NOAH

The offering will be made
from birds and many a beast.
On the altar they'll be laid
for our sweet Father's feast.

NOAH'S WIFE

A cow is what I'll install
upon the altar space.
May the Father Who made all
send us His loving grace.

SHEM

I have brought this sweet dove.
In honour of God's love,
It is my sacrifice.

SHEM'S WIFE

And now this plump pheasant
as our Father's present.
I hope He'll take a slice.

HAM

This 'andsome goose, it is my gift.
and on to my knees I'll shift
to offer up this bird.

HAM'S WIFE

God'll repay you for your deed.
This quacking drake I've brought with speed
and give for God's sweet word.

JAPHET

In honour of Lord God so great,
I dedicate this fulsome plate –
of lark and tasty partridge.

JAPHET'S WIFE

In honour to God and His word,
I'll sacrifice another bird –
this capon for his homage.

And then GOD THE FATHER *shall come to* NOAH, *and He says to him:*

GOD THE FATHER

Noah, because such love you bring,
no more will I take retribution
on the world, or give no warning,
of my vengeful persecution.
Now as I said, go forth, increase.
Fill the world once more with people.
Your own true goodness will bring peace
to fish, bird, insect, beast and cattle.

All animals that roam the land,
the fish that swim, the birds that fly,
they are your vassals, by my hand.
They are your food I verify.
But do not eat of bloody flesh,
until time brings the world to end.
Now go forth, work at it afresh.
You won't have time to rest my friend.

NOAH

Lord, what gain is there in labouring
if You wreak wrath once more on man?
With land finely tealed and growing
how could this fit into your plan.
You'll pass judgement without warning –
beast and plant will soon be dead.
Let me find some other dying
before your wrath falls on my head.

GOD THE FATHER

For all your love and for your sake,
Noah, I give you this promise.
Retribution I will never take
while you're here within my auspice.

NOAH

Excuse me Lord, but there's no token
of forgiveness in Your creed.
If by You, this word is broken,
there's little hope for us indeed.

GOD THE FATHER

I will not break in my lifespan
this covenant which is now made
between me and the race of man.
It will be lasting and not fade.

There, in the middle of the sky,
a wondrous rainbow I will place
and it, our trust will signify.
This bond is fixed, so is my grace.

A rainbow shall be the symbol
of that covenant which is made.
I will take it as my counsel
if my tolerance should fade.
If some bolts of wrath I wish to hurl,
I'll not forget this covenant
and never more the flood shall swirl:
Your tribe shall now be permanent.

And then GOD THE FATHER *goes away from him and* NOAH *says:*

NOAH

Father, whom I so regard,
all of Your wishes will be done.
I'll get on now, and work hard,
with children, wife, and everyone.

Here ABRAHAM *shall show himself, and afterwards he says:*

ABRAHAM

To the temple I will go and worship with great gusto
our dear God, as I ought.
For of all things, He is Lord.
His wisdom I move toward,
with fullest heart and thought.

Here, GOD THE FATHER *comes down.*

GOD THE FATHER

Abr'ham, come to me in haste.
There is not an hour to waste
for you to fulfil my wish.
A long journey you must make,
far from here, a trip you'll take.
My bidding you shall finish.

ABRAHAM

I am here, to do what You say.
Lord, for fear, on the judgement day,
remember my soul.
Tell me, what You would have me do.

I plea, at once, give me a clue.
It shall be my goal.

GOD THE FATHER

If you will fulfil all that I say
then you must, without any delay,
sacrifice your son Isaac this day,
whom I know you love deeply.
To you, a mountain I will reveal.
Go there, then prepare with zest and zeal.
I will never forget your ordeal.
Make this sacrifice for me.

Here GOD *goes up to Heaven.*

ABRAHAM

Dearest Lord, the sacrificial kill
shall be done, according to Your will.
The off'ring of Isaac, I'll fulfil
high upon the mountain.
Upon the altar I will bind my son
and burn him with firewood, as 'tis done.
I will not falter, nor this task shun.
Your will is my doctrine.

Here ABRAHAM *shall come to his son,* ISAAC.

'Tis necessary son, to be concise,
to make to dearest God a sacrifice,
because He is the Lord of heav'n and earth.
Fetch me a load of firewood.
Bind it up with rope and good,
and then, on your back, you can bear its girth.

ISAAC

Look, here's the firewood
bound tight as I could,
wrapped round by this cord.
Let's head off, this task begin
and travel to the mountain,
as willed by the Lord.

ABRAHAM

Both fire and sword. In each hand cup.
We're ready to go.
With one accord. We'll offer up
the sacrifice so.

ISAAC — Truly father, I have great wonder
about this task.

ABRAHAM — My dearest son, your words I'll not shun.
What do you ask?

ISAAC — Well, see here, I've got our fire
and some sticks to make a pyre,
and brought here from our hoard.
Where's the off'ring as you've learnt,
which God's grace must be burnt
in worship to our Lord?

ABRAHAM — God will send word of what must perish
in accordance with His will and wish.
I know my son, that it must be done.
Now I'll put all this hoarded wood
upon the altar as I should
to burn the sacrifice we've begun.

Here ABRAHAM *puts the firewood upon the altar.*

God's will must be done.
I tell you, my son,
that YOU are the one
offered up on the altar there.

ISAAC — If it is His will,
I bear Him no ill,
and me you must kill.
I welcome my death, this, I swear.

ABRAHAM — Lie down on the wood, as you've learnt.
Your body, it now must be burnt.
But lying there, I wish you weren't.
Oh sweet son, I am of no worth.
My heavy heart is full of dread,
but as I have already said
I can't say no to God instead,
for any person on this earth.

ISAAC — Be happy, make no fuss
since God's sweet will is thus.

I will take it as just,
to die for dear God in this way.
Beloved father, on this spot
my hands and legs, bind up the lot
and with a rope fasten a knot.
Make sure I cannot stand nor sway.

Father, bind me to the pyre.
Tight down is what I desire,
and when I feel that hot fire
I surely will not run away.
Father, may my death bring renewal.
It's sure to be painful and cruel
being burnt among all this fuel.
Please God, care for my soul today.

ABRAHAM

O Isaac my son. It can't be undone.
God will stand by you.
Our most gracious Lord. Will give your reward.
His memory is true.
Now with all my might, I'll bind you up tight,
The knot I will tie.
Then with my own sword, I'll cut your throat's cord,
watch you bleed and die.

Here GABRIEL *comes down, and shall come to* ABRAHAM, *and he holds his sword.*

GABRIEL

Listen Abr'ham to what I say.
My words speak of another way.
To listen, you'd do well.

ABRAHAM

Now who is it who speaks so strong,
who tells me what I do is wrong?
If you care, then please tell.

GABRIEL

I will inform Abraham
– an Angel out of Heaven I am,
sent to preserve Isaac, your lamb,
and your true fatherly joy.
God does know, for His part
the will of all your heart,
so withdraw from this, smart.
Truly, go and save your boy.

ABRAHAM

To God I will always yield.
Now that my son's life is sealed
my heart is most surely healed.
From you Lord, I'll never falter
In worship, Your love to keep,
'stead of Isaac on the heap
I will sacrifice this sheep.
Let it burn up on the altar.

ISAAC

The wood here ignite. Set it alight,
and I will blow.
In God, we rejoice. Hear our voice.
as we pray so.

ABRAHAM

Our offering's made, see the sheep's carcass fade.
Homewards, let's go.
Isaac my son. Our work is well done.
So come, follow.

Here MOSES *comes and speaks, and let* GOD THE FATHER *stand before him.*

MOSES

One special thing in my sight
– has given me quite a fright.
That rare bush there does ignite,
but it does not burn away.

I'll go closer, and see
if it's clearer to me
before I let it be.
'Tis strange, whatever you say.

GOD THE FATHER

Moses, please, no nearer push.
Don't move closer to the bush.
Even I will remain here.
Slip off your shoes, unhook their band
for on holy ground, you now stand.
'Tis the truth, you need not fear.

I am the true God of each forefather
– Abraham, Isaac, Jacob, all gather
and to you through history fall.

MOSES

For brightness, I can't look at Your face.

Besides Lord, I haven't got the grace
to gaze upwards to You at all.

GOD THE FATHER

In Egypt, some trouble has arisen:
my people live life as if in prison.
The Pharaoh oppresses them bit by bit,
and in toil, they cry out to be saved.
to soon be released from being enslaved.
But by themselves, they will never do it.

Moses, to Egypt you must go,
to meet the accursed Pharaoh.
Say, in fair warning – not as a whim –
that truly he must be more fair
to all of my good people there
or disaster will fall onto him.

After making this stand
then bring this escaped band
to a new promised land,
where milk and honey flows wide.
I do not want them to be
long there in such misery.
Now, can you my full plan see?
Let you, Moses, be their guide.

MOSES

Lord, they won't believe the likes of me,
nor hear what I've to say, don't You see?
I can speak to them all I like.
Tall people and short people'll say
God's told me nothin' like that today.
They will tell me to take a hike.

GOD THE FATHER

Speak to me bold. Quickly I vow.
What do you hold. In your hand now?
Say Moses, what you perceive.

MOSES

A rod of wood. This I do hold.
You're our chief good. My God, I'm told
and this I fully believe.

GOD THE FATHER

Cast the rod. Into the ground's sod.
Watch the spectacle.

Moses you will see. Full surely.
a fine miracle.

MOSES — O gracious God free. It is a serpent.
Terrible to see. I am vigilant.
I tremble on cue.

GOD THE FATHER — Take up the tail. Hold it in your hand.
Speak now and fail. Stay where you stand.
This is what to do.

MOSES — O dear Lord fit. I will take it
up as You say then.
From the serpent. Into rod bent.
It has turned again.

GOD THE FATHER — Now look after this rod by your arm,
and no one will do you any harm.
Moses, next I give you my grace.
If this grace you use,
you will never lose
to evil ones in any place.

Don't be sad at all, have no fear,
for constantly I will be near,
to offer help everywhere.
Away to Egypt tread
and do all that I've said.
My grace you'll be able to share.

MOSES — To Egypt then, by your will,
and there, your purpose fulfil,
my dear Lord God gracious and true.
I am happy, born in bliss
to offer You good service.
I'll remember what I must do.

Here GOD *ascends to Heaven.*

Here KING PHARAOH *shall walk about, and afterwards* MOSES *says:*

MOSES — You there, good sir, King Pharaoh,
to Egypt I've been sent so,

to enquire this: why do you
punish God's people so severely,
who live within Egypt, your country.
He is surprised at what you do.

PHARAOH

To what God today
must I now obey?
His voice I can easily shirk.
Talk of this God must instantly cease.
Israel's people I'll not release,
without putting them to hard work.

AARON

Moreover, dear Lord gives another vow,
that to his God, you will always allow
people to offer sacrifice somehow,
as He is very powerful.
If this deed you try to prevent –
stopping their service your intent,
His mighty anger he will vent,
and on you, he will be vengeful.

PHARAOH

Get out of here, y'scadgans!
You dare reprove me, my friends!
Here, now, in my own splendid hall!
Now these slaves will be worked twice as hard,
as long as they're in my country pard.
You party mean nothun' at all.

MOSES

Good Pharaoh, won't you even obey
God, who created all you survey,
and who created Heaven and Earth?
Trust in Him, free each slave,
or else He will not save
those whom you love, feel are of worth.

PHARAOH *comes down.*

PHARAOH

You crowd are properly mazed!
Gaa – You must think I am crazed!
In spite of this God, whom you mention,
His people shall not be spared.
By day and night, they'll be snared,
and set to work. Thas' my intention!

And mate, to top that, I offer a cure,
so no one is bold enough, or cocksure,
to offer this God sacrifice.
If someone does, by my sweet breath,
they shall be put to instant death.
As prevention, that should suffice.

AARON

In listening to God you will not start,
but go by the hardness of your heart,
which certainly, is very hard.
If you will not mend your ways,
He'll make sure punishment stays,
for how dear God, you now regard.

PHARAOH *goes up.*

PHARAOH

Get out of here mackerel-head!
Out of my sight, like I have said,
and don't stay in my court!
If I find you, I give warning,
I will kill you, before morning
with my own hands, for sport.

MOSES *walks in the plain.*

MOSES

This man won't turn to God above,
nor accept in his heart God's love,
in spite of all that we say.

AARON

We can do nothun' for him.
Certainly, things here look grim.
Disaster will come his way.

1ST MESSENGER

Hail Pharaoh, the whole world's flower.
I've learnt of great trouble, this hour.
A great sickness falls upon your land.
We cannot even begin to count
how many are dead, and their amount.
In this, Israel's God had a hand.

PHARAOH

Alas at this piece of news.
Go boy and leave me to muse.
So disaster on my country has fell.

Before you go my boy, can I quiz
you on the whereabouts of Moses?
Who is he with now? Where does he dwell?

1ST MESSENGER

He is with Israel's children,
teaching them God's law I reckon,
both during the night and the day.
I have heard he offers sacrifice
and that people follow his advice
to the same God. Thas' what they say.

Poisoned are both the water and the corn,
so many people are dead, or forlorn.
Here, our beasts die one by one.
Their God is not best-pleased I feel.
His punishment is very real,
for what you Pharaoh, have done.

PHARAOH

Alas! Alas! What should I do now?
You Counsellor, have you the know-how
of what I should do for the best?
My heart is heavy and numb
that such an evil has come,
making my country so depressed.

COUNSELLOR

If 'tis fear you want to prevent,
for a life that is more content,
Moses and Aaron must be sent
out of Egypt with their horde.
Let all the women and children
be banished, and likewise the men
so not one, will ever again
live in Egypt's fine accord.

PHARAOH

Gentle Counsellor, my thanks to you.
I'll follow your instructions through
without any hesitation.
I will go and speak with Moses.
I haven't had such fun in ages.
And I'll see Aaron's reaction.

Here PHARAOH *goes down.*

Friend Moses, I command you,
your large horde, and Aaron too,
to leave and go out of my country.
Men, women, children – 'tis clear,
shan't be able to stay here.
On return, there'll be no entry.

Let every man carry with him
all his property tight and trim,
as a bundle upon his back.
Now that Egypt's feeling is stronger,
we won't suffer you any longer,
so to another country track.

MOSES

You won't give us any peace Pharaoh.
We here, do you no harm though,
for just living in your land.
Severe will be your punishment,
for the way your anger is vent,
by the Lord of Heaven's hand.

AARON

We have to get out of this land.
No life for us in Egypt's sand,
or home for those in our band.
It seems we won't be left alone.

MOSES

O God of Heaven, on us smile.
Help us in the land of the Nile,
so we will have no treatment vile
at the hands of the Pharaoh's own.

CALEB

Here come our children,
the women, and the men;
their belongings on their backs borne.
There are a hundred thousand of them,
and each shall pass with no problem
as to God's worship, they are sworn.

JOSHUA

See here on my back. Is a fine pack.
'Tis a bundle well-borne.
God in whom we rejoice. Hear our voice.
Of danger please do warn.

MOSES — You're all precious to the Lord.
To the Red Sea, let's go forward.
Come children, women, men, come all,
to the Promised Land,
given by God's sweet hand,
for us to settle, our own call.

PHARAOH — Moses and his ragged band
have gone off, out of my land.
'Tis for the best, they'll learn.
Though I think I'll give pursuit
and slay them all on their route,
before I here return.

PHARAOH *mounts a horse.*

1ST SOLDIER — Pharaoh, you must hurry I plea
before they come to the Red Sea,
otherwise, they will be safe.

Here GABRIEL *comes down.*

I fear they are too far ahead.
They'll have reached the sea that is red.
Let's think before them we strafe.

PHARAOH — No sir. Hurry onwards each knight.
Squires too, who are here to fight.
Let's get after them, no warning.
For certain, each one I will slay.
Not one'll be spared on their way.
They'll all be dead by morning.

CALEB — Moses, to follow in your wake
from Egypt was a big mistake.
Your great plan has gone badly wrong.
By my soul, though we are free,
we'll never cross this sea.
There's no passage for our throng.

JOSHUA — Moses, Pharaoh is now close behind
with an army for us assigned.
See how his men form an evil shape.

What now? I am full of dread.
All of us'll soon be dead.
We'll never be able to escape.

MOSES

Have no doubt; in God rejoice,
for soon He will hear your voice.
Try hard to trust in His grace.
I say to you what is right:
for our passage, he will fight.
To such complaint, give no space.

GABRIEL

Moses, I come on God's behalf.
He commands thus: take up your staff
and with it, strike the sea true.
The waters then will open wide.
Your people can walk side by side
and have a safe passage through.

MOSES

Great worship to You, O gracious Lord.
You sent a message to our horde
to save us all from Pharaoh.
Whoever you are, whatever you haul,
Israel's people, I say to you all,
come forth and follow me so.

MOSES *smites the sea.*

In God's name, at this sea stretching wide,
with my staff, these waters, I'll divide.
Open up a pathway for us,
so we'n travel to the Promised Land,
ordained for us, by the good Lord's hand.
In truth, we may cross to it thus.

2ND SOLDIER

Lord Pharaoh, here's the update.
I will tell it to 'ee straight.
Moses has gone out into the sea,
striding out along his path, and goin' fur'n,
sea parting before 'un, as I discern.
It divides in two, the way I see.

A SQUIRE

All his people follow him across.
At what to do, we are at a loss.

The sea stands high on each side,
yet these two wet walls keep the water balked.
In this sanctuary, his people walked.
They'll not be drowned by the tide.

PHARAOH

I intend to follow them
and their very lives condemn.
Let me make it quite clear.
In their deaths I am compulsive.
Don't allow one of them to live
whatever happens here.

Get out! The waters join again!
The sea is falling on my men!
At this depth, we'll surely drown.
The God of Moses has done this.
We'll never reach the surface.
We're done for – my lungs'll shutdown.

A SQUIRE

Woe's me in dying! We are drowning!
We'll never escape!
What disaster! The waves come faster!
I can see death's shape...

And MOSES *and* AARON *shall come, and make themselves habitations, and* MOSES *shall say:*

MOSES

After our safe passage,
let us here, make a village,
so I can build myself a fine house.
We'll be able to live in peace
now our journey comes to cease,
and the waters, the Pharaoh did douse.

CALEB

Moses, let me an idea present:
While we are building our home,
let us make ourselves a splendid tent,
so we can shelter under its dome.

JOSHUA

Well Caleb, I've got just the tent
in all my belongings over there.
Now Moses, bless us this moment
before we start our shelter fair.

MOSES — May you have the Father's blessing.
Always be in dear God's keeping
and be forever in this peace.
May the Lord grant you His full grace,
and may you submit in your place
to Him, as your people increase.

MOSES *goes up on a mountain.*

Before me, see these three rods fine.
I've seen none finer, nor that shine
so bright, since I was born.
They are a token of the persons three
who in total, make up the Trinity.
To their form, I am drawn.

MOSES *cuts the rods.*

I think that I will cut them down,
whatever may happen,
and take them to our tent-town
for worship, I reckon.

AARON — Blessèd is each rod radiant,
since they are so fully fragrant.
From them, comes a wond'rous smell.
From all the plants of the earth,
there's not a scent of this worth.
Such a sweetness can here dwell.

MOSES — Blessèd is God of Heaven and earth
for revealing to us with reason,
these fragrant rods of such great worth,
full of virtue, every season.
So we may keep their grace,
the rods I will carefully wrap
and their fragrance encase
in fine linen, with a silk strap.

JOSHUA — I've been bitten by a snake,
and venom does its way make
around my blood, from foot to heart.
Woe's me for being born I suggest –

that I ever suck my mother's breast,
or from her womb, a course did chart.

MOSES

If such belief you've begun
that God is the only one
in whom people ought to believe,
you will recover from head to toe
through the virtue of the rods I stow,
as soon as they, your kiss receive.

JOSHUA

I believe in God and His plan,
and ask you in charity.
Moses, as you are a good man,
heal me by your pity.

MOSES

Immediately kiss each rod,
and God the Father's name assert.
Three persons, who are named one God,
will surely end all of your hurt.

JOSHUA

I'm happy to have kissed each rod
because He's prop'ly healed me.
It is right that you worship God
since He hears your voice so quickly.

CALEB

Of problems, I have a cartload!
I've been bitten by a black toad.
It got me here with its foul venom,
while I was sleeping up on the moor.
In charity, do you know any cure?
This inflammation's end would be welcome.

MOSES

Father of Heaven will hear your voice,
but Caleb, make sure that you believe.
In heaven, earth, sea and man rejoice,
and believe in what God did achieve.

CALEB

Moses, if the Lord will ease my pain,
then truly I can confirm here,
no other God will my worship gain.
Of me breaking this, have no fear.

MOSES

Now Caleb, go and kiss each fine rod,

in the name of our blessèd Lord,
and surely, by the power of God,
they will heal your pain, be assured.

CALEB

Lord and Father, You are most blessèd.
As You are God, and without sin,
my limbs are healed, as Moses said,
from the venom the toad put in.

JOSHUA

Moses, if you are a prophet,
give us some water that is fit
for all the people to drink.
If not, within our commune
many of them will die soon,
and that'd be awful I think.

MOSES

The Father of Heaven, by His grace,
will know your wish and have water sent.
Our one God, we won't need to replace.
In Him, His servants should be confident.

JOSHUA

Gaa! Your great God is worthless.
He won't be giving us drink or food.
Jove though, is a god peerless,
who offers us better servitude.

MOSES

Aaron, what advice can you give
about those who are disruptive?
Their strife is now gaining a grip,
for if they don't have any drink,
they will soon change their faith, I think,
and to other gods give worship.

AARON

Here's what I say brother:
Both of us will go and pray
to the dear Lord Father.
He has mercy, you did say.
Their thirst he will relieve,
finding water, so they'n drink,
and they won't disbelieve
what we have told them to think.

MOSES

Brother Aaron, you show great foresight.
Your advice I'll take onboard.
Above all, help me in our plight
to pray now to our Lord.
Hear the call of your people's strife.
Gracious God, who is constant,
give to them all the water of life,
so they may have refreshment

Here MOSES *prays in the mount.*

Give them no opportunity
to clamour for disunity,
and go against You, blessèd Lord.
When they no longer have a thirst,
their views of late will be reversed,
and to their gods, they'll cut the cord.

Here GOD THE FATHER *comes down.*

GOD THE FATHER

Moses and Aaron, on my behalf,
let the people see you take your staff
and go towards that rock just there.
With the staff, the rock twice brush
and there, a well-spring will gush.
Out of it will flow water fair.

Command it, before I leave,
so all, who me did condemn
and those who didn't believe
can see now how I helped them.

MOSES

Dear blessèd God, hear what I say:
You cannot worship You too much.
You always act in the best way,
and great pity comes with Your touch.
See, all of you who don't believe,
how foolish and wicked are your ways.
Worship to other gods retrieve,
and with a full heart, give one God praise.

Between us, I will bring out
water from the rough rock there.

The grace of Your work, I'll shout,
as the one God, true and fair.

And Moses *shall strike the rock with his rod, and the water shall come out. Here he strikes the flint twice and water flows.*

Caleb	Moses, I know now I am a sinner. Please, may I the Lord's ear win, and cry mercy upon God the Father, so He may forgive my sin.
God the Father	Because you did not honour my name, and some other gods praise and acclaim, on Israel's children I make a stand. Neither you, Moses, nor you Aaron shall lead these unbelievers hereon to a place of peace, to the Promised Land.
Moses	O my dear Lord, so kind of heart, who will lead them there if Aaron and I play no part? Please tell, this news share.
God the Father	Not one of you, by my hand, shall e'er reach the Promised Land, except those named Caleb and Joshua. The rest'll go no further on this trip, because only false gods they would worship, contrary to their faith and rescuer.

Here God *ascends to Heaven.*

Moses	I know it well enough now that I have no longer to live. The end has come I vow. Lord, I have no more to give. Into the ground of this grove, carefully, I will plant each rod. Woe to those who worship Jove, thereby offending dearest God.

Here Moses *plants the rods in Mount Tabor.*

In honour of God's eminence,
here I will plant these rods then,
and so live in His ordinance.
Take root and grow once again.
Dear Lord God, hear my dying voice.
Bring me to joy as reward.
To go into your hands my choice.
Receive my spirit O Lord.

And then MOSES *shall die.*

KING DAVID *shall play, and he shall parade.*

KING DAVID

After the work and talk here,
to my custom I'll adhere.
To lunch and drink I'll steer
afterwards to a little rest.
Butler, come quick without delay.
Bring me a fine wine on a tray.
Some sleep is in order today.
At this drowsiness I won't protest.

BUTLER

I'll get it milord (Don't get annoyed mind!).
'Tis in our wine hoard. The vintage I'll find.
Fit for anything – that is me in truth.
To his Lord I'll wing (all play for that youth!).

Parlez! Vous êtes seigneur of mine...
Lord, you will not taste a better wine.
From the cork, such a bouquet sprang.
There's not a finer wine in this land.
Such spices, such taste... and in your hand.
'Tis piquant, yet without a twang.

KING DAVID

My good man, you're so right.
The wine is clear and bright
by dearest God, the Father wise.
But now I'll sleep for a goodly bit.
Tiredness comes to me where I sit.
I feel heavy in my eyes.

COUNSELLOR

My Lord, go, lie down and rest,
Then all here will cover you

with rich sheets upon your chest
fit for a king to accrue.

GOD THE FATHER

Gabriel, to Jerusalem go.
On you angel, a task I bestow.
With King David, these words share:
In Arabia, on Mount Tabor,
he will find three rods, with some labour,
which Moses once planted there.

He should bring them to Jerusalem,
for there will be born in Bethlehem
a son Who shall redeem the earth.
Although one day, a cross shall be won
to kill and crucify Christ, my son
He will bring peace right from His birth.

GABRIEL

O Father, as You are full of grace,
I will do all that You wish.
Your command I'll complete apace.
Truly Lord, have no anguish.

And then GABRIEL *shall come to* KING DAVID, *he being alone, and* GABRIEL *says:*

David, to Arabia journey.
There, go to Mount Tabor, I decree.
Moses planted three rods there.
Carry them to Jerusalem with speed,
since of these three rods, we have a great need.
Bear them to us with due care.

In the future, the human race
will have important need of them.
A day will come, which they must face
when a cross is made from each stem.

Then KING DAVID *waking up, says in astonishment:*

KING DAVID

Bless the Lord God Supreme!
I have seen in my dream
an angel before me, clear as a bell.
He has commanded me to labour

to fetch the three rods from Mount Tabor.
In their virtue, our salvation does dwell.

My messenger! Fetch my charger!
Quick, make it ready to ride!
All my household, all nobles bold,
to Tabor, come at my side!

1ST MESSENGER

My Lord David, by God's day,
your noble steed gives a ready neigh.
Your tawny war-horse is in the count,
and standing in noble array,
are the hackney and the palfrey.
They are all ready for you to mount.

KING DAVID

My thanks to you messenger.
I will ride at once thither.
So that we may be led the right way,
and not in the wrong direction
let's ask God for a solution.
To the merciful Lord we all pray.

Here let KING DAVID *come down.*

In God's name, as is fit,
I will mount this trusty horse.
May His noble Spirit
guard my soul in due course.

Then KING DAVID *shall ride.*

Blessèd was the moment
when the angel gave me this news.
Ah here, in my judgement
is the mount that we should peruse.
Men, all of you dismount!
See them! The three rods count.
They grow green on this mound.
Glory I vow. To our God true.
By cutting now. The rods of virtue.
Which grow up from the ground.

COUNSELLOR These are the rods of virtue.
Anywhere, I would argue
a like fragrance you'll not meet.
Dear God is with us here.
To me it's very clear,
since their odour is so sweet.

KING DAVID Let us all celebrate this wondrous find!
Make music minstrels! Drum if you're inclined!
Let's hear the trumpets and plenty of the harp.
Psaltery, fiddle, viol and dulcimer.
Hit the kettle drum, the shawm and the zither.
Play loud organs, cymbals and recorders sharp!

To the riders.

Everyone get on your horse,
in the name of dear God the Father,
and homewards make a direct course,
where both knights and squires may gather.

BLIND MAN King David, dear lord, please help me
with your rods of virtue in some way.
for I am blind and cannot see.
Don't bear me a grudge, cure me today.

LAME MAN I'm crippled up. The pain please relieve.
Give me strength to walk straight and true,
and truly, I will always believe
that they are rods of great virtue.

DEAF MAN Your help dear king, I'd appreciate,
to a deaf man who cannot hear.
The more I will give thanks to God great
if the virtue rods cure each ear.

KING DAVID Every one of you I will cure,
if you have a faith complete and pure
in the power of the rods of virtue.
Let you be cured, each and every one,
in the name of the Father and the Son,
and the Holy ghost, Who are always true.

BLIND MAN — Father, You are the blessed Lord.
We are cured as our reward.
With no doubt, the disease has gone.
In God, worship and rejoice
that He has heard our voice.
These are rods to put praise upon.

Here let KING DAVID *alight from horseback.*

KING DAVID — Let everyone on horse alight,
but before I climb the tower's height,
tell me now, all of you in tow,
where's best for the rods to be planted,
so honour on them can be granted?
Where do you think they will best grow?

COUNSELLOR — Whilst we are considering
for security and safe-keeping,
place the rods on the grass near this bracken.
Then my lord, two guards appoint,
who'll watch them, as sentries joint.
Punish them if the rods are then stolen.

KING DAVID — With that good advice, I won't argue.
Butler and Messenger, I'd like you
to ensure the virtuous rods guarding.
Make certain mind, and past the rods pace,
so they won't move to another place,
on penalty of drawing and hanging!

For I wish to sleep awhile
before I have something to eat.
Travel, mile after mile,
has near worn me out, got me beat.

KING DAVID *goes up into his tent.*

1ST MESSENGER — Near to the rods of virtue I'll cling,
so that not a person on this earth,
or even an emperor or a king
would be bold enough to take their worth.

BUTLER — An emperor, or king of a country,

or a sultan, however great they be,
those men will steal them never.
Though their eyes may fall on this lure,
I'll keep the precious rods secure
in Jerusalem forever.

1ST MESSENGER — I reckon we should sit apart mate,
and keep a look-out while we wait.
Let's keep our eyes peeled for a starter.
If the rods, somebody does steal,
we'll make a turn on fortune's wheel,
and the king'll have our guts for garter.

BUTLER — Dun't be s'addled in your brain bonehead!
no one'll steal the rods from this bed
unless they were this huge and strong.
Relax, and sleep if you can.
Boy, I'n get you a woman
with whom, you'n do of sorts, some wrong!

Then KING DAVID, *waking from sleep, says:*

KING DAVID — Refreshed after a morning's sleep,
energy's easy to gather.
Faith in God's work, I'll always keep.
Honoured be dear Lord the Father.
Some Grace from Him we might expect.
The rods I left in the guard's sight
I will plant them with great respect
in some nearby place fair and bright.

2ND MESSENGER — Lord, here's something for you to comprehend.
A most miraculous thing had happened –
'tis hard to take into my head.
Last night, the three rods rooted in the ground
each other found, and into one rod wound,
after you left and went to bed.

KING DAVID — Lord of Heaven, I worship you here,
and pray to You, with a loving heart.
Your power'll never disappear.
In such marvels You play a full part.

KING DAVID *shall go to the rods.*

In this place, the rods, now as one, shall stay,
since they have been planted through the Lord.
Woe comes to those who don't follow His way.
Sorrow'll find them as their reward.

In honour of this wondrous tree,
a garland of silver rise
and put around its spread and spree,
so we may know its full size.

BUTLER

Lord, I have done this errand
and made a fine silver garland.
I'll put it round the tree so.
Around it, I will climb
and see, in a year's time
to what great size it will grow.

And KING DAVID *says to* BATHSHEBA, *washing a garment in the stream:*

KING DAVID

Give me some of your love
gentle damsel, pretty maid.
All other women I'd shove.
My feelings for you won't fade.
No other girl compares to your grade.
I will give you all of my tower.
then my chamber and my parlour
to be your husband and lover.
Once we're together, you won't be afraid.

BATHSHEBA

My dearly beloved lord,
you are king over all of the earth.
This would be our reward.
I know of your wishes and your worth.
I'd be with you more, no fuss
but I fear that we will be found out.
If Uriah know of us,
he would kill me without any doubt.

Let BATHSHEBA *go home with* KING DAVID.

KING DAVID

Bathsheba, sweet flower, soft breath.

World's joy. I'll do it for your sake.
Uriah shall be put to death.
Loyalty to you, I won't forsake.
To make love again, let us conspire.
Quick, come to bed with me now,
as for you I feel such desire.
You'll always be mine I vow.

BATHSHEBA

I won't refuse you all your pleas,
but Lord, grant everything please
that I have asked of you.
If Uriah hears of our game
he will certainly put me to shame.
Kill him first in the queue.

KING DAVID

My dear beloved heart,
God's made you such a flower.
Uriah's death I'll start,
using my kingly power.

Uriah, my best knight of all,
here's something to give you glee.
Take a strong army at your call
to fight a battle for me.
See, there is a powerful foe
threatening over my land.
I would go, but I can't ride though.
I feel sick when I stand.

URIAH

Sir Lord, I'll battle them so.
I'm daggin' to hit this foe
with all my strength and power.
And as I am your trusty knight,
I will not return from the fight
until I've made the foe cower.

KING DAVID

Uriah, you are an obliging knight.
I've always admired your skill and might.
That you serve me well, it is very clear.
Make sure that you lead from the front,
so you're no coward, to be blunt,
else at the back, some may think you have fear.

URIAH I swear my lord, my King so good,
by the order of my knighthood,
no man'll call me a coward.
I will be the first on the plain
to give a scat in this campaign.
Proving my prowess won't be hard.

Farewell David, my dear lord great.
No longer will I delay fate,
but bless me I pray, before I leave.

KING DAVID Uriah, my full blessing on you this day.
Take the butler and messenger for the fray.
Of their duties here, them I relieve.

URIAH Well... my wife Bathsheba must be heard
before the battle I depart.
If I went without saying a word,
she would surely break her heart.

URIAH *says to* BATHSHEBA:

Bathsheba, my pretty sweetheart,
I have to leave 'forenoon.
To a battle I must depart,
but I will be home soon.

Here URIAH *is prepared and armed.*

BATHSHEBA Do not go, on my soul.
To this war, don't walk!
My heart I can't control,
when I hear fighting talk.
I'll commit suicide
if you go dear husband.
I will not eat, I confide
if you leave this second.

URIAH Sweet Bathsheba, my faithful wife,
I must enter this war and strife.
Our sovereign lord wills it so.
Here, I can no longer stay.

Come, kiss, and your fears allay.
Pray that I return from this foe.

URIAH *kisses her and leaves. Here* URIAH *comes down.*

BATHSHEBA

O, I wish I had never been born.
While you're away I am lovelorn.
I yearn for you my sweet lord.
But then Uriah... I will pray
for you not to return this day!
That would be a fine reward!

Here GABRIEL *comes down.*

URIAH

Messenger, you are allowed
to hold up my banner proud,
like you know we'll win on the heath.
Butler, normally you're prim,
but here, make your face look grim,
like a brave knight armed to the teeth.

Here URIAH *mounts a horse.*

2ND MESSENGER

I say to you Uriah,
have no doubts, I'm no liar.
I have a heart tough as tin.
I'll perform well my role,
I tell you on my soul.
I'm confident we'll win.

And then URIAH *and the* 2ND MESSENGER *shall ride out of the play. Afterwards, the* 2ND MESSENGER *comes, and says to* KING DAVID*:*

My lord, here is the score!
I have survived the war,
and have returned home alive,
but brave Sir Uriah is slain
and your butler's life they did gain.
Alas – that they won't revive.

KING DAVID

What! Sir Uriah is dead?
Tell me, in all the bloodshed,
what sort of death Uriah had,

and how exactly he was slayed.
for he was a strong knight by trade,
a mighty soldier, a brave lad.

2ND MESSENGER

I will tell how he died, by God's thanks.
He aimed to break the enemy's ranks,
and scat the squared-up foe flying,
but a knight of theirs, had Uriah downed,
hacking to pieces our poor knight renowned,
and left him on the heath dying.

Then GABRIEL *shall come to* KING DAVID, *and ask him a question; and he says:*

GABRIEL

In this puzzle king, of your life take stock.
A man has one hundred sheep in his flock.
yet his neighbour only one.
If he did steal his neighbour's sheep,
on him what punishment would you heap?
Tell me what you would have done.

KING DAVID

On the question I won't delay.
An answer I'll soon offer.
A just and right verdict would say
that death he ought to suffer.
I know of no such crime hereat,
but I'll repeat my statement.
For stealing a man's sheep like that,
death is the right punishment.

KING DAVID *comes down.*

GABRIEL

David, this is what you've done in your life,
taking from Uriah, his only wife,
but you'll receive the same treatment.
You had, I determine
more than enough women.
For this, suffer your own judgement.

KING DAVID

Lord God, please forgive my soul!
Woe that I made sin my goal
with the body of a womanfriend.
O God, have some mercy upon me

according to Your grace and pity,
so I won't have torment in the end.

And then under the Rood-Tree, KING DAVID *begins the Psalter namely 'Blessèd is the man...'.*

KING DAVID

Good counsellor, teach me I pray
to make amends for my offence?
How can the Father, in some way
be given due recompense?

COUNSELLOR

To make amends somehow. And your sin stifle,
order to be made now. A shining temple,
and make the structure large and broad.
Then sir, go and find. Skilled masons aplenty.
Notify all mind. And tell the whole city.
Make everyone work in accord.

KING DAVID

The Lord God's blessing on you,
for this is the right thing to do.
You truly give good counsel.
Thus, according to advice,
and to atone my sin's price,
I will build this great temple.

KING DAVID *goes up.*

Messenger, and holder of the bell,
come over here, I've something to tell.
I'll explain in full my plan.

2ND MESSENGER

By God the Father, my dear lord,
serving you is enough reward.
What errand do you want ran?

KING DAVID

Go command, and give some warning
to all the masons in the city,
to come here tomorrow morning,
or be hung without any pity –
to bring mortar, bricks and a hod
to the very centre of the town,
for I wish in honour of God
to build a temple of some renown.

2ND MESSENGER — Lord, I'll get on it right away.
I'll drop everything else today.
Masons'll be my priority.
I will not delay this anymore.
Compared to war, this is a fine chore.
Farewell, I'm off around the city.

KING DAVID — Find the masons and good luck with your task.
For a better envoy, I couldn't ask.
Messenger, you're both quick and witty.
Before you go, have a drop of mead.
You'll be nimbler then, and go with speed
on my errand around the city.

Here GOD THE FATHER *comes down.*

2ND MESSENGER — Oggy Oggy Oggy Oi Oi Oi!
Oggy ! (Oi!) Oggy! (Oi!) Oggy (Oi!)
Oggy Oggy Oggy Oi Oi Oi!
O yez O yez O yez Oyez!
Here Boys, listen up the lot of 'ee.
If you want to live and be free
make sure tomorrow that you'm in town
working on the king's new project,
or else a hangin's in prospect.
He plans a temple o' some renown.

And the 2ND MESSENGER *shall come again to* KING DAVID*; and he says to him:*

Lord, in your task I've taken some pride.
All the masons have been notified.
I gave the brickies your warning.
Your wish for labour they won't shirk,
and they'll be ready to start work
on the temple in the morning.

KING DAVID — Well done messenger for your service.
Some reward I will give to you.
Have the charter rights to Trehembys,
and in addition, take Carnsew.

2ND MESSENGER — Proper job my gracious lord

for giving me these places of worth!
This gift is 'andsome reward.
Your grace is beyond people on earth.

1ST MASON — You boy, mix up the cement,
and find brick, wedges and a sledge,
and I'll get on, as I'm meant
to build the walls inside the edge.

2ND MASON — I've got the foundations laid
with hand-rammers bit by bit.
Let's make 'iss with trowel and spade,
or else boys, we'll be in for it.

KING DAVID — Let's go Counsellor my pard
and oversee the workmen's pace.
If they are not working hard
ruin will be what they'll face.

COUNSELLOR — Graceful sire, sweet lord so grand,
on the worksite you will find
the finest builders in the land.
No bodgers have we assigned.

Let GOD *be in the plain.*

GOD THE FATHER — I'm sure David, despite your endeavour
that you will not complete my house ever.
Your role as a murderer outright
has destroyed, by your disgrace
an image of My own face:
Uriah, who was your trusty knight.

KING DAVID — Then dear Lord, who is the one
who'll complete your house's construction?

GOD THE FATHER — Solomon, your dearest son
will finish my temple's erection.

Here GOD *goes up.*

KING DAVID — I must be strong and tough,

now that my end is here.
I have lived long enough.

KING DAVID *shall go to the tents.*

Lords, ladies, have no fear,
just crown soon Solomon, my dear son,
and view him as your king everyone,
as long as you live upon this earth.
And like myself, honour him most true
for God has revealed him to you.
'Tis God's will, so know Solomon's worth.

2ND MESSENGER

Lord, I'll do 'zactly what you've said,
and make Solomon king instead,
hoping nothing else'll happen here.
I know that it is God's will,
but I'd rather serve you still.
We will miss you, that much should be clear.

KING DAVID

Praise be to God and know His full worth.
He wishes me not to live on earth.
I understand his will.
Lord, into your hands whole
here, I commend my soul.
Save it from the devil!

And then KING DAVID *shall die.*

COUNSELLOR

This is terrible! I feel such dread.
now our unmatchable lord is dead.
Let us bury his body in the grave
and then we'll pray for his soul,
that pity comes from God whole,
hoping a way to His Kingdom he'll pave.

And the COUNSELLOR *shall bury him, and carry the body under some tent, and shall go to* SOLOMON*; and the* 2ND MESSENGER *says:*

2ND MESSENGER

David's son Solomon we should meet,
so he'n be put on the royal seat
as a new king upon his throne.
The crown'll be placed on his head,

as his dear father commanded,
who now lies under a gravestone.

Here SOLOMON *shall parade.*

2ND MESSENGER

Come quick Solomon, our new lord!
The king's throne waits as your reward,
as willed by your father David.
You are the chosen king for us,
so we'll crown you quick with no fuss.
That you're our king, I do not kid!

KING SOLOMON

Gladly people, I will be king.
Thanks for this honour that your bring,
and that you desire for me.
If for just one year I live,
a reward for this I'll give,
whoever may object, I decree!

Here, let SOLOMON *go down.*

2ND MESSENGER

Solomon, go into your palace.
You'll make a governor peerless,
soon Israel's king true.
Also sit on your throne,
which your father did own.
He has left it for you.

Here the 2ND MESSENGER *shall enter.*

KING SOLOMON

Sirs, many thanks for all of this.
Messenger, you are tireless.
As my body-guard, you shall dwell,
and because you have crowned me,
I will give your Lanerghy,
Bosvena and Lostwithiel.

KING SOLOMON *shall parade here, and afterwards he says:*

Messenger, my courteous envoy,
proper service from you I enjoy.
Come here, I have something to ask.

2ND MESSENGER — King Solomon, as you're a lord fair,
not for love nor money anywhere,
will I fail you in a task.

KING SOLOMON — Messenger, go into the city
and say to workmen, for their pity,
on pain of being hung by my mob,
for the masons and carpenters,
the roofers and skilled stonecutters
to come back here, and finish the job.

2ND MESSENGER — Sir lord, by Saint Gylmyn,
I'll do what you outline,
and give them enough warning.
I will notify the craftsmen
to get to the temple garden
by tomorrow morning.

Here the 2ND MESSENGER *shall come in.*

Oggy Oggy Oggy! Oi Oi Oi!
Oggy! (Oi!) Oggy! (Oi!) Oggy (Oi!)
Oggy Oggy Oggy! Oi Oi Oi!
Listen up again all of 'ee.
Put down your pasties and tea.
The king – through me – gives sufficient warning
that all the craftsmen, carpenters
masons, roofers and stonecutters
should be at the temple in thc morning.
There, they'll continue with the project,
which the late David did entreat.
Any delay is not in prospect.
He wants his father's work complete.

Let the 2ND MESSENGER *return home.*

The workers I did summon
and lord, I've given them warning.
All of your finest craftsmen
will be here tomorrow morning.

KING SOLOMON — My thanks to you for your work Griffin.
You've helped the project no end I think.

If wine or mead you can't find therein,
go to the well for a cooling drink.
Meanwhile, I'll go and have a look
how all my workmen are progressing.
I will study the plans and sketchbook
and clarify what still needs building.

1ST CARPENTER

What a beauty tree for a rafter!
He's straight-edged and just what I'm after.
Its end is ideal for the design.
From the branches and the slender stem,
I will cut some beams, plenty of them,
as well as lots of laths and corbels fine.

KING SOLOMON

God's blessings on the two of you.
You're working hard at what you do,
as far as I can see.
Make sure the walls are cemented in
and the top-course isn't too thin.
Good pointing – that's the key.

1ST MASON

Lord, I've much sweat on my brow,
but the walls are finished now.
By my faith, they're straight as a die.
I'll tell 'ee lord, no bugger
will find fault with my rigour
as a mason, else here I lie.

KING SOLOMON

Right well said, gentle comrade.
For your work, you'll be well-paid.
You do a proper job from where I stand,
and because your work's fine, tis my wish
to give you all of Budock parish,
and the Seal Rock, with all of its land.

2ND MASON

Ha! Oh many thanks my lord!
This is a fitty reward!
I can't stop grizzlin' at such a gift.
We can be our own bosses now,
and not have to lift our hat's brow.
The lord's given our district a lift.

2ND CARPENTER

Well boy, let us each carved rafter now test,

to see if on the walls they neatly rest,
so we'n fasten it altogether,
with struts and beams at the angles
and roof it over with shingles,
so it will look sweeter than heather.

1ST CARPENTER

Never mind about testing now!
Give all us a hand here somehow
to put up this geat timber,
so it can be fixed into its place.
In the middle, 'tis always the case,
you need a good strong lumber.

2ND CARPENTER

By dearest God, you'm right there boy.
The timber fits well, for our joy.
'Tis even accurate for the wall.
All o' you roofers, get in the fray
n' roof the temple without delay,
so through the rafters the rain won't fall.

KING SOLOMON

Workmen, other than finishing the roof,
of your skill at building, you've given proof.
You are truly experts of your craft.
But workers, tell me, where in our scheme
can we find the timber for the roof beam,
that is as straight as a spearshaft?

1ST CARPENTER

I'll tell the truth, according to my team.
In all the woods, there idn' a single beam
that for a roof, is of the slightest use.
Nor is there one in this country,
except I've seen one special tree,
with a silver garland, we should peruse.

KING SOLOMON

I am most reluctant, can you see,
to cut down that particular tree,
but since no other tree can be found,
in God's honour, take your axe and saw,
and make it fall down onto the floor.
Before it falls, mark it from the ground.

2ND CARPENTER

I'll measure it up good n' proper
and lord, though the tree is a whopper,

have no fear of our chopping.
We'll use rules, compass and a set square,
so it'll be the right length I swear.
Not short nor long with our axe swing.

SOLOMON *shall go home.*

1ST CARPENTER
That 'ee's well-measured tis clear.
We wun't ever improve that site.
With precision, I'll cut here.
Hold un steady with all your might.

2ND CARPENTER
You'm a pilchard-head! You proper twit!
Your measurement was so accurate,
that 'tis too short by a good cubit,
marked by your maths, on the wood hereat.

1st Carpenter
'Ave it down from its height.
We'll soon have 'un set right.
I'll put in a hiding scarf joint.
There's no need to be angry with me,
for 'tis the correct length surely.
Let us heave the wood to its point.

2ND CARPENTER
Heave it up the devil's arse!
Fitting this beam is a farce,
for 'tis now a cubit too long!
Cut 'un right in the middle of the joint,
and if 'tidn accurate to the point,
then I really dun't knaw whas' wrong.

1ST CARPENTER
We'll cut 'un right here, as you've just said.
Thas' the middle 'less I'm a bonehead.
Anyone on earth would mark 'un there!
By dear Lord God, with me saw true,
I'll cut 'un evenly in two.
This time boy 'twill be proper and square.

2ND CARPENTER
Let's just raise it up for God's sake!
Now we've made another mistake,
for 'tis a whole cubit short again!
Boy, this 'ere bit o' wood is some queer.

Let's go and tell the king of our fear,
and that measurement's proving a pain.

Here begins 1ST CARPENTER*:*

1ST CARPENTER — Cap'n, we've come here by our reckoning
to tell you of the queer things happening
with the geat beam we cut down!
When the wood's too long we'm distraught.
Another time it comes out too short.
Measuring 'un makes us frown.

KING SOLOMON — Since this wood has caused such anguish,
it is my most considered wish
that with great honour it must be placed
in the newly-built temple to lie.
On pain of you being forced to die,
make sure that with honour it is graced.

Helpful carpenters, men good and true,
go out in my woods and for a beam scan,
and find a tree that won't deceive you.
Get on with that job as soon as you can.

2ND CARPENTER — Here boy, I d'knaw where there's one
cut down, and all the shaping done.
It might even be the right length for us.

1ST CARPENTER — Well, for God's sake, let's go and get 'un,
and fetch 'un to finish what's begun,
so it can be measured with no fuss.

2ND CARPENTER — Here 'tis look! Ee'll fit in there nice.
I've already measured it twice
for the beam job in the roof.

1ST CARPENTER — Heave it up boy! Your shoulder brace!
Carry it back n' set it in place.
This time the mark, we won't goof.

2ND CARPENTER — Let's put the timber in its spot,
and hope that in there it does slot.
A good fit'll give me joy.

1ST CARPENTER

Lovely job! We couldn't find, let's be fair,
a straighter bit o' timber anywhere.
See, 'twas made for it boy.

2ND CARPENTER

There 'tis boys! The finished temple looks great,
and done well-inside the completion date.
Let us tell Cap'n Solomon, our lord.

To KING SOLOMON*:*

Greetings Solomon, on your throne s'rich.
The temple's all finished without a hitch.
We ask (ahem!) for financial reward.

KING SOLOMON

The Father's blessings upon you.
You shall have, by dear God true
a fine reward for all your effort.
Jointly share all of Bohelland Field,
and care of Penryn Wood, you will wield.
And also, for your future comfort,
I give to you both, all of Gwerder,
the places Enys, Arwennack,
then Tregenver and Kegellick.
Draw up an appropriate charter.

1ST CARPENTER

A lovely charter, our matchless lord!
We'm some pleased with all o' that.
Without doubt, this is a fine reward.
What proper gifts, by my hat!

KING SOLOMON

I will now ordain, and reveal
to the Clerk of my Privy Seal
that he's the temple's bishop, who must vow
to maintain here the canon law,
and intone service to God's awe.
Therefore, I will consecrate him right now.

The COUNSELLOR *shall be* BISHOP, *and he says:*

COUNSELLOR

Sir lord, may dear God give you His thanks
for promoting me to such high ranks.
I'm pleased that you feel I'm of worth.
You know that I will serve you faithfully,

and promote to all your servants truly
that there's no equal to you on earth.

Here the COUNSELLOR *puts on clerical dress.*

KING SOLOMON

I made my mind up long ago,
for all the loyalty you did show,
that you should have this position.
Now, as bishop, I consecrate you.
Be faithful and keep your service true.
This mitre's your acquisition!

Here KING SOLOMON *gives the mitre to the* BISHOP.

BISHOP

Since this role for me is your desire
I accept it fully Solomon sire,
in honour of the dear Lord Father.
If this, for me, is God's will and reward,
then I will hold a service to the Lord,
and in the temple, people gather.

Here the BISHOP *goes down and he shall cross over to the Temple.*

In honour of God and this temple,
I command you – all of the people
to give Him our full prayer and praise.
Afterwards, let us in this line,
here drink deep a draught of this wine,
and the comfort of our hearts raise.

And then KING SOLOMON *and the* BISHOP *shall pray, and speak low, as if saying prayers; and* MAXIMILLA *shall come into the temple, and she sits upon the log, and her clothes are set on fire by the log; and she cries out, saying:*

MAXIMILLA

Father God, by your mercy,
please improve my health for me.
Of an end to disease I dream.
Aaaaah! Help! I'm burning! What a fright!
I'm on fire, my clothes alight,
caused by me sitting on Christ's beam.

My dear Jesus Christ and Lord true,
God of Heaven, by Your virtue,

please end the heat of the flames and fire,
just as Adam and Eve, so I've dreamed
shall, by your body, soon be redeemed,
and brought to heaven with song and lyre.

BISHOP

What did you say just then, you stupid maid!?
On 'Jesus Who' do you put accolade?
There is no god called Christ on this earth.
I've read Moses' law,
and there, from what I saw,
His name's not written nor felt of worth.

Nor does it say, give another God your love,
you full wench of a maid, you evil crone,
save the dear Father of Heaven above.
Nor must you make up a god of your own.
May I be hung till I breathe no more,
if you say such blasphemy again.
Expiate what you did before
and take back your horrid words just then.

MAXIMILLA

Fool of a bishop, no, I'll not recant,
for the three rods that David once did plant
and which then turned into one,
are thorough evidence most certainly
of the three persons in the Trinity
– one in three and three in one!

Here the BISHOP *goes up to his tent.*

The Father of Heaven is one.
Another is Christ, His only son,
Who will of a Virgin be born,
and the Holy Ghost is the third.
Three and One then, as you have heard:
so One Godhead that three adorn.

BISHOP

Get out of here, you brazon hussy!
Caring for witches I'm not fussy.
Though you're proud now, you'll pay for it!
I swear I'll have you sorted out.
You boy, advise me well in this bout.
Shall she be put on the gibbet?

CROZIER BEARER

I'll be straight with you bishop sir,
and to an honest end refer.
If it's her death you want for sure,
order your men to strike her with stones.
Don't let them cease, 'till they've broke her bones,
and that she is dead upon the floor.

BISHOP

Well said, by her insolent breath!
That's a great method for her death,
You know when to say the right thing.
For all the executioners call!
Stop hurling around that silver ball,
and to my palace your way wing.

1ST EXECUTIONER

Lord, you've a task for us I bet.
Oooh see – I'm drippin' 'ere with sweat
from hurryin' over to you.
What role for us can you see?
What can us do for 'ee?
If we'n kill it, we'll kill it true.

BISHOP

Go and drag the maid, if you please
– who has been making up stories –
out of our glorious temple.
Stone her, I do not lie
until this witch shall die.
Honestly, the job's that simple!

2ND EXECUTIONER

We'll get on it then, by God's soul,
for it is our profession's role
to 'ave stones 'til our arms ache.
You maid, come out, in the devil's name!
We 'ent playin' no cat n' mouse game.
Death's the route for you to take.

3RD EXECUTIONER

Watch out! Let me her head soon split
as I scat her with this mallet:
right on the hussy, it'll thud.
Her sweet life, we will soon spoil.
She will stink like pilchard oil,
or rot like estuary mud.

4TH EXECUTIONER

I'll strike the strumpet with such a blow

that she'll never think there's a scat so,
nor a bludgeon or a whack given as hard.
I'll pound into her, under the skin,
crushing her bones and her death win,
bruising like an apple 'aved across a yard.

1ST EXECUTIONER
I'll hit her with this piece o' slate.
It'll strike like a massive weight
straight onto her stomach and breastbone here.
She will topple to the ground,
and I'll batter her around
crushing her like malt into mild beer.

MAXIMILLA
Dear Lord Jesus Christ, Your love display,
and have mercy on my soul I pray,
as I am being tortured for You.
Just for speaking of Your name,
I'm being killed by their game.
Forgive me, please help in my rescue.

2ND EXECUTIONER
Hear of 'er boys and what she d'say!
What a hussy, by Chewidden day,
naming that which dun't even exist!
With the bishop she would dare to wrastle,
trying to trick 'un at the great temple,
and the worship of one God desist.

3RD EXECUTIONER
For all the rubbish she packs,
scat her hard on the chacks,
and with stones at her limbs shower.
Baissly maid and her foul lies!
We'll make certain that she dies,
even if she calls on her God's power.

4TH EXECUTIONER
I couldn' give a fart for her God,
nor the mum and dad of the sod!
This hussy'll soon be dead...
Things 'ent looking good for you maid!
As I finish my fist's tirade,
it looks like life from you has fled.

Here MAXIMILLA *dies.*

1ST EXECUTIONER

'Ang on y'lobsterhead,
the maid's already dead!
The blaws from my fist didn't miss.
A stream o' blood runs from her heart.
Let us get to the bishop smart,
and we'n tell 'un the gist of this.

2ND EXECUTIONER

Hush your bal! We 'ent over this brawl.
Not for all of the tin in Cornwall
do I believe she's dead yet.
Before we go, let me give one last whack
with this geat granite stone n' her head crack.
That'll end her as a threat.

3RD EXECUTIONER

A'right Bishop! To you we've sped
to confirm that the maid is dead.
Any threat from her has now passed.
In spite of us saying she'll be dead,
she didn't retract what she had said,
from the first stone 'aved, to the last.

BISHOP

Never mind my stoning experts!
The maid has got her just deserts,
and had her full come-uppance!
For all your work, I'll give you land.
You can have Bosanneth and Bohelland.
Take control of them at once,
by nightfall and before stars begin.
Also, for making her comatose,
I give you the proud town of Penryn,
and all the Canonry of the Close.

4TH EXECUTIONER

Sir, a fabulous reward for our work!
What a prize Sir Bishop, for goin' berserk
with a few lumps of granite and slate.
We're always up for this kind of sport,
to serve a kind Bishop of your sort,
truly so gracious and so great.

BISHOP

Will you do me a favour Gebal?
Take the cut tree out of the temple,
and with Amalek's intervention,
go, sling it, by my rule

deep into Bethsaida pool,
as the log's a source of contention.

Here the log is carried to Bethsaida.

GEBAL

Sir, we'll carry it there this minute.
Have you got a grip for definite?
Amalek – stop acting the fool!

AMALEK

Right Gebal, no lash-up!
Let's take a good run up
and 'ave the wood into the pool.

The 3RD MESSENGER *comes to the* BISHOP

3RD MESSENGER

Sweet lord, what you are doing with this tree
is of no advantage, from what I'n see.
It brings indignity, from where I'm stood,
for my lord, the word out there, on the street
means that people go to the log to meet
since all the sick are healed by its wood.
The people are angry, and are blaming you
for dragging it out of the temple
since they feel it has a great virtue.
To it, the sick and weak still stumble.

BISHOP

That doesn't make me fret.
I know a good plan yet,
for me to carry out, by this day!
There's no bridge over Cedron water,
so let it be fixed there with mortar.
My men'll drag it there right away,
so underfoot it'll be damaged,
and by crossing, its virtue pillaged.
That should defile this 'tricky' wood.
You two! Alter the course of your haulage
and use the timber to construct a bridge
over Cedron Water, if you could!

AMALEK

Gebal, you'll face a 'anging
unless you start carrying
one end to the water of Cedron.
Get on then! I'm ready this end boy!

For sure, the Bishop'll have no joy.
With this log, his bliss'll soon be gone.

Here the log is carried back from Bethsaida and put over the water of Cedron.

GEBAL

'Tis no wonder I'm browned off with this job!
All we do here is this lump o' wood lob.
If there's even wages for this, we dunno!
From here to there, is all we face...
Phew! I'm shattered. 'Ave it in place.
My worn-out arms do ache from Fowey to Padstow.

KING SOLOMON

Good folk, you've seen demonstrated
how God the Father created
Heaven and this earth as He did wish.
After that, He created by His good grace
Adam and Eve, in an image of His face,
telling them to go forth and flourish,
and God's world always share.
He gave them all of this fine earth
to live there, and know their full worth,
and see in time, their children's birth,
who shall always live there.

May God's blessing be on all of you:
men, women and children, to be true,
but for the time being everyone,
the Creation play has come to its end.

Don't even think of staying home,
for the play of the Passion will stun.
It shows how Jesus Christ suffered for us,
so be here on time, each and every friend.
Now my beauties, let's all head home!
In the name of the Father proud
all minstrels about the Round roam,
make sweet music and pipe up loud!

From the Creation Window of St Neot's church, Cornwall, 16th Century.
The Death of Adam.

Passio Christi

The Passion of Christ

Cast in order of Appearance

** before the character indicates a role in Origo Mundi*
 # after the character indicates a role in Passio Christi

JESUS CHRIST #
PETER #
ANDREW #
* SATAN #
JOHN #
BARTHOLOMEW #
* GOD THE FATHER #
MICHAEL #
GABRIEL #
JAMES THE GREATER #
MATTHEW #
KEEPER
1ST BOY
2ND BOY
3RD BOY
4TH BOY
5TH BOY
6TH BOY
7TH BOY
BISHOP CAIAPHAS
CLOTH DEALER
TRADER
PILATE #
BLIND MAN
LAME MAN
JUDE #
SIMON THE LEPER #
JUDAS ISCARIOT
MARY MAGDALENE #
CROZIER-BEARER
PRINCE ANNAS
HEAD OF THE HOUSE
HOUSE SERVANT
JAMES THE LESSER #
SIMON
PHILIP #
1ST TORTURER #
2ND TORTURER #
THOMAS #
3RD TORTURER #
4TH TORTURER (MALCHUS) #
PORTRESS
1ST SOLDIER
1ST MESSENGER
1ST DOCTOR
2ND DOCTOR
2ND MESSENGER
2ND SOLDIER
HEROD
COUNSELLOR
GAOLER #
GAOLER'S BOY #
* LUCIFER #
* BEELZEBUB #
PILATE'S WIFE
BARABBAS
DISMAS #
JESMAS

Mary #
Veronica #
Mary, Mother of James #
Mary Salome #
The Smith
The Smith's Wife
Centurion
Longius
Joseph of Arimathea
Nicodemus

Here beginneth the Passion of our Lord Jesus Christ.

Here JESUS *stands on the Mount of the Forty Days Fast, namely in the desert between Jericho and Jerusalem.*

JESUS

One and all, my disciples, to you I say.
right now is the very time to pray,
to Him above all else – God on high,
Who sent grace to those who occupy
this earth, so at the end, you are saved.

With the angels who are bright
in Heaven your souls shall reunite
and live forever, I recite
in unending joy, and pain waived.

To preserve us from the Evil one
who craftily tempts each and everyone
always in every place to work his evil
and to good work, to cause upheaval,
as I tell you the truth.

The Devil labours hard, is so depraved
to make man condemned, enslaved
to pain, that he might not be saved.
That's fully his desire's sooth.

Though young and old are deceived
through his persuasion, let them call for mercy:
His power lessens in my prophecy.
Mercy's a shield to him who believed,
whosoever he may be – I profess.
Prayer from a full heart
protects from temptation's dart,
so his soul will have no distress.

Here, let ALL *come down from the mountain.*

JESUS

To My Father's full grace, I pray for you all
so you are saved from the Fall
and are all brought to Him and His Kingdom

to live in lasting joy and freedom
with the angels flawless.

Oh, you cannot conceive
the bliss you will achieve.
It will be endless.

PETER

Master, we worship you today!
There is wond'rous teaching in what you d'say.
Both schooled and lay, we all desire to pray,
for God's sweet mercy this day!

ANDREW

We all will pray, both young and old,
to God for mercy, through our cause now told
so we may be guarded from the Devil bold
and be saved forever. This, I behold.

JESUS

Penance is needed for his destruction shrewd
so his power can be hewed.
Through my fast of forty nights' solitude
I now have such a craving for food.

SATAN

Ha – if he do long to eat,
I knaw for sure he's a cheat
and for certain, he 'ent no God.
Anyway, I'll go and tempt him,
in case I can induce this victim
to commit gluttony with my prod.

But surely, in spite of all my power,
in my trap he's tricky to devour,
to make Him commit any sin.
He seems like a man to redeem everyone:
but for His teaching – in my view, overdone,
all shall perish and head into ruin.

Here SATAN *comes down and says to* JESUS.

Yew! You, with Your mouth abroad:
if You are the Son of God – and no fraud,
act up, command, and say
to these stones to turn into bread.

I'll know then that what You said
about Your power is not hearsay.

JESUS

People have other needs aside from bread
to make their lives whole.
Rathermore the good words read
from the Trinity's scroll.

To the DISCIPLES.

My disciples, by such action
now you can see clearly
how the Word of God feeds with satisfaction
those who accept it sincerely.

JOHN

As you have just said,
dear Master, I believe in His love
and that our souls will be fed
by the glorious words of God above.
As it is written in the scriptures,
the puffed-up devils we'll overcome,
and dreckly go to Heaven's chambers
and eternally joyful we'll become.

SATAN

Ga, if you are God from Heaven bright,
of wonders, let me have some sight?
Do one now that I can see!
Go to the Temple's pinnacle
and there perform a miracle.
That's a tricky place for 'Ee.

JESUS

Alone, I'll go unequivocal
up upon that pinnacle
indeed, to sit in peace.
Not that I am hostile.
I have, for a while,
to attend there, and matters release.

Again, SATAN *shall tempt* JESUS, *saying:*

SATAN

Your position You heighten,
but it is a precarious view.
In the scriptures it is written

that there are angels guarding You
for fear that You will be thrown down
and hurt your foot 'gainst a stone.
If You are the Son of God renown,
descend to the ground on your own.

JESUS

It is written in the scripture's text,
that you shan't tempt God – make him vexed
at all in any way;
but Lord God of Heaven worship
in your continued fellowship
in each place you stay.

JESUS *descends.*

Companions, let us go for sure
to wander upon the towering Tor
and to pray
to My dearest Father Who
with love, will guard you
from downfall's way.

ANDREW

Dear Lord, Your wishes I'll complete,
and everywhere, Your will repeat
while in this world we are alive.
With fasting and praise joyous
I'll pray to God so virtuous
and from him grace we'll soon derive.

BARTHOLOMEW

Fittingly, You should be given worship
by all of the world's citizenship,
for Your teaching is most excellent.
Forever happy will be they who do abide
in Your service, and there reside
for sadness shan't be present.

Again SATAN *shall tempt* JESUS, *saying,*

SATAN

Jesus, here's a high tor,
and a sight for eyes sore
this country, Kernow.
All of this world you'n take
if you'll listen to me, no fake

no lie, you know.
Do 'Ee see the world's joy
rich towns and cities ahoy,
great castles 'mongst lofty trees.
All of these you'n have right now,
if you'll worship me – make a vow
down low upon your knees.

JESUS

Satan, you accursed devil,
'tis written in many a text,
that in every way you will level
and worship God and His name next.
Go away, evil one,
into the wilderness of darkness:
your power will be undone
forever over the souls you possess.

SATAN

Sick as a shag I am that I went to Him,
since thrice he's beat me on a whim.
Gaa – I've come off worse
And all that great power I had,
I've lost it, he's made me mad.
Now all I can do is curse!

SATAN *retires.*

GOD THE FATHER

Rise up! My angels gather round.
Now, make yourselves bound
to serve My dearest Son
Who has three times this day
overcome the false fiend's way.
And be happy when His worship's done.

MICHAEL

O Father God, most powerful,
to Your command we are faithful.
Your work we obey.
With great honour I will observe
dear Jesus, Your only son and serve
his mother, Mary, this day.

Here let the ANGELS *descend.*

GABRIEL

Jesus Christ, joy to You I bring!

You are Heaven and Earth's King
and Lord most powerful – this, I here cry.
Praise upon Your dearest Father
for sending us – and here gather,
since Your work pleases his eye.

JESUS

To God my Father, thankful I'll ever be,
and full of mercy too,
since He's sent honourable servants to me
of great stature true.

And then sending TWO DISCIPLES *to a village to seek for an ass and foal.*

JESUS

Quickly, and without delay
disciples, two of you, this day
go into the village before us.
There, tied up by a tether
are an ass and a foal together.
Straight-away bring them to me thus.

And if anyone has any opposition,
put across your position.
You should answer there:
'The Lord has in his wisdom
a proper purpose for them.'
He'll give them up fair and square.

JAMES THE GREATER

Lord, I won't fail Your wish
I will it accomplish,
as you have asked us to.
So 'ave her on, sweet brother,
the Lord's said we'll have no bother
if we speak proper, beasts we'll accrue.

JAMES *and* MATTHEW *go for the ass and the foal.*

MATTHEW

I'll gladly go with 'ee boy,
and we'll find the foal and enjoy
bringing the donkey down from the carn.
In the name of God the Father,
they village animals let's gather.
You first – into the barn.

JAMES THE GREATER

Dear God, who made all the creatures
I hope we'n be goodly preachers,
Amen, I pray hard where I stand.
The foal's tied at that hook,
and there's the donkey look...
Get on and give us a hand.

KEEPER

Boys – now whas' on here?
Why are 'ee both acting so queer
and leading my animals away?

MATTHEW

I'll answer with no omission:
the Lord with your permission
has need of them this day.

KEEPER

With pleasure, take 'em, you men of mirth,
since He wishes this s'bold.
For Him, I hope that they are worth
a thousand pounds of pure gold.

JAMES THE GREATER

Well, 'tis true He is the Lord,
and His work here surely proves this.
He who don't worship Jesus is a fraud
and as I see it, is mindless.

And then JAMES *shall come with the ass and the foal to* JESUS *and* MATTHEW *says (Here* MATTHEW *and* JAMES *kiss* JESUS*):*

MATTHEW

Master, whom none can surpass!
See, here, I do have the ass
and here, see, the foal.
For comfort, I have spread a throw
and if 'tis time, off you go.
Climb on, if that's your goal.

JESUS

May My Father in all His splendour
be of help, a great defender
against temptations from the devil's crew,
so that when I die, for each and every soul,
in Heaven's joy you will enrol.
Oh you faithful twelve are a chosen few.

Then the HEBREW CHILDREN *come and let them bear palms and flowers towards* JESUS, *and the* 1ST BOY *says:*

1ST BOY

There's news. I do hear it said –
that to this place Jesus is led.
The Blessèd one coming here to our city.
I want to go and meet Him,
gladly see 'Un – this is my whim.
Like God, He's a man who shows some pity.

2ND BOY

Agreed, we'll go see Him,
give some respect.
Everyone's God of Mercy
is what I expect.

3RD BOY

Hebrew brothers, you'm right.
Without delay, let us proceed
and meet Godly Jesus in town
with great speed.

4TH BOY

That's it boys, make 'is, make a row
When we find olives we'll place a bough
before Him on the earth.
We'll honour Him the best we can:
All will kneel before this fine man.
We'll sing worship to His worth.

5TH BOY

Mind – if good branches I can't find,
then these, my clothes I'll unwind
and lay them beneath his feet.
I'll sing to our Saviour's face:
'Blessèd is the Son of Grace
who, in the name of God, you should meet!'

6TH BOY

Well said. I think I'll follow your aim
and strip off my best clothes the same.
Down before Him, these garments I'll cast –
I have here a 'andsome flower hoard
in honour of my sweet Lord
– to strew beneath him as he walks past.

7TH BOY

I have palm, bay, herbs,
and box branches whole.

Lord of Heaven – from all evil
guard my soul.

Now JESUS *shall mount upon the ass and foal and shall ride to the Temple, and* JESUS *says:*

JESUS

My blessing is upon all of you
for coming in My homage anew
with branches, beautiful flowers I see.
Indeed there will come a day withal
when I will repay it to you all –
for the honour that you've given me.

1ST BOY

Proper Son of David, joy to You!
To save us, I ask You true
and take us to Heaven's Kingdom!
In God's name, He who comes is blessèd
praise to Him shall be widespread!
King of Israel, mighty Lord of Wisdom!

2ND BOY

Joy to 'ee David's son I tell!
You are God's son and yet a man as well.
Please save all Your faithful servants!
You have come in the name of God
so blessèd upon earth's dank sod
that You are indeed in my observance.

3RD BOY

Jesus, You'm blessèd indeed!
Happy he is, the one who follows Your creed,
and be sure to give You faithful worship.
Only without treachery, a belief never waived
that through You we'll all be saved.
Son of God, joy to You upon your trip!

4TH BOY

So joy to You, Lord of Heaven
and earth's spinning ball!
Give me the grace to come to Your place
'mongst your angels all.

5TH BOY

To Him Who is both God and man
I give my love!
Truthfully, through you, we'll all
be saved above.

6TH BOY

Graceful Jesus who is Son
and merciful Father,
Certain joy to You,
all our prayers gather!

7TH BOY

Sweet Jesus of Nazareth town,
unhindered joy to You who came down,
and great honour to You I do give!
You are the World's Saviour
That I believe it so, no odd behaviour.
So have mercy upon me, my sins forgive.

JESUS

Now My Boys, all of you listen,
My blessing on you in unison.
Your desire shall be heard.
Requiting you with a view to judgement
for the honour at this moment
you party have given me in your word.

Then let JESUS *dismount and go into the Temple, and He says:*

JESUS

I'll dismount from these kindly creatures
and go see what this fair features
inside this grand temple.
If there is a market in God's house,
I'll drive them out, the fellows arouse,
and cast out their wares and jumble.

Here BISHOP CAIAPHAS *shall parade.*

CAIAPHAS

Tell me companions, do not clown,
who is that who's come to town
on the back of an ass with a foal
going to the Temple, in that direction?
Looks like there'll be some friction
before he dies and his bell doth toll.

Here CAIAPHAS *goes down.*

CLOTH DEALER

Aw 'ee? He's the prophet Jesus,
Who do say He's the Son of God
from Heaven's high reaches:
come from over Nazareth way,

from down Galilee they d'say
Thas' the Kingdom – 'es 'tis.

The CLOTH DEALER *shall go the Temple.* CAIAPHAS *goes up into a tent.*

JESUS

Get out you traders! Scram!
You are making a sham
of God and his Holy Church
when you erect your market eaves
and this den for foul thieves.
My House of Prayer you all besmirch.

TRADER

Say now, Jesus, You despot,
what right have You got
which You can show to all gathered here
since you're behaving all mazed
scattering our wares so we'm all dazed
and destroying the fair's cheer?

JESUS

If no apparent sign is to you bound
then if the Temple was raised to the ground
destroyed so that nothing stood,
I will raise it up by my faith's ways
before the end of three days,
up better than before in likelihood.

CLOTH DEALER

Thas' all mockery and scorn in my ears,
for it took forty-six years,
before this place was finished:
and He thinks three days is ample,
to raise it up from the rubble,
even though its structure's diminished.

Here PILATE *parades.*

PILATE

I will head over to my Temple's trove
and pray to my god Jove.
There I'll give him praise.
I believe that this fellow Jesus
has a manner most righteous.
He'll destroy this fair with such malaise.

PILATE *comes down.*

Now let PILATE *go over to the Temple of Jerusalem and the* TRADER *says to* CAIAPHAS:

TRADER

Yew! Caiaphas, haughty Bishop Sir!
Help me! Jesus, all puffed up and full of stir,
has been bedolin' and blustering in the stan'un:
and He has said to us straight
that if the Temple was in a demolished state,
in three days He'd up and raise 'un.

CAIAPHAS

The rascal speaks falsely of it!
By Saint Jove, he shall pay for it,
if He does not retract His nonsense.
Now, here comes Pilate, the Justice!
Let him deal with this artifice
when he hears of His impudence.

CAIAPHAS *comes down and meets* PILATE *on the plain.*

Then PILATE *shall come to* CAIAPHAS, *the chief priest and says:*

PILATE

Joy to you Sir Caiaphas!
But what events in the Temple alas
led by Jesus, the false vagabond!
He has destroyed all the stalls.
With great bravado He drawls
because He is of honour so fond.

CAIAPHAS

A hearty welcome to you Pilate!
Such disorder's been caused by this braggart.
He is so very arrogant
that if the Temple were demolished
'twould be rebuilt in three days instead
and truly 'twould be most extravagant.

PILATE

Good priest, He does but boast.
Everyone knows the truth
that nobody could raise it uppermost
in only three days. Old's truth!
I will examine this builder.
If He can raise a temple so grand
we all ought to worship this intruder
on both sea and land.

Here PILATE *and* CAIAPHAS *shall come to the Temple. Then let* ALL *go to the Temple, and the* BLIND MAN *says:*

BLIND MAN

Lord of all graceful behaviour
in as much as You'm a Saviour,
I pray to You charitable lad
to heal me – on these eyes take pity.
I can't gake at any in this city,
never saw anything good nor bad.

LAME MAN

I'm all proper crippled-up now
so Blessèd Lord show me how,
I may walk again by Your grace,
and I'll always believe without scorn
that You are from a virgin born,
the Son of God, our Redeemer in place.

JESUS

I will heal both of you gladly:
in nomine Patris et Filii
et Spiritus Sancti, Amen.
Transite a me mani.

BLIND MAN

O sweet Jesus, full of grace
with my eyes I do see Your face.
In truth I can see!
You are Lord of Heaven and Earth:
most truly I believe Your worth
absolutely.

LAME MAN

Lord to you I yield. For I am healed
– my disease has gone!
You are beyond all. To Thy power I fall
blessed hereupon!

1ST BOY

Son of David, joy to You forever!
You are beyond a blessèd soul!
I ask You to write my soul's endeavour,
when I'm dead, within Your roll.

2ND BOY

Joy to 'Ee, Son of David!
You'm beyond all blessèd fame!
A man, yet the Son of God gifted,
when You come in His name.

3RD BOY — Jesus, King of Israel whole,
I find Joy in Your gospel!
When dead, I'm dagging for my soul
to be fetched by an angel.

PILATE — Come Jesus, take a peek
at the children who sing Your praise.
The young I've seen often speak
in such fanciful ways.

JESUS — In the Scriptures it is written
that joy is made true
from the mouths of good children
and suckling babes anew.

PILATE *says to* CAIAPHAS:

PILATE — That doesn't mean a thing,
but Caiaphas, we can't succeed here:
all the people think Him a King
and will follow Him far and near.

CAIAPHAS — You don't know what you're talking about
prattling on throughout.
I'll tell you straight Pilate:
'Tis better for one man to die
shall we say, than the people's faith untie
or be lost to a bigot.

PILATE — Jupiter! Lord of the world,
what you say will be unfurled
to this filthy stubborn fellow.
I will catch Him out
in all that His throat will doubt.
Let none listen to the Word he lets flow.

Let PILATE *and* CAIAPHAS *retire.*

And then ALL *shall go to their tents and* SIMON THE LEPER *shall come to* JESUS, *and says to Him:*

SIMON THE LEPER — Sire, Lord, I'd like 'Ee
to eat a meal with me,

if You and Your disciples willing are;
for there's good crowst made
if You and them, I'n persuade.
'Tis in a place nearby, not far.

JESUS

I will gladly go with you,
and disciples do not argue,
over his tale.
Peter, Andrew, John – don't be slow
and Simon and Jude – let us all go
without fail.

JUDE

Proper job Lord. I'm impressed.
You do knaw whas' best
for You to get on and do.
You'm better than all the world's folk,
the origin of all things at your stroke.
You do give counsel true.

MARY MAGDALENE

I will anoint so neat
my Lord's hands and feet,
with some ointment, a brave bit,
and stream it upon His head weary,
heal him from being so leary
and salve His sore spirit.
Joy to You, Master so Sweet!

I wish to kiss Your fine feet,
if you'll let me, though I don't deserve it.
For love itself, you fret
Your feet are with tears a wet,
but I'll wipe them with this ringlet.

I wish I could break this box instead
'tis worth a fair old whack,
and I'd pour it over Your head
and Your foot's front and back.

SIMON THE LEPER

Now were He really a blessèd prophet,
surely He would knaw
that she be a sinner, the strumpet:
Wouldn't let her anoint Him with her paw.

JESUS

Simon, as I am resolved,
I have in faith right now
something to say to you who are involved:
do please hear what I vow.

SIMON THE LEPER

Master, tell me at once what ever 'tis
and quickly with no apprehension
say what in Your mind blazes:
I shan't raise any objection.

JESUS

Once upon a time in this droll
there were two men in debt.
The one creditor had two loans as his goal.
One man owed from his sweat
five hundred pence in cash,
and fifty to the other so they say.
The creditor gave both their stash
because they had nothing else to pay.

Of these two in such trepidation,
who had the bigger obligation
to love him? Now tell me.

SIMON THE LEPER

An answer soon I'll give to 'Ee.
Yes – he who's been most forgiven it'll be.
He'll love most, everywhere.

JESUS

That's a true decision, for certain, you've made.
Now Simon – do you see this maid?
Since in your place I've been housed,
you've given no orders to wash My feet.
But this woman, who you mistreat,
has my toes and ankles doused.

She wiped my tears with her hair.
You've never kissed my feet there,
and this woman has not ceased instead,
since I came into your dwelling,
to kiss my feet in manner compelling,
and she anointed me all over my head.

And surely, on account of that,
all of her sin, in concordat

shall be then absolved,
because she so loved My soul.
Your faith has made you whole.
So, go in peace, now that we're resolved.

JUDAS ISCARIOT

Have you any prior arrangement
to spill this precious ointment?
I'm sure it could have been sold
for more than three hundred pence
and then, swiftly it dispense
to the poor, whom we all love and hold.

JESUS

Judas – bear no grudge in your heart
against her who's anointing Me,
for in truth, soon my suffering will start
for I may not abide with thee.
Folk – poor as coots, you'll find
will cry upon you always:
when you yourself wish, mind,
you can make the bad into good days.

This same balm which she has anointed proud
upon me, will be for my burial shroud.
She did it through her adoration.
So whenever this gospel may be read
make sure she's revered – that it's said
and this, the truth, for her narration.

Here ALL *arise and walk and* SIMON THE LEPER *goes with* JESUS. *Words of the play go on to* CAIAPHAS.

CAIAPHAS

Clerk – fetch Annas the Prince,
so I may hear in this province
what is the best thing to do
against this traitorous brigand
who many a wife and husband
are speedily turning to.

CROZIER-BEARER

Sir, faultlessly this I'll do.
Farewell – my blessing to you!
(Well would false prophets of Nazareth
be done away with before the Sabbath).

And then the CROZIER-BEARER *shall go to* PRINCE ANNAS *and the* CROZIER-BEARER *speaks and he shall parade if he wants. Here* ANNAS *shall parade and furthermore the* CROZIER-BEARER *says:*

CROZIER-BEARER

Alright there, splendid Prince Sir!
Sir Caiaphas (to he I do refer),
sends greetings most plenteous,
and asks you to come to his abode,
to put him on the right road
over what's to be done about Jesus.

PRINCE ANNAS

I will go to him I swear,
for he is my father-in-law,
to do away with the villain there
if illegally he decides to craw.

And then PRINCE ANNAS *shall go to the* CAIAPHAS. *He goes down.*

Mighty Caiaphas, Sir Bishop. Hail!
May a thousand joys prevail.

CAIAPHAS

By Mahomet's blood! Welcome.
Come, sit and share our wisdom.

ANNAS *goes up*

A certain fellow, if He could
would convert all the city
from Mahomet, by my hood!
Harming our doctrine's integrity.

PRINCE ANNAS

Send out spies to search for Him
to see if He's in a house somewhere;
bind His foot and forelimb
and bring Him to our care.

Here JUDAS *shall come to them and he says (*PRINCE ANNAS *waits with* CAIAPHAS*):*

JUDAS ISCARIOT

Cap'n – tell me now straight
what are you willing to give me,
and I'll have, if we'n negotiate,
Christ for you to see.

CAIAPHAS

Ah sweet friend. I'll be loyal to you!
You can have anything you ask for.
No delay – come to the front of the queue.
How much to settle the score?

JUDAS ISCARIOT

Thirty pieces for success!
I won't take a penny less
for it – alright?
But I'll need some help from you
if we're to see this through.
We'll act at night.

CAIAPHAS

Judas, all that you demand
will come by your command:
I've got the money pinpointed.
Tell me, my good friend,
when shall men do the fetching you intend?
Make sure we're not disappointed.

JUDAS ISCARIOT

Just when He's at supper
I'll warn you proper.
Make sure that your men are wise
carrying swords, truncheons
and each with their lanterns
so they won't give us surprise.

CAIAPHAS

By my faith! You are a good chap:
I'll put gold in your cap
as your price.
Now we've got weapons for a tussle
and men with some muscle
we'll seize Christ.

And then JUDAS *shall come again to* JESUS *and the* APOSTLES. *Now let* JESUS *send disciples to prepare the Lord's supper.*

JESUS

Go into the town and order our
Passover meat without delay.
Peter and John, go within the hour,
so it may be ready today.

PETER

Tell us, dear Lord
where, amongst the town's ward

do You wish us to order the meat?
And I will provide it fitting,
so we may eat as permitting,
and sacrifice to the Father sweet.

JESUS

When you're in the main street
there you soon will meet
a man bearing a pitcher of water.
Wherever he goes, you go.
Into the same house also,
and say, with no quarter

to the man of the house there
that your Master asks with haste
where He may find food fair,
for Him and His disciples to taste;

and he will show you for sure
a spacious barn secure.
In it, prepare enough food
sufficient for our multitude.

JOHN

Precious Lord, we'll do this deed
and follow Your precedence.
Peter, my friend, let's go with speed
and complete our errand with diligence.

PETER

Agreed. Let us quickly speed
without further telling.
If we find such a man indeed
we'll follow him to his dwelling.

HEAD OF THE HOUSE

Dear servant, you, I compel,
to fetch me water from the well
to prepare food today
for our supper to behold,
as is the custom old
on Maundy Thursday.

SERVANT

For clear water, I'll be your fetcher:
See, I have here a pitcher
ready to fill.

And then the SERVANT *shall go and fill it.*

SERVANT

On my shoulder I'll carry 'un,
and hasten home, get the job done
with a speedy will.

JOHN

Peter, I see a brisk porter
carrying a kibble of water;
I pray to you – let's go after him.
Our Lord's word – without question
has truth in His suggestion,
for He's both God and man in His trim.

And then JOHN *shall go to the* HEAD OF THE HOUSE, *and* PETER *says to him:*

PETER

Give this house God's peace!
Our master – Jesus, sent me as mouthpiece,
as a wishful rover
to find a comfortable shed,
this night, in which we could place a spread
to eat the meat of the Passover.

HEAD OF THE HOUSE

Come with me. I'll show you Mister
a house for your Master
in which He can prepare His supper,
so roomy it could hold every mother's son –
He and all His disciples one by one –
can relax there fit and proper.

See, here's a fine outhouse
with plenty of straw on the floor:
Dun' matter what sight you arouse,
be it clerics or laymen poor.

JOHN

It is a beauty house sir.
May the Great Father of Heaven above
to that place grant transfer
to you and your wife by your love.

And then PETER *and* JOHN *shall prepare the Supper.*

PETER

John, help with vurze to kindle this fire,
but surely no more food we need to acquire

for our evening meal,
if it were all cooked-up.
Giss on – so we can sup
and the brothers' hunger heal.

JOHN

The fire's burning, 'tis goin fur'n!
When a mind to, they'll join our sojourn:
their food's ready on the skewer.
But it's brave and early yet:
The meat mustn't too brown get
or else the lamb won't be tender.

Now JESUS *arises and shall go to the Supper.*

JESUS

We should be going now,
for do you see how
Peter and John have prepared our food?
By the time those two, we greet
it will be time for us to eat.
Simon – blessings to you in plenitude!

And then JESUS *withdraws from* SIMON *and they shall come to the* DISCIPLES, *and He says (*JESUS *kisses them):*

JESUS

Grant God's peace in this place,
and My blessing be yours in such a space!
Is the Paschal Lamb ready for us
so we may go to supper now?
Peter, as I care for you
tell Me the truth with no fuss.

PETER

Dear Lord, it is all complete.
God the Father we are in receipt
of Your love and serve You alone.
And all my brothers gathered here
sit down in peace – come near,
for soon, hunger will atone.

And then ALL *sit at supper and* JESUS *says:*

JESUS

Truthfully, I'll tell you here,
I have been eager – friends dear
to eat with you tonight,

the Passover meat before I am dead,
and to torture and pain led
in tomorrow morning's light.

Now, all of you, drink the wine,
which I'll not touch 'til my Last Day's design.
I'll be unable to drink with you anymore;
until I go into My Kingdom
– you with Me and My Father's welcome
in a joy forever secure.

JOHN Lord, I hear your words fine and clear.
As long as You'm upon this sphere
we'll never suffer sadness.
You're our God and our Cap'n,
and if You'm ever undone,
we too, shall be in distress.

JESUS I'm not telling you a lie:
one of you, beneath this night's wond'rous sky
has to enemies, sold me for a fee.
There is one amongst you all
who'll betray me in Cornwall
and therefore to My death quickly send Me.

ANDREW O my blessèd Lord,
at this news You say
my mouth drops abroad
– which one of us does stray?

JUDAS And Lord – please – do tell me
if you – think – I am he,
so no other man be accused.

JESUS With us here is one we face
eating at this very place
who has already sold Me.
God's Son sent from this world we see,
as in the written decree
that many scriptures have foresworn.
I pity forever he who has Me betrayed!
A thousand times better, 'twould be, I'm afraid
if, into this world, he were not born.

JUDAS

Sweet Master, in the Father's name,
– don't tell me dreckly –
am I the one who's sold your fame
to Jews, to be slain so wrongly?

JESUS

I've already given you show,
but I will say to you again:
Judas, you've said it, you know,
and that's the truth, amen.

Here JESUS *gives the Host to the* APOSTLES.

Here – come and take this bread
for yourselves, everyone,
and all eat, so you are fed,
for Eucharist, for My body as God's son,
exactly as I said to you all;
I'll be sold and slain upon the cross:
but to you redemption will fall,
to all My people in pain and loss.

JAMES THE LESSER

Who's thought of as the greatest man
along the route that disciples chart?
He who knows should answer if he can,
however stubborn is his heart.

JAMES THE GREATER

He who's of most important rank here
will clearly be called the greatest
by a lesser man of a lower tier
as every man of the world knows, honest.

SIMON

Then brothers, come and us enthrall,
since you are considered wise,
ask for him, amongst us all
to pull down his disguise.

JESUS

Stories say that people's Kings
have always been lordly things.
It's been like that in the past,
and its them who have the power
who look at old and young with a lour.
As great people they are cast.

But you are not like them.
Here, importance is our item,
and he who has most power I shout
will be like he with the least clout,
and he who is the first to eat
shall be equal to his waiter's feet.

Answer me, men well-read!
Who is the most exalted –
he who eats, or he who's the server?

SIMON

The Eater? Is it not he?
That's the answer, it's got to be.
A lord is greater than a butler.

JESUS

But I have sat amongst you
as a servant in attendance
and you've continued in this crew
despite temptation in My presence.
And to you I have given
Heaven's Kingdom in which you may dwell,
that which My Father has riven
for My own blissful farewell,
so that in such bliss
your lips will kiss
food and drink at my table on high.
You shall sit on Judgement Day
to judge the world and its way,
each according to conduct's eye.

BARTHOLOMEW

Master, You should be blessèd
– your teaching is learnèd
for us this day and always.
No person can criticise
Your answer and words so wise.
For fine reasoning, You, I do praise.

Here JESUS *gives wine to the* APOSTLES.

JESUS

Now, all of you should drink this wine,
which stands as the clear blood of mine
shed for you soon
to make amends for everyone's sin.

You will remember me brethren,
when wine is opportune.

PHILIP — Allow us to be worthy, dear Father above,
to receive Your son's blood pure,
on this precious day of His love.
Please Lord, this kindness do assure.

Here water is got ready for washing the APOSTLES' *feet, and a towel.*

JESUS — If the water is warm at the fire,
then after supper, when you tire,
I will stream off all your feet,
and with a towel of clean linen
I'll wipe them clean I determine.
Your toes I will make so sweet.

Then JOHN THE APOSTLE *comes with warm water and a foot-bath, and* JOHN *says:*

JOHN — Lord, here's the water nice and hot,
for each man's ankles, toes... and whatnot.
Now, You'n wash their feet.

JESUS — John, pour it into this bowl
and I'll wash, where they do stroll,
so though dabbered up, they won't fret.

And meanwhile JESUS, *girt with a towel, shall begin to wash the feet of the* APOSTLES, *and when He comes to* PETER, PETER *says to Him:*

PETER — Whas on? Lord, if You my feet wash,
I'll be some ashamed, I 'ent nothun posh.
Dun't want it, no more'n a toad do want a sidepocket.

JESUS — Well, Peter, you won't know what I'm doing yet.
But you'll know it in the end, don't forget
as I am elsewhere set.

PETER — Dear of 'Ee Lord. My feet are baissly
and have never had a proper wash.
For certain, there's no need, You'm too holy
to give my ten toes a swash.

JESUS

Don't worry Peter. You don't know
exactly what I'm doing here.
But if I don't wash you so,
you won't go to Heaven I fear.

PETER

A'right Lord. Wash me
head to foot, will 'Ee?

JESUS

He who's been cleaned is fully clean
– no need for washing inbetween
except for dust which'll clean feet demean.
You are cleaned of all corruption,
but sadly, you are not all clean:
One here, offers defiling disruption
dulling your company's sheen.

JOHN

Dear Master, Heaven's Cap'n,
I am filled with scorn.
This foul man for certain
was the most wretched ever born.

JESUS

Master by you I am called,
and Lord: what you say is principled.
So, if I can wash your feet
and then wipe them dry,
wash each other's hereby.
This of you, I now entreat.

And you whom I love, beware,
for Satan is determined in his deceit
to sift your souls anywhere
like corn in the winnowing-sheet.
And you, dear Peter
many times have I prayed
that your conscience won't teeter
for fear of being killed.

PETER

Dear Lord, I am always ready
to suffer being slain with 'Ee
and holed-up in prison.

JESUS

Before this night is over
you shall be offended however

by Me – each of you a mother's son.
When the shepherd is the smitten one
the flock then undone
and all the sheep will disperse.
But I will rise again,
surely meet you then
and in Galilee all converse.

PETER

And though all will offended be,
I will never turn from 'Ee,
in spite of being slain.

JESUS

Then, here is something you should know:
three times, before the cock will crow,
you will deny me, I am certain.

PETER

If I were cruelly slain
by great affliction and pain,
I would never deny You!
In response to this dreadful threat
You're Lord with no equal, from outset.
That I'll never deny You is true.

JESUS

All of you gathered here,
say, if you needed anything
when I send you far and near
night or day, with no staff or sharing.

ANDREW

Good Lord, we needed nothing.
There wasn't a thing we did lack:
at our very need everything
was ready, not one item slack.

JESUS

Now he who carries a staff tall
away from him, his shares should fall,
and he who hasn't these
should his own cloak sell
to buy himself a sword swell.
The Gospel has truth as its bases.

Here are made ready two swords, and let PETER *bear one.*

PETER

Here's two swords as aides,

ready for my comrades.
See – they'm tough as ling.

JESUS — Blessings on you forever Peter!
Truly they are enough meeter
to control the world's wanting.

Then JUDAS ISCARIOT *shall go to the* CHIEF PRIESTS, *and he says to them:*

JUDAS ISCARIOT — Ah, hail, Sir Bishop, sitting there in
your lovely cloak!
Hail, Prince Annas, a thousand joys
you do evoke.

CAIAPHAS — By my faith, welcome Judas!
Welcome by Mahomet's creed so joyous,
a thousand greetings to you in my lovely hall!
Say if it is the time then
to send with you my armed men
to fetch the vilest knave in Cornwall.

JUDAS ISCARIOT — It is, Sir, by God's foes!
But let everyone who goes
carry a staff, or a good sword.
And you maids, with lit
lanterns, make sure you'm fit,
to get on and join our horde.

JUDAS ISCARIOT *waits in the same place.*

CAIAPHAS — Upon you, may Mahomet's blessing never be null,
since certain you are trusty and faithful,
and so steadfast in each promise.
Now my torturers, without delay
come into this delightful fray.
I need you for... a little malice.

Let the TORTURERS *have swords and staves.*

1ST TORTURER — Proper. You want us! You got us!
Now, for calling thus
– something dreadful is it – in your utterance?
Well, tell me secretly

what you want us to do for 'ee
and will do 'un at your convenience.

CAIAPHAS

Yeees. Each man ready for the ruckus,
go along with my friend Judas
to fetch the laughing... pisky
pretending to be God's son:
He'll have woe rather than fun
when He comes into my sight so risky.

PRINCE ANNAS

Say there, my comrade wise,
how shall we be able to recognise
this... pisky... amongst these men?
I fear they will resemble Him
indeed making these men's job grim
and we'll not recognise the prophet then.

JUDAS ISCARIOT

You'll see Him with my signal:
I'll salute Him – thas' plain and simple,
when I reach His form,
then straight-away I'll kiss Him.
That's Him, in the middle of the swim!
Get hold of Him in the swarm.

JUDAS, *standing, waits with* PRINCE ANNAS.

CAIAPHAS

And you, Annas, my dear son-in-law,
show that you are a prince excelsior
for undoing beliefs Christian.
Bring Him right here to my place
and let Him say straight to my face
that He is the Jews' Chieftain.

PRINCE ANNAS

Sir, I am sure I can;
for I have a cunning plan
for capturing the King:
As soon as He receives the kiss
He shall be caught without miss,
for his false fiddling.

CAIAPHAS

Well... hasten then, son-in-law,
and mind the rogue does not escape.

Violence, you know that I deplore,
but a little's appropriate in this jape.

2ND TORTURER

We'm way to go your grace,
by Mahomet, lord of all the place,
in spite of this mazed miracle man.
A'right, let's get on boy.
I'll scat at 'Un, give our lord some joy,
according to his plan.

JUDAS ISCARIOT

'Tis best for you to be cautious.
This boy's very crafty, proper treacherous,
and knows many a trick, mind.
Slink up to 'Un, feeling your way.
If He sees you, we've lost the day,
for He'll hide if He's inclined.

PRINCE ANNAS

That's good advice, for sure.
As soon as you kiss His cheek pure
grab Him by the throat,
and grip so hard,
that He'll have no guard.
In His feeble efforts we'll gloat.

Then JESUS *shall go to the Mount of Olives to pray, and shall take with Him* PETER, JAMES THE GREATER *and* JOHN.

JESUS

Disciples, sit down by this stile
and rest here awhile
whilst I am praying:
all except James and Peter,
and John, three, who for their meeter
must with me go on walking.

Here PETER, JAMES THE GREATER *and* JOHN *go away with* JESUS.

THOMAS

No problem Lord. As you want it,
as you are Lord over everything.
Master, I'll always do my bit,
as long as I have zest and zing.

JESUS

Come with me, you three,
for even in my soul you see

I'm saddened over my end.
Assuredly, work for me here
and watch me with no fear,
my beloved ones, you each a friend.

JAMES THE GREATER — My heart now feels ill
at what You do say:
If agony enters Your will,
I'll be dead with you, 'afore day.

Then JESUS *withdraws from them and He shall pray. And they shall sleep.*

JESUS — My sweet Father, full of graces true,
all things can be made possible by You:
I pray to You, as Your son,
that if it is possible,
prevent my death probable
so no slaying will be done;
if you can this instil
in our future's clime,
Lord, then Your own will
is surely followed every time.

JESUS *waits there at prayer.*

GOD THE FATHER — Gentle messenger, to the earth descend down.
And as firmly as you might,
direct Jesus, My Son renown,
Who prays to Me this night.

GABRIEL — Father, You are blessèd,
To Him, my wings will be led,
as He is my Lord dear.

Then GABRIEL *descends.*

And GABRIEL *says to* JESUS *praying:*

Worship and joy to You!
Your dear Father true,
says 'be of good cheer'.

JESUS — I adore My Father sweet,

for comfort he does greet
me readily in His way.

And then JESUS *shall come to the* THREE DISCIPLES *and He shall find them sleeping and He says to them:*

Peter, couldn't you for one spell
just have watched Me well
before My severe agony this day?
Watch with Me again awhile
pray, to My Father be now servile
that you won't enter into temptation:
the spirit is so ready,
but the body's unsteady
from sickness and resignation.

PETER

O, dear Lord, we will,
if we'en do it still.
I know we are amiss.

JOHN

Lord, our eyes sore and hurt
with watching we assert.
Though to watch was our office.

And again JESUS *withdraws from them into the garden to pray, and they shall sleep.*

JESUS

My father, if there's truth in what You say
that death won't turn away,
and that I must suffer it,
then Your wish will be done;
for Scriptures tell the fate of your son
and they are truly writ.

And again JESUS *shall come to them and shall find them sleeping, and He says to them:*

JESUS

Awake my friends once more,
and together pray, and implore
that you will not enter into temptation.
Judas does not sleep a moment,
but hastens this instant
to take me to the Jews' fabrication.

Here PRINCE ANNAS, JUDAS *and the* TORTURERS *shall come walking onto stage.*

JUDAS ISCARIOT	All of you remember the sign which you should know fine my beauties: The one that I do kiss, that's He – the one s'worthless. Dun't give 'un any ease.

Again, JESUS *shall pray a third time, saying:*

JESUS	And yet, if it is in your possession dear Father, give concession that death will not visit Me. But if it can't be otherwise, Your will I'll vocalise. This fulfilment is My plea.

And then JESUS *shall come to them a third time saying:*

My good friends, now you should sleep,
and together your resting keep.
I have prayed to My Father enough.
The time is drawing near
when I'll be delivered as mutineer
and given my Jewish rebuff.

And again JUDAS *shall come and shall meet them:*

Here we are surplus. Let's go you three
away from this place,
for false Judas, who sold Me
is near our space.

Here PETER, JAMES *and* JOHN *go away with* JESUS*:*

JUDAS ISCARIOT	Ah, Master renowned. In every Hundred joy to 'Ee.

And he kisses JESUS.

JESUS	Friend, this is impromptu. Why are you kissing me? You've surely come to kiss me, to sell me for the traitors' glee.

Here JESUS *says to* PRINCE ANNAS *and the* OTHER JEWS*:*

A kiss on the cheek. Whom do you seek,
all you Jews?

PRINCE ANNAS

Jesus, my pard, – Nazareth's trump card,
He with the Christian views.

Then they shall retire backwards and fall upon the ground, and again JESUS *shall ask them, saying:*

JESUS

Look at Me, now, directly:
I am Jesus of Nazareth.
So say again – you eager men
whom do you seek so?

PRINCE ANNAS

Jesus, by my breath, he of Nazareth:
We'll not let Him go!

JESUS

I have told you straight
that I am Jesus whom you hate:
And if you're looking for Me,
having hunted your kill
by My Father's will
let My people walk free.

PRINCE ANNAS

All you crowd, bad luck to 'ee!
Now – catch hold of this rogue you see
who says He is the Son of God.
Let's take him back to Caiaphas the Bishop,
to see now what will develop.
Worst luck to this wretched clod.

3RD TORTURER

I'll hold 'Un nice an' tight,
I'll grip Him with my hands' might
so 'Ee wun't escape.

And they shall seize JESUS.

Let's get over to the Bishop's place:
Dun't dally with the boy s'base.
Take 'Un by the neck's nape.

PETER — Lord, tell me straight-away
if, in this affray,
You and Your Father might wish,
me to scat with this sword
those who hold you Lord:
the evil villains so oafish!

Then PETER *cuts off the ear of a torturer by the name of* MALCHUS.

4TH TORTURER — Aargh!! Boys! Help! Help!
He's cut the ear off me scalp!
Cleaved 'un right off me head
quicker than duck's muck.
This disciple'll come unstuck
and pay for this in sorrow and dread!

Here JESUS *shall take the ear of* MALCHUS *and shall heal him.*

JESUS — Hold on. Stop this tomfoolery!
I'll repair the misery
of your cut ear.

The ear of MALCHUS *is healed.*

In the name of My blessèd Father,
let this ear and head bind together,
so they may adhere.

And Peter, your sharp sword return
to its scabbard, and there, the blade intern.
It is written in the Bible,
that 'He who lives by the sword
will perish by its accord,'
and its word is good counsel.

In my prayer – do you believe
that My Father won't relieve
Me and send from Heaven's gate
in full succession, twelve legions
of angels to this land's regions?
He won't refuse Me in this state.

In many places, one reads thus:
that it is requisite,
for the Son of Man to suffer the world's fuss
and enter His bliss exquisite.

JESUS *says to the* JEWS.

With weapons you come in glee,
to slash and stab the life from me,
as if right now I were
the biggest, boldest thief around.
But when I taught at the church renowned
no one did I then bestir.

Then all HIS DISCIPLES *shall take flight except* JOHN, *wrapped in fine linen, and* PETER *follows Him from afar.*

1ST TORTURER

Rascal's son, through and through,
we'm glad to have 'Ee in our crew.
Bind his arms some tight
so 'Ee can't escape and we'n relax.
Give it to 'Un on the chacks:
Let dread sin no one fright.

Then the 2ND TORTURER *shall lay hold on* JOHN THE APOSTLE, *and he, leaving the linen cloth, shall flee naked.*

2ND TORTURER

Gah! You youngsters, by my creed,
are an irresponsible breed.
Better fit if you left this fellow.
Leave Your clothes as a deposit:
I'll have it for me pay and closet
and You'n hang on the gallow.

3RD TORTURER

However tough You think Your arms be,
I'll tie them hard so You wun't break free.
I'll bind You like a common thief,
and take You back to Caiaphas' lair,
in spite of Your mean stare.
If You were wise, You wun't have grief.

4TH TORTURER

You lead this rascally drip,
and I'll drive 'Un with me whip

to give 'Un a bit for a start.
Get on! You vile disgrace!
Here – I believe by God's face
He's let fly a loud fart!

And then they shall come to CAIAPHAS *with* JESUS, *and shall say to Him:*

PRINCE ANNAS

Bishop Caiaphas, hail, O hail!
This fellow here, we did nail
and brought Him to your hall!
To Judas, we owe some debt
for he led us from outset
right up to our windfall.

Here let THOMAS *be present and ready to act:*

CAIAPHAS

You're so welcome to this house!
The coals do not douse,
for the weather is so very cold:
I will examine Him, His people,
what they teach in His 'chapel'.
And why such a toehold?

Here BISHOP CAIAPHAS *goes down.*

1ST TORTURER

Certainly dear Lord and sire
'twould be proper to have a fire,
for the wind has a bravish hold:
and I'm cold as a quilkin
with feet chillier than the moor past Bodmin,
and teeth chattering in the cold.

Here a fire is got ready in the hall.

2ND TORTURER

Fetch us some furze boy,
and I'll blow hard for some joy
so soon the fire'll catch ablaze:
In truth the chill near has me beat
– I can't even feel me feet:
I'm numb leastways and longways.

Here let the damsel that kept the door be ready to play. Here THOMAS *shall bring* PETER *in and* THOMAS *says to the* PORTRESS*:*

THOMAS

In your kindness somehow,
I ask you here, to allow
me to bring my friend inside;
and if he can come in, I'll
make it worth your while.
To you, this, I confide.

PORTRESS

Friend, I'll do more than that.
I'm no autocrat:
Come forward in Jove's name!

The PORTRESS *says to* PETER*:*

Are you a good friend then
– one of this Man's men?
I ask you to disclaim.

Here PETER *shall for the first time deny Christ, and* PETER *says:*

PETER

I'll answer you right away:
I was never part of His brace,
nor in faith His protégé!
Never seen his gait nor face.

3RD TORTURER

I've got fuel enough.
Blow hard all you crowd,
or fan like the wings of a chough,
with your hems up good and proud.

Here CAIAPHAS *says to* JESUS*:*

CAIAPHAS

Tell me hereupon:
where have Your disciples gone?
Why have they not come in the door?
And right now, give me one argument
from Your teaching's sentiment,
so I can learn from Your lore.

JESUS

I have openly always taught
My doctrine to the Jews:
into quietness, I never bought
or in a whisper gave my news,
but in the synagogue

I loudly told many mother's sons;
and in the temples had dialogue,
with my disciples, the listening ones.

But do not ask this now of me
speak to those who heard the word free,
for they can tell you
everything I said to them.
Therefore don't ask for each item
in secret for their value.

4TH TORTURER

Way to go there wretch!
The bishop's patience You'll stretch!
Such answers will gain You abuse,
and because You're rude and that,
I'll give 'Ee a good ole scat:
Take that! God give 'Ee the noose.

And then the 4TH TORTURER *shall give* JESUS *a slap in the face.*

JESUS

If I've said something falsely,
you've witnessed me lately;
but if I speak so uncouth,
why do you slap Me so?
The maltreatment you show
is for telling the truth.

Here the TORTURERS *go away from Him. Here the* PORTRESS *that kept the door taunts* PETER *and says:*

PORTRESS

Upon my soul, this man
was part of Jesus' clan.
He lived with Him!

Here let the CLOTH DEALER *and the* TRADER *be ready to play.*

To deny it is useless for 'Ee,
for the man's from Galilee.
I know His trim.

PETER

Maid, dun't be s'mazed,
for I have never served
this man – upon my soul!

You do me misplace.
I wun' recognise His face
'mongst Him and His patrol.

CAIAPHAS

Tell me who You cherish,
why are You so foolish
sweet, sweet Jesus?
By Jupiter, I do apologise
but Your words retract, if You're wise
to make me joyous.

JESUS

I've done nothing foolish,
and I always let you flourish,
and helped with your every need;
but to send men of this sort
– with weapons – as my escort,
was not your best deed.

CAIAPHAS

I stand by all of this,
and I'll find many a witness
about Your unlawful speech.

CAIAPHAS *speaks to the* CLOTH DEALER.

Now speak up each trader
– what was said by this invader?
Fair men it's time for you to preach.

CLOTH DEALER

Definitely, I heard Him,
and His crazed whim:
Better than before – he said in the stan'un
– thas' the words he said to us straight
that if the temple was in a demolished state,
in three days, He'd up and raise 'un.

TRADER

And I am witness to that too
that if the temple became a lash-up
in three days – thas' true,
He'd raise 'un back up.

CAIAPHAS

You cannot say a thing
against what trusty witnesses say.
The truth begins to sting

as You stay silent and obey.
I dare you, with all my power,
and God's true name defy,
for You to tell me, this hour
if You're the Son of God on high.

JESUS

It is, as you say it is.
But in addition, I'll tell you this:
Very soon you will see
the Son of God sitting
at the right hand, truly fitting
by the Father God, next to He;
and He will come to you on Judgement Day
and you will certainly see Him
in the sky, judging your way
and the world's people, both poor and prim.

And then the BISHOP CAIAPHAS *shall rend his garments in anger and says (He goes up into a tent and* PRINCE ANNAS *with him):*

CAIAPHAS

The imposter's made a jig of us.
There's no need now
for you all to testify against the tuss.
Your heard the devil's vow.

CAIAPHAS *speaks to* PRINCE ANNAS*:*

What's the best way to deal
with this slippery eel?
Pray, lend me some bliss.

PRINCE ANNAS

In this world, for my breath
he deserves to suffer death,
if there is justice.

CAIAPHAS

By my faith, you are right!
He'll pay for it with my might,
I'll be revenged for His speech untrue.
Here boys, in the devil's name,
let us play a little game!
Come along, each of you.

1ST TORTURER

Right on! Time for our 'hinds to haul!

Tell everyone, tell one and all.
Whatever 'tis proud Bishop,
remember we'm your men:
for we'll do whatever's needed when,
and we'm ready to wallop.

CAIAPHAS

Torturers, kind fellows now.
Without blowing a horn or making a row
fetch Jesus to us:
And give His ears a scat
using your fist as a bat.
Slap Him one thus.

Let the TORTURERS *have whips. Here a garment is put ready for the blindfolding of* JESUS.

1ST TORTURER

Sir Caiaphas, what a great task.
I'll do what you ask
with the greatest of pleasure!
Well met, little pisky!
I've some scat for 'Ee
on Your chacks for good measure.

2ND TORTURER

Boys! Boys! Hang on:
With a cloth I'll cover this woebegone
and someone hit His face,
then let Him guess
whose punch brought success
'gainst us boys s'base.

Here JESUS *is blindfolded.*

3RD TORTURER

In faith – that sounds a good game!
I'll blindfold 'Ee who you name.
Now let one of you strike
so that He may now see
if He's the Son of God of mercy,
when we scat the tyke.

4TH TORTURER

Ha – you rogue, have that!

Here the 4TH TORTURER *gives* JESUS *a slap.*

Say now, you little sprat,
if You're Christ, Son of God
and guess who scat You:
and if Your guess is true,
I'll blindfold that sod!

1ST TORTURER — Though he wun't guess the name,
let's carry on with the game,
and give Him a good 'ole scat
with your fists and your whip.
Give his ears some gyp
for the lying stories of the brat.

2ND TORTURER — I'll strip His kit
and to insult 'Un, I'll spit
upon His eyes and face.

Here let the 2ND TORTURER *spit in* JESUS' *face.*

And boys, this lad maltreat,
then your fun repeat
and put Him in His place.

3RD TORTURER — Now, at 'Un I'll give a gob
– in His eyes some spit lob
and it'll drip down His face.
He thoroughly deserves this –
for cheeking Caiaphas' office.
Some harm, He'n now embrace.

4TH TORTURER — And this 'ere chap
followed Jesus' claptrap –
and dun't try to deny it,
for what You do say s'free
proves you'n from back Galilee.
They all d'knaw the varlet.

PETER — No, I didn't serve the man
and knew nothing of His plan
nor His face or form.
I ask of you to understand
that if I ever followed his band
on me, a curse'd be the norm.

And then JESUS *shall look back on* PETER, *and* PETER *says:*

Oh woe! My misery does multiply
that so shamefully I should deny
my Lord, who so loved me!
He forewarned me of this,
but I was proud and mindless
and swore different upon my knee.

My grief cannot run deeper.
Now I feel cheaper
than any person in the world.
I feel sick in my heart:
All joy does me depart!
This woe won't be unfurled.

I shan't dare to speak a word
to all my brothers, who've heard
by now, of my shame.
And alas – what course is best
to bring this matter to rest?
What woe upon my name!

Think of me still sweet Jesus,
I, who stand here, s'callous,
and forgive me my trespass!
My folly fills me with disgust:
But in Your mercy I will trust.
Remorse is now my purpose.

My trespass was so terrible
when I denied God's parable,
and all His work as well.
Alas – that it went that way!
With a full heart, to you, I pray
to forgive me, my fear dispel.

CAIAPHAS

Annas, what plan is best
now for our guest
– this snivelling traitor?

PRINCE ANNAS

I'll tell you right away:

Let's examine Him – He'll obey
– the vile agitator.

CAIAPHAS
By my faith, that's a good idea!
To this, I'll be an overseer.
Let's go – there'll be none faster.
I have a servant – a crozier-bearer –
of dogma, he's a good declarer.
At debating he's a master.

CROZIER-BEARER
I'll ask Him – the little sod:
if He's the Son of God
or the devil's boy. I don't give a fart!
Whoever He is – the vagabond,
I'll confuse Him in a second.
So, He thinks He's smart...

They come down

CAIAPHAS
Bring the... ahem... prophet inside,
for we're ready to preside
over His examination again.
If He doesn't truthfully speak,
I swear we'll not be weak
so before His death, He'll pay with pain.

1ST TORTURER
Sirs, I'll fetch the prophet.
You deserve all You get!
Woe for Your misfortune boy.
We've tried with the sneak,
to make 'Un speak.
He wun't, despite many a ploy.

And then they shall lead JESUS *into a corner, that is, in the plain between them.*

CAIAPHAS
Now tell us nice and clear,
without evasion, and be brief.
if You are Christ, David's son dear,
and over all the prophets, now chief?

JESUS
Though I do not lie,
not one of you believes me.

If I question why,
an answer is never given free.
But soon you will behold
the Son of God, surely sat
at the Father's fold
in eternal bliss thereat.

CAIAPHAS

Well, obviously then, over us... You tower
You really must be the Son
of God of great power,
full of mercy and pity – You're the one.

JESUS

You have said that I am
and it is no lie
You shall find it no sham;
Judgement Day will the fact simplify.

CAIAPHAS

Why should we bother to wait,
or find another reference,
since You acknowledge it... mate?
See, He speaks his own sentence.

PRINCE ANNAS

For His irreverence,
to Pilate take Him, and explain,
so He can have His sentence,
then before the Sabbath, be slain.

JUDAS ISCARIOT

Oh, I was perverse, 'tis true
when I the lifeblood of God sold.
Therefore the best thing to do
is to give up this sinful fold.

CAIAPHAS

What's that to us,
since you were willing to sell Him?
You know the truth Judas,
no one forced you to be a victim.

JUDAS ISCARIOT

You know your words aren't funny.
Every penny of this money
I'll throw upon the ground,

Here JUDAS *shall throw the money on the ground.*

and now go and hang myself;
since in selling Christ for wealth
in utter sin I now abound.

A tree is made ready, and a halter for hanging JUDAS.

Oh yes, so great has been my sin
in making Christ my bargain
to be slain by these Jews.
There's no mercy, I am depraved.
No way for me to be saved.
In faith, I have no excuse.

I'll make a running knot,
so this loop may garrotte
the wind from my throat,
and so swiftly strangle me.
Suicide's the only way to flee.
A hideous end for a turncoat!

Here JUDAS *hangs himself.*

SATAN

Ha, I'll have you for my mission.
Come to us in perdition
for strangling yourself in sin.
Your soul, ya' traitor shoddy,
will not escape your body
for kissing Christ's chin.

CAIAPHAS

This money, I'll look after
and in glee and laughter
keep every penny for the present.
It shouldn't be given to the treasury
because, by its mastery
death to a noble man was meant.

PRINCE ANNAS

With the money in your hand
we should buy some cheap waste-land
as a Christian burial-place,
so they won't stink out
or injure, or kill those devout
of the great Jewish race.

CAIAPHAS

Oh, most excellent advice.
I'll find them somewhere nice.
We'll do it right away.

CROZIER-BEARER

I own some nice waste-ground.
I'll sell it to you for thirty pound,
if you complete the deal today.

CAIAPHAS

Oh, I'll buy it from you.
Here's cash of the value
to pay upfront.

CAIAPHAS *shows the purse with the money.*

In sight of many a dignitary
I'll pay you for this territory
(Do it now, to be blunt!).

CROZIER-BEARER

Gladly I accept this sum
and consent that this land'll become
forever a Christian burial place.
I'll sell it so that after death's shout,
they won't stink the place out,
or reek in a Jewish place.

Then CAIAPHAS *pays him the money, and afterwards he shall go over with* JESUS *to* PILATE.

CAIAPHAS

Sir Pilate, joy to you.
Here's Jesus for you to view.
We've bound Him, see.
I found him offering perversions
to our people on many occasions.
With their faith, He does disagree.

PRINCE ANNAS

I've heard that He does forbid
any accounts so splendid
of tributes to Caesar,
and boasts, the roughshod,
that He is the Son of God.
There's none equal to this loser.

Here the TORTURERS *shall go home.*

And let them all go up except JESUS *who shall stand before* PILATE*'s tent.*

PILATE

Well... welcome, Caiaphas so true,
you, your company and crew.
Yes... welcome to my hall!

PILATE *speaks to* JESUS*:*

Now, tell all, and me enthuse
if You are the King of the Jews.
Speak out, and us enthrall.

JESUS

Pilate, you have said
the right thing there:
To the truth you've been lead
by me, on this day fair.

PILATE

I see no grounds on earth
why this man should be slain.
Clearly, He is of some worth.
To keep Him alive would be more sane.

PRINCE ANNAS

But all over the Judaean Kingdom
He spouts perverted wisdom.
He began in Galilee,
then came here, always teaching
getting all to believe His preaching,
to worship Him as God's pedigree.

PILATE

So tell me correctly,
if He's from Galilee
He's from Herod's vacinity?
I'll send Him, make Him trot
back to Herod the despot,
if He is from his authority.

PRINCE ANNAS

Sir, I'll tell the truth.
This boy so uncouth
was born in Bethlehem, in Judaea:
send Jesus to Herod, that's sensible,
if this plan is permissible.
Herod is our overseer.

PILATE | I will delay no longer:
He'll go there, as you infer.
Soldiers, using your skill
immediately take Him to Herod.
Say that I send Jesus homeward
to do with Him what he will.

Here PILATE *goes down and* CAIAPHAS *shall go into his tent.*

1ST SOLDIER | I'll take Him to him, by my soul!
If not, may devils from Hell's hole
snap the bones of his back,
so He can't sup Morgy broth!
Your blood'll run to a cold froth
when this plan, I unpack!

PRINCE ANNAS | Sir Caiaphas, may I go along?
'Twould be well for us to join the throng,
so we can accuse Him.
Send word to our doctors there
so they are on our side, sat fair
to argue against this victim.

And then let them go away with JESUS *and they shall walk about awhile on the stage while the* 1ST MESSENGER *goes after the* DOCTORS, *and* CAIAPHAS *says:*

CAIAPHAS | His future is told, by God's foe.
He'll suffer yet more woe.
Sweet Annas, by the Lord God,
go light-footed as a messenger,
tell my two doctors, of the danger,
to speak against this slipshod.

1ST MESSENGER | I hear what you say.
I'll do it now with no delay,
else the devil take me home!
If I don't bring your doctors here,
so in Jerusalem, they appear,
then ill-fortune 'mongst you roam!

Now the BISHOP *and* PRINCE ANNAS *and all the* SOLDIERS *go away with* JESUS *and walk to and fro on the stage.*

CAIAPHAS Well then son, fare you well:
To them yourself propel
quickly now, give them your message,
and you'll receive your reward
and be paid, no fraud,
by the month's end for your carriage.

Here the DOCTORS *shall parade. Here* CAIAPHAS, PRINCE ANNAS *and the* SOLDIERS *go over with* JESUS *to* HEROD.

1ST MESSENGER Doctors and masters hail to you all!
Bishop Caiaphas has sent me to tell
each of you to come to Jerusalem
to debate with Jesus, everyone,
the man who says He is God's son,
and was born back Bethlehem.

1ST DOCTOR We're ready at his command
to shortly join your band.
Both of us, without fail,
will confuse this rascal,
who spouts such babble.
His ideas, we'll soon assail.

2ND DOCTOR Like the 'Obby 'Oss, we'll make Him spin.
He won't believe what confusion He's in.
He won't be able to reply
a single answer to my argument.
How stupid He is, how innocent
to argue 'gainst us, to even try.

2ND MESSENGER Well... He speaks very boldly
and says to all proudly,
that He's definitely God's son,
Who'll judge us, our souls weigh,
in the sky on Judgement Day.
This aim, He has, for everyone.

Then the DOCTORS *shall come and they go over to* HEROD *after the others.*

2ND SOLDIER 'Ave on, Jesus, Y'proud fool!
Now, to avoid ridicule
I hope You d'knaw the Scripture.

If You wish to beat
the Doctors You'm about to meet,
and defeat their dogma.

Here HEROD *shall parade if he likes.*

HEROD

No – I won't love myself, for
the idea of it is no use:
no one can honour me more,
however much vanity I produce!

Here BISHOP CAIAPHAS *speaks to* HEROD *and the* PRINCES, *saluting him:*

CAIAPHAS

Greetings, Emperor of all things!
Hail to you, the King of Kings.
Of our world, the overlord,
most mild and intelligent!
Ahem... Pilate, has, with honour, to you sent
a prophet, an evil fraud.

JESUS *here walks in front of* HEROD*'s tent awhile.*

HEROD

Well... by Jove, welcome Caiaphas!
And you, my cousin Annas.
To your company good cheer!
Now, briefly tell me
who is this rogue I see
whom Pilate has sent here?

PRINCE ANNAS

He's the son of Joseph the smith.
His name is Jesus, and like a myth,
He says He's the Son of God:
that the Temple He can demolish,
then raise it again, upon a wish,
better than before, on His nod.

HEROD

Ah, so it's Jesus, I've heard about.
A warm welcome to this poor lout.
I've longed to meet His sort;
and Pilate, for sending this victim,
long will I love Him,
even more than I thought.

1st Doctor — Hail Emperor of all the land!
May Jove give justice in your hand,
to rule your Kingdom well.
Hail to you Sir Caiaphas!
and greetings also Annas!
And a nod to Jesus You rebel.

Let all go up into Herod*'s tent, and* Jesus *alone.*

Herod — My friends, welcome to my humble tower!
May Jove offer you much power,
all throughout your lives!
Relax here, as men of rank
and let me be very frank,
don't be hasty over how He thrives;

for I'll come to the right decision
over Jesus' division.

Herod *speaks to* Jesus*:*

So to You, who in Nazareth does dwell.
Now tell me, if You're Christ, God's son,
how are You a man as well?
Come, give reply for everyone.

Caiaphas — He has told us that before
at my palace and plenty times more,
so He can't deny such libel.
The Son of God, a man too,
and born of a virgin true!
Now that would be something special!

2nd Doctor — Jesus is being so ignorant
since God and people are different,
and quite contrary by my troth:
God is a spirit, of a body no need,
but people have limbs to show their creed,
so He can't ever be both.

Herod — Alright then Jesus, my friend.
You'll be careful over whom You've trod

and whose ideas You defend.
Tell us next, if You are God.

1ST DOCTOR — I'll step in here first:
From me a joke does burst.
He might be half-God, half-man.
The Mermaid of Zennor is half-human;
a fish forms the rest of that woman.
Jesus fits this merry clan.

2ND DOCTOR — Ha, and do consider this then!
He says He would rise to life again
after three days in the grave:
But when someone is dead,
their spirit is there and then shed,
never more His bones to brave.

1ST DOCTOR — But in addition today:
He didn't only this say,
that His body would rise once.
He said it would rise many a time
from the granite and grime
after those three days thence.

HEROD — Why won't You answer Jesus?
Or do You remain so joyous
because You told us the score
that if the Temple became unfit
in three days you up-raise it
much better than before.

2ND DOCTOR — If that's been said and done,
then you're a son of the evil one:
Nobody, except using witchcraft
could raise it up in three days.
Such sorcerers, for their ways
ought to be burnt for being so daft.

And JESUS *shall continue to hold His peace.*

HEROD — If it's the Son of God I meet,
then come on, show me some great feat,
so that I can believe in You:

and by my father, if You can,
I'll know You are a holy man,
and will worship You anew!

And JESUS *continues to hold His peace and answers him not a word.*

What?! Will you not speak?
The rascal's afraid, gone all meek,
since if he speaks He'll be confused.
He is nothing but a dunce:
before He leaves, at once,
clothe in Him in white, to keep Him bemused.

Here a white coat is made ready for JESUS *and let it be handed to* HEROD'S COUNSELLOR.

I'll show He is a fool,
and those of His school,
that He dares not acknowledge it.
Fetch Him an overcoat of satin:
I'll give it to this cretin,
'cause He's come far, I'll admit.

COUNSELLOR

I've got it ready sir;
the garment to which you refer.
Let Him put it on.
It's as white as china clay.
But what a pity, I'd say
that it goes to this woebegone.

HEROD

Well, I grant it to Him anyway!
So go back all of you today
to Pilate the justice again.
And take Jesus away with you.
He has done nothing to construe
me to put Him into death's reign.

CAIAPHAS

Right you are, our ruling doyen.
We'll take him home to Pilate then,
and let him decide the right course.
Farewell dearest Lord of all Jewry;
blessings to you and your company.
Your wisdom... I'll endorse...

HEROD — Well then... take care Sir Caiaphas,
and you too, dear cousin Annas!
See if you can advise Jesus
to stop being so foolish
and forget all this rubbish,
or else, it'll end disastrous.

PRINCE ANNAS — I've advised Him to do that,
but not for many a scat
will He abandon His heresy.
For all the offence He's committed,
I'd pardon Him for what He said
and forgive Him for his idiocy.

And then they shall go over with JESUS *to* PILATE*; they shall come to him, and say:*

1ST SOLDIER — 'Es, y'baissly beaut;
a good 'anging'll make 'Ee mute.
(Do 'ee see how crafty 'Ee were?
when 'Ee wun' reply at their request
in the presence of they who knaw best;
even the Doctors are in a stir!)

1ST DOCTOR — Time for us to disappear,
the job's finished here,
so all the best then friend!
From what I've seen of this freak,
and given that He don't speak,
He'll come to a bad end.

CAIAPHAS — No, hold on. You must stay,
until we conclude this affray.
Come and travel with us:
for this pisky has a glib tongue;
from Him some shame will be wrung.
I promise this as a bonus.

2ND DOCTOR — Alright. I'll gladly go with you
and offer help to your crew.
We won't leave anywhere:
and should He choose to argue
He'll find us a stickier glue.
His words we'll soon ensnare.

And then ALL *shall come to* PILATE *in* CAIAPHAS*'s tent, and say:*

2ND SOLDIER

Good day Justice Pilate Sir!
King Herod, in a bit of blur
has sent Jesus back to 'ee,
all in white clad.
And to this, Herod did add...
'Pilate, my love is for thee'.

PILATE

Mmm... May sweet Jove love him true!
And everybody else love him too,
as he well deserves.

PILATE *comes down.*

So it seems, my dear Bishop,
you again, come in a gallop,
and your captive, to me, now swerves,

as if He were some perversion
to whom only you have an aversion.
When I talk to your 'evil wizard'
and question his words and fame,
I can't see any blame!
And neither, it seems, did Herod!

When you all accused Jesus,
instead, Herod found Him innocuous
and he sent Him back.
It's best to let Him go
if a new life He can show,
without us as a hunting pack.

PILATE *speaks to the* GAOLER*:*

Gaoler, quickly over here slip,
you and your skidder of a son... Arsewhip.
Come here, as fast as possible.

GAOLER

Lord, we've come straight as a die.
We went fur'n fast, no word of a lie.
Arsewhip & Son: Good rates, very reliable.

PILATE — Open up your prison door
and place upon the straw
Jesus, so He can rest awhile.
And fetch, if you can,
a wenching woman
to make Him smile.

BOY — Right on, Sir and Lord
– the prison's open for a bawd.
I swear, with the maid I know,
she won't give 'Un no peace.
Oh no... from her, there's no release.
Night or day, she does go!

PILATE *and all the* JEWS *go over to* CAIAPHAS*'s tent.*

GAOLER — Proper job! Hold 'Un tighter,
for 'Ee's a tricky bugger.
He do knaw how to deceive 'Ee
with cunning and crafty ways,
so make sure He never strays,
and doesn't try to break free.

BOY — I'll bind 'Un at the waist,
so He'll have no time for haste,
and beg our forgiveness.
By the Buccas, I'll tame Him
so 'Ee can't run on a whim.
This dirt, I'll soon oppress.

GAOLER — Come on mate, inside the cell!
And I'll advise You well,
ask Jove to be merciful.
Don't talk any more nonsense
and then in an instance,
the Lords'll knaw You'm faithful.

BOY — Get on an' do that fartface
and you shent 'ave no disgrace.
Have some joy instead!
Forever, You'll have honour,
and You'll stay in favour,
and love for 'Ee will spread.

LUCIFER *shall parade if he pleases.*

LUCIFER
Gaa! This has all gone too far!
Our power He will mar.
Christ's goin' to lessen our power.
But I don't knaw what to do:
He's the Son of God, that's true,
and His vigour, none can devour.

SATAN
Right. I didn't knaw this clod
was indeed truly of God!
What the hell shall I do now?
All those who don't worship Jove
will join His nice little grove.
It'll cause a fine row.

BEELZEBUB
I know how to end our strife.
Go and tell Pilate's wife
that some vengeance will fall
upon her husband, if Jesus Christ
is slain and sliced.
And get her kids n' all!

LUCIFER
My bold, bad, brazen Beelzebub!
You are this merry band's hub.
You're wiser than this crew.
Now go to Pilate's wife;
make her think of her husband's life.
Advise her on his rescue.

BEELZEBUB
For this 'andsome bit of play,
I'll go there straight-away.
I won't fail in what I'm to say.
My errand will her thoughts sway.

And then BEELZEBUB *shall go to* PILATE'S WIFE, *sleeping in the tent, and says to her:*

BEELZEBUB
Yo! How is it great maid?
I've come here as your aide.
Now, tell Pilate, vengeance'll come
to you and your children
if the Innocent's death does beckon.
Does this beat upon your eardrum?

PILATE'S WIFE

Are your words really the truth?
Because if this is sooth
I would do anything not to see
my children given harm
or destroy their world's calm,
else a broken heart you'd give to me.

BEELZEBUB

I'm telling 'ee the truth maid.
Your husband's life'll be paid.
He and your children'll be slain.
To those lovelies, vengeance'll be done,
for you'm dealing with God's son,
sent down from 'eaven's reign.

PILATE'S WIFE

Because of what you say
I'll send a messenger on his way
to warn my Pilate, so he'll obey.

BEELZEBUB *retires.*

PILATE'S WIFE

Messenger, go without delay,
tell Pilate my word not to betray.
He mustn't condemn Jesus this day;
for in my sleep I've seen
that if Jesus is killed clean,
by Jove's sweet breath,
there'll be no release, no pardon,
for my husband and children.
All'll suffer a painful death.

2ND MESSENGER

My Lady, I'll do it right now,
and to your husband go;
to you, I'll make a vow
to tell him what to know!

PILATE

Tell me, right away,
what accusations have been said
against Jesus's display?
– since you long for Him to be dead.

CAIAPHAS

It's easy enough to answer that,
Yes, I'll explain all the row.

If He wasn't such an evil rat,
there'd be no need to bring Him here now.

PILATE

So then, here, upon your whim,
and according to your law
and your conscience do you sentence Him
to death, to settle your score?

PRINCE ANNAS

Well, we've no right, in my belief
to kill a man this instance,
even if he's a criminal or thief,
without a proper sentence.

Then PILATE *shall go to the prison alone and says:*

PILATE

Come Gaoler, open the door,
for I wish once more
to make it known to Jesus
that it would be pity indeed
for Him not to recede
this folly and ruckus.

GAOLER

Yep – I'll get on and open it:
and you'd some honour fit
if you could change round
Jesus to see things another way.
Yes – what He has to say
has made many move from faith's ground.

And then PILATE *shall enter the prison alone and he says to* JESUS*:*

PILATE

Now Jesus – no time to peruse,
are You the King of the Jews,
as You've been accused?

JESUS

That depends, if what you've said
is the truth, and from your head,
or has it come confused?

PILATE

Tell me if I am a Jew!
and Your nation review,
for it's those like the chief priest,

who've brought You here.
Why have you given them fear?
Give me the truth at least.

JESUS

Well... I'll untie the knot:
Of this world, I am not,
and in My eternal Kingdom,
my servants wouldn't have sold me
gladly to Jews in mindless glee
to show I've no place or wisdom.

PILATE

So then, by your logic,
You must be a King in some way
since You have a Kingdom... idyllic.
Jesus, is this what You say?

JESUS

Then you do understand:
I'm a King over the land
in which I was born.
I came into the world for that,
to give good service hereat
and the truth never scorn.
Whoever is on the side of truth
shall hear on earth, I'll say sooth,
be they Jew or Saracen.

PILATE

And answer this snippet:
The truth, what is it?
– since You speak it so often.

And He answers him not, as PILATE *goes out and says to the* JEWS*:*

I'm telling you all,
I find in Him no gall,
no cause for condemnation.
So, as is the custom at Passover
I'll end His forced hold over,
and give one prisoner cessation.
So agreed, as a showpiece,
for the Passover I should release
Jesus, King of the Jews?

CAIAPHAS

No Sir Justice so righteous.

We'd rather plead for Barabbas
who lies in the prison's mews.

Then CAIAPHAS *shall go home with* PRINCE ANNAS *and then* PILATE *turns to* JESUS *in the doorway of the court and says to Him:*

PILATE

Oh Jesus, see how stupid You are!
Disaster and You are on a par.
Torturers, in the devil's name,
stop fussing around like blue-assed flies!
With whips take this, your prize.
Jesus can now take the blame.

Here whips are got ready for the TORTURERS *and a pillar for the binding of* JESUS, *with a cord and chain, and a crown of thorns is prepared.*

1ST TORTURER

Right on Sir Justice!
No – We wun' miss this!
We'm here on your shout.
Please make sure that in a moment
we shen't be put off his 'treatment'
by drolls expressing doubt.

PILATE

No. To that pillar tie Him
bind each hand and limb
with the rope and cold chain;
then beat His belly and back
black and blue, give Him a thwack
without mercy, again and again.

And if He doesn't retract his lying
begs for mercy with His crying
or make amends for His treason,
on Him a crown of thorns place
and for His pretence and disgrace
the King of Jews will have a reason.

And then PILATE *goes up into his tent.*

2ND TORTURER

I'll get on that, like a long dog!
With this whip, I shall flog
to bring 'Un to death's door!
Oh, my boy so foul,

I'll hush Your bal.
Some blows upon 'Ee pour!

3RD TORTURER — I'll bind 'Un right up so,
and He'll wish his cake dough.
Snatch away his coat,

The TORTURERS *take off* JESUS' *white coat, and a purple one is got ready.*

so He won't have no clothing
n' we'n give 'Un a good slapping.
Don't spare Him a smote!

Here JESUS *is bound to the pillar.*

4TH TORTURER — Bind 'Un brave and tight
to make the most of His plight
and to give 'Un a better blow.
Now, all of 'ee scat 'Un.
He deserves this fun
so He'll tingle and glow.

1ST TORTURER — I'll give 'Ee a slap m'andsome!
A broke back'll be a problem!
Have that, for You'm s'scabby!
See, my fists are good enough:
yet You d'like it rough
else You'd shout for mercy.

2ND TORTURER — I'll give 'Un a good whacking,
so that others'll have a warning
when they see His body drop:
I'll tan His ass,
make Him a mass
of blood, before I stop.

3RD TORTURER — Yeah, Y'rogue. Go and hang!
'Ave a geke at our gang.
We'll do 'Ee a bit of harm!
I'll whip s'fast over your eyes,
You'll see sparks in surprise,
Your skin smoking in alarm.

4TH TORTURER — Thas' it. Beat 'Un like a dirty bugger:
Fragrant farts float like a lugger
from your arse to His face!
You'm look any way You like,
but You'll feel my strike,
to put You in Your place.

1ST TORTURER — Ga, you'm only boasting!
Just givin' 'Im some hitting
'ent goin' t'finish Him off:
He's a rascal through and through,
and in spite of what you do,
He wun't lie in death's trough.

2ND TORTURER — A'right. So, if He wun't end,
a crown to Him, I'll lend
and make 'Un King of the Jews!
The prickles and many a thorn
Will make 'Un wish he'd not been born.
His brain they'll prick and bruise.

Here thorns are made ready for a crown for JESUS.

3RD TORTURER — And I say, though He's bare,
rich purple He should wear,
so He's fit to be a King,

JESUS *is unbound from the pillar.*

enthroned and newly crowned.
King of Jews! I fall to the ground.
Salutations to 'Ee, I d'sing.

He kneels.

4TH TORTURER — Yes, here's a purple gown
to remove his frown
and enclothe His lovely skin.

Here they put purple on JESUS.

A shame though, 'tis on this lout,

for 'tis a beauty bit o' clout.
But I'll clasp it with a pin!

1ST TORTURER — And since the gown is let,
His crown shall be set,
King-like, upon His head.

Here JESUS *is crowned, and they put a white rod in His hand, whereupon one of them strikes* JESUS' *head.*

And push it down hard
so each prickle and shard
may make His brain go dead.

2ND TORTURER — I'll knock it down like a bal
so the sharp spikes do fall
and enter His soft skull,
scattering His stupid brain.
Hail, Jew King and Your reign!
Does Your misery now dull?

Here CAIAPHAS *and* PRINCE ANNAS *come down.*

PILATE — Torturers, you're a fine unit!
Now take a break for a bit.
Go home and get some sleep:
Meanwhile, I'll interrogate Jesus,
and root out why He's so righteous,
why still, counsel He does keep.

The TORTURERS *go away home and* PILATE *shall go to* JESUS *in the courtroom where he stands.*

Now Christ, listen to me:
If I am capable
I will try to set you free.

Here PILATE *takes* JESUS *by the hand. Then he shall come out to them, and* JESUS *held by His hand.*

Sirs (most inescapable!),
Look who I have here with me.
He's earnest, as you can see.

I can't find anything wrong with Him;
not enough to be slain.
Let us Him unchain,
the best plan for this victim.

Here CAIAPHAS *and* PRINCE ANNAS *and the* DOCTORS *shall come to* PILATE.

PRINCE ANNAS

Put Him to death I say
on the cross I vow!
and so He won't stray,
nail His hands n' feet now.

PILATE

Here's your man of treason!
So, go, and crucify Him!
But I can't see any reason
to kill Him on such a whim.

CAIAPHAS

As you yourself saw,
we're just abiding by the law.
He ought to be killed,
for Him saying before, so sly,
that He's the Son of God on high,
for the new faith He tries to build.

PILATE

Well friends, look, if He has said this,
I'll examine him as your Justice
in private, to dig 'neath the surface.

And then PILATE *fears the more and he shall go again with Him into the Courtroom, and he says to Him 'Whence are Thou' and again* JESUS *shall be silent, and* PILATE *again says to Him (Here he shall go with Him into the courtroom):*

Jesus, for all this Kingdom,
for honour, end this storm,
and tell me where are you from?

Let me make it quite clear.
You will respond to me here
for today, I can make a choice:
I can crucify Thee,
or I can set You free.
Say which, and give me Your voice.

JESUS — You won't have any power over Me
– yours comes from a higher authority,
granted and sized to your trim;
He, who's sold me for more than a score,
has sinned a good deal more,
and an evil end'll greet him.

Then PILATE *shall go outside, and the* 2ND MESSENGER *shall meet him, saying to him:*

2ND MESSENGER — Sir, Lord, a'right there!
My lady s'good n' fair
has sent me to tell you
that it is not wise to kill,
the prophet, or His blood spill,
for if He's slain, to be true,
vengeance will fall on you.
You'll see what is due
to you and your children.
She was told this by an angel
who to her, came a light all ethereal,
woke her, and told her, I reckon.

PILATE — Messenger, what a juicy snippet!
Is what you say the truth?

2ND MESSENGER — Sir, upon my soul I do swear it,
by the tin of Redruth.

PILATE — I'll protect Him if I can,
and prevent Him being killed:
I'll be able to excuse this man
if I am strong-willed.

And then PILATE *says to the* BISHOP CAIAPHAS *and* PRINCE ANNAS *and the* DOCTORS*:*

Lords, I'll give it verbatim,
There's no reason to kill Him.
I find in Him no fault.

Here a chair is made ready for PILATE, *and forms for the others.*

Therefore, here's what I say.

Let Him go upon His way,
and stop our assault.

CAIAPHAS

If you let go this loser,
then you're no friend of Caesar,
who is our Lord and King.
You're stupid to go 'gainst Caesar' word
and carry on here undeterred.
This fool's crazy; he's nothing.

PILATE

Arrange a jury to sit
and I'll preside over it.
We must sort this out.

1ST SOLDIER

Sir – it will all be done –
plenty of seats for everyone.
Sir Justice, please sit hereabout.

And then PILATE *shall go and sit before the bar, and he says to the* GAOLER*:*

PILATE

Immediately, bring over
one by one, each prisoner,
Dismas, Jesmas and Barabbas,
so we may judge them.
Gaoler! Bring over each item,
and your boy, who whips each ass.

GAOLER

Right on sir! And to save mayhem
We'll move 'em over as a mass!

Here they shall all sit before the bar; to wit, PILATE, CAIAPHAS, PRINCE ANNAS *and the* DOCTORS.

Now Arsewhip, don't look agog.
Make out those release charters;
for Pilate's angry as a dog
and'll have our guts for garters.

BOY

I dun't care one iota
if his heart's broken.
You'll get beaten in his rota
if you follow his token!

Pilate — Does my patience have to flicker?
See how these rogues bicker,
so they can't hear me spout.
Whatever their status inside,
bring the prisoners to my side,
so some judgement I can shout!

Gaoler — See, Pilate's in a hell of rage now:
so will 'ee please stop yer row
and bring out those who thieve.

Boy — But it's been ages
since I've had some wages.
I think I'll take me' leave.

Gaoler — You'm a pain in the neck;
you'll get your cheque.
Get on and do your job.

Boy — 'Tis no good forcing me:
for I 'ent goin' t'set 'em free.
'Tis the same old fob.

Gaoler — Listen you hogshead.
I'll have you arrested
and 'aeve 'ee in prison in a scat.

Boy — I couldn' give a foul fart
for what you're trying to start.
You'll fail to do that.

Gaoler — Oooow. See how stubborn he is,
and how he thinks I'm full of swizz.
That boy is full of cheek.

Boy — From here to the Hundred of Trigg,
for you master, I cun' give a fig.
He'n be such a geek.

Gaoler — Dun't 'ee talk such twaddle.
Bring 'em out in a huddle,
or else we'll be in ruin!

BOY

Oh, go and hush your bal!
I'm not your slave, pal:
Fetch 'em y'self, and Pilate win!

GAOLER

Serving his master with no care,
the bad servant does always air:
'Do it better yourself then!!'

BOY

So, slave, I say without fear
have a clip round the ear,
and dun't be s'cheeky again!

Here two swords are got ready.

GAOLER

With the prisoners we ought to go:
so get an' bring them out to show,
with no more fuss.

BOY

I'll tell 'ee; when they're watched,
they might well be snatched
by men from us.

GAOLER

Good point. We can't say
if this'll happen on the way,
so they slip from our reach.
So, if men us do harry
we better had carry
a good, sharp sword each.

BOY

Well said. That's clear.
We'd better test ourselves here
before we do set off with this band.
To check, before we'm gone
if anyone can take us on,
so we'n make a public stand.

GAOLER

Look out all about 'ee now,
for I'll test 'ee I vow,
to see if you'm man enough.
And watch out for yer elbow
or on 'un, I'll rain a blow.
This sword's proper tough.

BOY

Don't worry, I'll 'ave 'ee back,
and give 'ee such a smack
you'll fly across the Tamar.

GAOLER

No you wan't, upon my soul.
I 'ent takin' no stroll.
Dun't think you'm a star.

PILATE

Oi, gaoler! Hurry along!
Quick, bring over your throng! –
He can't hear a thing! –
See the pair of them fighting,
each giving the other a beating.
What idiots they're being!
I will separate you both
for being so stupid, by my troth,
and knock your heads together.
Get me the prisoners now!
You blockheads furrow my brow.
You have the brains of a feather.

GAOLER

Have mercy on us Master!
I promise we'll be faster
and bring them before you.

BOY

'Es, we wun't dally any more:
We'll complete our chore
before darkness is due.
Come on Barabbas and Jesmas,
You too Jesus, and you Dismas,
its your very own judgement time!
For by Saint Malan, right now,
taking you to Big P is my vow,
for 'ee sits to hear each crime.

GAOLER

Greetings to you Justice Pilate!
and Caiaphas, – state's stalwart!
Hail to you too, Prince Annas!
Hail to you, doctors and masters!
Hail to all of you soldiers!
In fact, Hail to all this mass!
See here's Jesus and Barabbas,
who we've sped to you,

and here too, Jismas and Dismas,
now to judge and view!

PILATE — By Lord God, our thanks are due!
Behold, standing before you
is Jesus, the new king.

CAIAPHAS — Kill Him! Kill this dross!
Put Him on the cross,
as He's so deserving.

PILATE — You're certain then, sure inside,
that your king be crucified
– this Jesus of Nazareth.

CAIAPHAS — There is no king I conceive,
save Caesar, so I believe
and swear it upon my breath.

PILATE — To a different view, I am swung:
Better that Barabbas be hung
and set this prophet free.

PRINCE ANNAS — For the right of freedom in my view
Barabbas should be first in the queue
by Passover's decree.

PILATE — If Barabbas is set free,
what of Jesus, I plea?
Tell me that for a start.

CAIAPHAS — Upon the cross, He should be stuck;
nails through His feet and hands struck
and then pierced through the heart.

PILATE — If He's such a flaw,
tell me by which law
He ought to be killed by.

2ND DOCTOR — Such small concerns we will quell.
One law proves it very well.
My friend here'll say why.

1ST DOCTOR

It doesn't seem right by the law,
that here, as a man condemned:
He'n remain silent evermore,
as when He was first accused.
He – whose silent is so adamant
before a judge, and judgement's force –
proves it then, by sound argument:
Crucifixion isn't the right course.

2ND DOCTOR

I go against that decision:
I can't believe what you say –
a doctor with such lack of vision
in favour of that wretched way!
Truly, He has pretended throughout,
to be both God and a man.
Though He doesn't speak, without any doubt,
He ought to reach the end of his lifespan.

1ST DOCTOR

Sir, that is not the reason,
nor can it ever be so –
that He should die for such treason,
for some goodness, He did show.
For example, look at the mermaid
down Zennor, half-person, half-fish:
Of such a split, don't be so afraid.
Give it credence, that's all I wish.

2ND DOCTOR

Sir, I am telling you straight
it is fitting that He should die.
'Twas all started at the Temple's gate
when into the traders, He did pry.
Their business was regulated
by those who know best:
but by Him it was destroyed.
Outside He cast them! In jest!

1ST DOCTOR

I'm surprised at the colours you've showed.
You know what the scriptures say:
how along every single road,
you seem to want to go astray.
A market is not appropriate
in the House of God at any time.

Thus God we should appreciate
Our Lord of the land, the sea's rime.

2ND DOCTOR

Yes, but it's the truth that this man
has perverted many with his lore.
Our land has suffered all it can
with such wilful breaking of the law,
so right here I'll make my stand.
He ought to die without delay:
All the doctors of the land
in faith, cannot save his skin today.

1ST DOCTOR

I hear this unfriendly malice
and how this has all culminated.
Good conscience won't follow this:
The man is not even incriminated.
This soul, I have heard, who you so pan,
a single crime would never shout.
A sad end for an innocent man,
to be unfairly taken out.

2ND DOCTOR

He so boasted many a time
that He would – being so vain –
knock down the Temple in its prime
and in three days build it again
as good as it was before.
He'll never do it I vow.
His life can't be saved – that's sure.
In truth, He's got to die now.

1ST DOCTOR

It's the truth we need to find out
of this all too terrible matter,
and justice too, must here be stout
for they share a similar patter.
Certainly, if 'tis to be done,
according to the way these two fall,
We will never destroy this one
by logic's pure reasoning at all.

It seems you wish to have Him slain,
executed after custody.
He who kills Him will get no gain,
since He has done wrong to nobody.

Disaster will surely occur
if His blood is shed;
and God of Heaven, we'll stir,
for He is God's son indeed.

2ND DOCTOR

Then I'll tell you the real cost:
'Tis better that He should be dead
than for the people to be lost
and in spiritual darkness tread.
No need to argue it anymore.
We've all seen enough idolatry;
so let the Justice decide the score,
with the commoners of the country.

Sir Pilate, you have heard our advice.
Deliver your judgement on Jesus Christ.
Hear our maxim:
We've made our request and reasons why,
and all of us will surely cry:
'Crucify Him!'

And all the JEWS *say: 'Crucify Him!'*

CAIAPHAS

Let their opinion be a guide,
that Jesus should be crucified –
the fellow who's the son of the smith.
Barabbas should be set free.
There's no better plan, as I see.
People – tell me He's a myth!

'Crucify Him!'

PRINCE ANNAS

In the name of Satan, Sir Justice,
deliver and set free Barabbas.
This is what we beg you to do,
and crucify this fool Jesus,
then the thieves, Dismas and Jesmas.
This is the right plan to pursue.

And ALL *say 'Crucify Him!'*

PILATE

Since this is the sound of the law's breath

then all you three shall proceed to death,
and Barabbas is now free to go.

DISMAS — Mercy Sir! You do terrify!
Please, please allow me to reply
as all our lives ebb and flow.

PILATE — The sentence was given just then.
Thus I will not give it again,
but as a symbol that I am clean
from the blood of Nazareth's Jesus,
I will thoroughly wash my hand thus,
so see where my sympathy does lean?

And then let PILATE *wash his hands.*

CAIAPHAS — If there is any vengeance for it,
let it come soon, and us, try to hit.
Let it fall upon our children.

PILATE — Then I judge that three should be crucified.
Dismas, Jesmas, Jesus – to the cross tied.

And then sitting, PILATE *calls the* TORTURERS *and says to them:*

Torturers! Come here, you men!

Here the TORTURERS *shall come.*

1ST TORTURER — We torturers are up for it!
But I have been wrasslin' a bit
and now, I'm all knackered out.
I ran quicker than a hurdler.
Now, I'm panting like a hurler –
sweat from me' armpits does spout!

PILATE — Torturers, with no more fuss,
up on the cross, place Jesus,
right now, if you would:
Stretch out His arms and feet,
and let the four nails meet
there against the wood.

Here is made ready the timber of the Cross in Cedron, and two crosses for the thieves.

Put Dismas on His right,
and with ropes good and tight
bind him to another Cedron cross.
Place Jesmas on the other side.
String him up there, make sure he's tied.
Quick about it – or it'll be your loss!

2ND TORTURER

All in our capable hands Sir.
Their escape's easy to deter.
To their death they shall remain.

The 2ND TORTURER *holds* JESUS' *hand and says in derision, 'Hail, King of the Jews!'*

Get on Jesus, what news
for the King of the Jews!
Time for miserable pain.

3RD TORTURER

Take off His coat for a hoot
for in His own birthday suit
the pisky now we should dress.

Here the TORTURERS *strip* JESUS *of the purple coat, and He stands naked.*

But hang on boys, where's the wood
we'm s'posed to make good?
Where 'tis, is anyone's guess.

4TH TORTURER

No – I just can't think of where
we'n find wood straight and square
and it into a big cross transfer.
Each of us think I implore
and perhaps then, they might knaw
where we might find some sound timber.

1ST TORTURER

Here's a thought – I'n save the day,
since back over Cedron way
there's a fair timber stack,
but no one's been able yet
to some good use from it get.
The planks we can up n' whack.

2ND TORTURER — Then there, our task we'll uptake.
From it, a good cross we'n make,
since it is not needed
and Christ is not needed either.
Now boys, each can meet the other.
Cursed wood to cursed Christ lead!

3RD TORTURER — Let's go and get it boys,
so Christ can shout some noise
on the cross before Sabbath's day.

The TORTURERS *go over to Cedron for the timber of the Cross.*

The timber's here! Give me a hand!
There is none finer in this land.
Let us make the cross right away.

4TH TORTURER — Let us cut it in two, the wood split
to make a horizontal for it,
and fix it with a wooden dowel.
I've got a fine axe on me
to make the two tough halves free
and I want throw in the towel!

1ST TORTURER — You'm some skilled boy, I can tell,
for you've cut the timber well.
They couldn't have a better fit.
Here soon, a deep hole, I'll bore
for a dowel in the core
so to securely fasten it.

Here two crosses are made ready for the thieves.

2ND TORTURER — Now the timber's bored through.
Let them be fastened true.
Put the dowel through the hole.
Now a second problem vexes –
boys, we still need two more crosses!
Finding extra wood's our new goal.

3rd Torturer — 'Ere, I knaw where there's some more wood
ready for them in likelihood,
so no need for 'ee to vex and frown.

Now lads, put the cross we've made
up onto Christ's shoulderblade,
so He can carry it into town.

Here the TORTURERS *place the cross upon* JESUS' *shoulder.*

4TH TORTURER

Now, hold the cross upon your back!
And don't say a single wisecrack.
It's enough of a burden.
Now make 'is. Get on with it,
and you rogues, help as fit.
Your pace increase and quicken.

MARY *goes over by another way because of the multitude of the people.*

MARY

For my dear son, I feel so sorry.
See what agony He must suffer.
For His pain, I'm near faint with worry.
With sheer fear for His life, I stagger.
Oh, how on earth does He cope?
He needs my blessing through this.
Yet I know not from which stope
to watch such awful madness.
I can hardly bear it though.
His hurting they oversee.
Watching my son being abused so,
will completely destroy me.

Here MARY *shall meet* JESUS *at the gate.*

No! No! No! I am filled with lament
to see my son given such treatment!
It's proper shameful.
Your sorrow hurts me inside,
so I can scarce see Your stride.
My eyes are tearful.
I feel so helpless!
My heart sick of this;
the deep-felt pain I hold.
I can barely stand it any more,
for the sorrow of what's in store.
His end I can behold!

Here VERONICA *comes and speaks. And then* JESUS *falls to the ground and they shall meet* SIMON THE LEPER *and shall say to him:*

1ST TORTURER	Come Leper, you, wrapped in a sack. Carry this cross upon your back, for Jesus is exhausted: He's brave n' knackered out you see. Relieve Him – you're His devotee. Take over from Him instead.

Here JESUS' *hands are tied behind His back.*

SIMON THE LEPER	I will its weight duress to save Him from distress. Over my shoulder sling 'Un. Don't you realise what villains you are? This man's innocence whom you mar, and upon you vengeance'll be done.
MARY, MOTHER OF JAMES	Oh, what a sight for sore eyes, to see Jesus in this guise. To see 'Un treated so badly. I hope that our Father above will them some proper vengeance shove before they eat s'greedily.
MARY SALOME	I am top to toe full of woe that You are treated so, when You have done so much good for them s'needy and sick. My heart's heavy as a brick for Him and all this falsehood.

Then JESUS *shall turn to them, and He says (and* JOHN *shall be with them):*

JESUS	Jerusalem's daughters – my tearful supporters don't weep for me at all. For yourselves only, give a tear and for your children's future fear; weep for what shall befall. There will be a time kindred, when wombs will be blessèd

which never had children.
And likewise, your breasts thereat
which babies haven't suckled at,
will be so happy then!
Then you'll wish anew
that the moors will fall upon you
placing you in such a terror,
and you'll pray for the tor
to cover you ever more,
so you'll end misery forever.

2ND TORTURER

Stick Your stories up Your ass!
No good from them'll pass.
That's the truth of it.
To Your death you're bound
so stick the cross in the ground.
There make it sit.

3RD TORTURER

Hang on boy! I have a fear
we've forgotten something here.
Where are us goin' to find each nail
to fix 'un upon the cross of wood.
There is a smith whose s'pose to be good
in Marghas Yow. Tell 'un our tale.

And then the 4TH TORTURER *shall go to the* SMITH, *and he says to him:*

4TH TORTURER

Yew! You there – farrier by trade.
Have you three great long nails made?
Or else we'n in some lash-up.
I want to nail Jesus to the cross,
that there false prophet we have come across.
If not, can 'ee make 'em up?

SMITH

Sorry boys, I can't do the job.
I can't hold tools, my hands are so leprous.
Me fingers do so hurt and throb.
For nail-making I must be dexterous.

Then the SMITH'S WIFE *scolding him, says:*

SMITH'S WIFE

Gad, you and your addled brain!
Both of them were right as rain

when you got up this morning!
Take 'em out from under your coat,
or else have rope round yer throat.
Husband, thas' yer last warning!

SMITH — Wife, you are so quick to condemn:
but there idn' any skin on them
that 'ent blistered or flayed.

The SMITH *shows his hands.*

Here now, each of you have a gake,
see how my skin begins to flake,
so please, end your tirade.

SMITH'S WIFE — O you fool! I sense your crime!
You have worshipped at some time
Christ, the false knave:
Yes, your hands were all right this morning!
His evil magic's been here hanging,
to you enslave.
So, leprosy on each hand does grow,
but surely you've got some nails though?
No? Typical males!
Give the fire a blow,
the forge needs more airflow.
I will make the nails!

The SMITH *withdraws from them: his hands are healed.*

SMITH — O, I'm healed! I see His plan.
I know You are both God and man.
I'll worship Jesus forever now.
Believe it and you'll be thankful;
there is no need to be fearful.
His servants make this very vow.

1ST TORTURER — I'll blow on 'un brave and strong.
For your air, I'll do no wrong.
None'll blaw better in this country.
I dun't knaw a smith in all Kernow
who do blaw better than me you know.
My motion's like Glasney poetry.

SMITH'S WIFE

Go easy y'fart! Not so fierce!
Blaw careful or the bellows you'll pierce,
and in the forge, a spark wun't stay!
Stop that, you bladder of lard,
beat the iron now, nice and hard.
Get on with 'ee. Do as I say!

1ST TORTURER

My strikes have a certain flare,
and I'll do it with great care,
so the iron'll stretch like wax.
There is none in all Cornwall
who can match the way I maul.
Missus, I won't let my blows lax.

SMITH'S WIFE

Hit it on the tip. You dull drip!
Will 'ee do as you're told!
Scat at 'un right. Hit it with might.
Tidn' no use if 'tis cold!
They should be dented with the hammer
but this way, they'll make the toad tremor.
They'll be rougher than rats in His hands.
This one here gives a hammer's hit
like a cow handlin' a musket,
like 'Geagle makin' a rope of sands.

1ST TORTURER

I shan't be worrying about that;
rough nails are vittie for this brat,
the more dishonour for the man.
For each hand, go, measure the hole,
and for His feet, give us the toll.
Go on, do it, quick as you can.

2ND TORTURER

I'll bore the hole for the nail.
There idn' a man west of Hayle
who could bore 'un better than me.
Bring me a nail, as we planned,
and I will fix up His left hand
safe and sound, for all you to see.

3RD TORTURER

I'll bore the hole for the other hand.
That'll tame 'Un, make 'Un understand.
I've no guilt, upon my soul.
Yes fool, it is best to look sombre

so stretch out your arm on the timber.
Oh hell! It won't reach the hole!

4TH TORTURER — Did you say His mitt won't reach the hole?

3RD TORTURER — Nope. It wun't boy. I knaw 'tis droll,
but there is near a good foot to go yet!

4TH TORTURER — It dun't matter if it wun't reach;
in the wood a new hole, we'n breach,
or... we'n stretch His arm with a bit of sweat.

Here a cord is made ready to stretch JESUS' *arm.*

1ST TORTURER — Soon, this sturdy rope in my fist
will be tied to the rascal's wrist,
and you three stand there, heave mighty hard
until His right hand reaches the hole,
then one hit a nail in, as our goal.
Bang 'un in sweet, like rhyme off a bard.

2ND TORTURER — I'll heave His hand hard and fast,
so 'twill reach the hole at last!
All hands haul! Show your manhood!
For certain, His joints we'll dislocate,
test to see if He's elasticate.
Now, nail 'Un into the wood!

JESUS — O sweet Father, forgive them so;
for they're innocent, they don't know
whether they do evil or good.
And if they only knew the truth,
these men would not be so uncouth.
Forgive those pinning me to wood!

3RD TORTURER — For forgiveness, I don't give a fart.
And in despite of Your mother's heart,
I will put a nail through Your feet.
I'll knock it in and it'll hurt,
and come on boys, put on a spurt
get up them two, so for crib we'n meet.

Here the TWO THIEVES *are bound to the crosses.*

4TH TORTURER	I'll bind up the first then. I've got the rope again. I'll make sure the knots are tight.
1ST TORTURER	When you've finished, I'll do Him, then we're done, as is our whim. Very soon, they'll have no fight.

Here is written the superscription of the cause of death for JESUS.

PILATE	I have written on this maxim all the reasons for killing Him, ready to nail it o'er His head on the wooden cross where He is maimed. He is Jesus of Nazareth named The King of the Jews'll soon be dead.
CAIAPHAS	Do not write 'The King of the Jews', but the wording will more amuse if you write that the villain said that He was the King of the Jews. You'n tell everyone the news, that these fine words came from his head.
PILATE	I will give answer to that brother: What I have written, I have written, and won't write anything else either, enough of a mouthful I've already bitten.
PRINCE ANNAS	Now, bring it to me so I can nail it quickly and rightly above His head, so that men and women can read what is writ and understand why He will be dead.
2ND TORTURER	In the name of the father Satan, raise up this g'ate cross boys, I summon. Put it into its correct place!

They raise the Cross.

	Haul hard! Each of you, the strain take. Allow 'Un for the devil's sake to fall snugly in its right space.

3RD TORTURER

This boy's the devil's own little pest;
but His body's jolting like the best.
See 'Un there, feelin' the strain.
Now, get the other crosses up,
so we can head off home to sup.
Yes, God'll give 'Ee some pain.

4TH TORTURER

Us two'll set Dismas up on high,
so he'n peer over this Cornish sky.
Over here and give us a hand!
And then you raise up this boy sly,
so that the two villains may die.
Do 'un quickly so we'n disband.

1ST TORTURER

A'right! I'll do it. No problem.
Up there, dun't 'Uh look some 'andsome.
Time for us to home, be flying.
Leave them here, their arms all outspread,
but before we leave the blockhead,
let us hail Him as a great king.

The TORTURERS *kneel mocking* JESUS.

CAIAPHAS

King of the Jews, as You are known,
hail to You upon Your new throne!
You look so elegant upon Your seat.
And would You like a bit of skirt?
I know one who's your sort of flirt.
If so, I will fetch her for You to greet.

Here lots are made. Here JESUS' *clothes are distributed by lot.*

2ND TORTURER

Now I will distribute amongst us
all of His lovely garments and gear.
I'll share them out, without any fuss.
Trust me, you needn't have any fear.

3RD TORTURER

I'm proper loathed to tear His coat,
or to divide it, so each has a strip.
Doing a hand of lots gets my vote.
A torn-up coat heads straight to the skip.

Here let the 3RD TORTURER *be blindfolded and he shall give out lots of* JESUS' *coat.*

4TH TORTURER	Proper! See here, I have three lots.
1ST TORTURER	Take one more then, you clever clot. It will add a fourth to the tote.
2ND TORTURER	Now show 'em on your palm. He with the longest charm wins, and gets Jesus' fine coat.
3RD TORTURER	For certain, as I'm no sinner that straw of yours is the winner. Gidgy! That length there's the best.
4TH TORTURER	By Saint Jove, I will come on down. I can't believe I've won his gown. Take what you want from the rest.

Here the CHIEF PRIESTS *and* SCRIBES *begin to salute, kneeling before Him and deriding Him.*

CAIAPHAS	Fie on You! While you're up there, be humble. You said you would destroy God's great temple, and before the end of three days, raise it up again, better than before. If, of Your father God, You are so sure, let him save You now, by His ways.
PRINCE ANNAS	If we have God's son truly found, come down from up there to the ground. Show us all a bit of Your power: and then perhaps, beginning this day, we shall believe in what You do say. Above us, a hero You'll tower.
CAIAPHAS	He has been able to before. I've been told it over the moor, but hark now, listen how He groans. I heard the dying He revives and can save other people's lives, but now He can't save His own bones.
PRINCE ANNAS	If He's the King of Israel, then let there be no betrayal.

Let Him come down from the summit.
If he does it and makes this vow
we will be convinced here and now
that He is a holy prophet.

CAIAPHAS

Oh, in His God He did so trust.
He will deliver as He must
if He's not hapless.
He boasted – the country clod
that He was the Son of God,
Lord of the worthless!

And then PILATE, CAIAPHAS *and* PRINCE ANNAS *go off home, and then the* THIEF *on the left hand, railing at Him, says:*

JESMAS

If You're Christ and therefore God's son,
save Yourself before anyone,
so you won't cruelly die here.
But if You're saving Your own soul,
place us in that same role,
for a hideous end we fear.

Then the OTHER THIEF *on the right hand rebukes the* 1ST THIEF, *and says to Him:*

DISMAS

Shut up y'fool! How silly you are
that you don't fear God's mercy so far,
and you condemned to death up here!
Like Him there, we are crucified,
given sentence when we was tried
for the evils we did this year:
this man's never given Good a wide berth,
nor performed an injury to the earth.
He's no sinning, evil man.
Lord Christ, I ask of 'Ee
to maybe think of me
when You'm in Your Kingdom.

JESUS

For your faith, I have this to say –
Though your present state has a price,
before the closing of today,
You'll find yourself in Paradise.

4TH TORTURER

This boy thinks He is so smart!

Of that place He'll be no part.
The vile upstart.
Let' go get Longius, him who's blind
to spear this poor criminal s'refined
and pierce His heart.

1ST TORTURER

A'right boy, there's none better I feel!
With this waste of space he'll soon deal.
I'll get 'un right now for a start.
We will put a sharp spear in his hand
then he'll upward thrust at our command,
piercing this Christ right through His heart.

JESUS

Mother – do you see Your child,
a thousand times defiled?
Chased like a badger by a long dog.
John, do you see My poor mother:
look after her like no other
as together through this life you slog.

MARY

O what sorrow comes to one!
My heart's filled with such consuming dread
when I see Jesus, my own son,
with a crown of thorns 'pon His head.
What an end this Son of God must meet.
This true King, this dying lion.
On each side up there, his hands and feet
are pinned down with nails of iron.
Now there can be no parole
But this way, on Judgement Day,
misfortune will 'pon them pray,
to those who have sold His soul.
My heart's weary, my thought's grim.
See how poorly they treat Him.
He won't be set free.
I wish my own end might come,
rather than watch what He's become.
I'd rather go than He.

JOHN

Dear lady, do not grieve,
for certain, please believe
I'll be at your service Madam:
as is your brave son's joyful dream,

and all the world's good redeem
since the creation of Adam.

JESUS — Eloi, Eloi, lama sabachthani?
You, Who is My dear God and Father:
why do You show me no pity
and leave me here this moment to falter?

1ST TORTURER — Hear of 'Un calling for Elijah:
Now let's watch this procedure
in case 'lijah comes to deliver.
If he does this after all He's done
I swear it, I will believe in 'Un,
and I will worship Him forever.

Here a sponge is made ready with gall and vinegar and then a CENTURION *comes out from his tent, and he says:*

CENTURION — Bored of being on guard, I will go see
how Jesus copes with this situation.
Some pity that a good old boy like 'Ee
should be given a bad reputation.
You could understand if He was evil,
but He idn' in any way I do think.
They do treat 'Un very uncivil
for saving people on death's brink.

The CENTURION *goes down.*

2ND TORTURER — Tidn' 'Lijah He's calling at this cull.
The boy must be thirsty as a gull.
I've got a special brew for 'Un.

The 2ND TORTURER *holds out the sponge.*

Perfect drink for this kind of weather:
Bile and vinegar mixed together.
Drink up if you're thirsty son.

JESUS — A great thirst is in me.

3RD TORTURER — Well, here's a drink for free.
Our wine, boy is off His menu.

	You used to do miracles and things; now come down from the cross on some wings. We promise, we will worship You.
JESUS	O Father, into Your hands I commend my spirit: by Your will take it back to Yourself, as once You sent it to the world.

And then JESUS *shall die. Here the sun is darkened.*

4TH TORTURER	O save us God Jove, full of grace as a great darkness fills this space. We can't see to journey home now. All the light has gone from the sun. I believe some sin we have spun today in killing Christ somehow.

Here occurs an earthquake.

1ST TORTURER	Here boy, feel this tremendous earthquake too. I can't even stand up any more. On such a scale! We'll never get home you! Our killing of Him made the ground uproar.

Here the graves stand open.

2ND TORTURER	The graves are opening their store. Bodies burst out from the slit. If we hang on 'ere any more, we will live to regret it.
3RD TORTURER	Longius, you must come with me. Come with me, as the quake you flee. The Justice orders it.

And he leads LONGIUS *to the crosses and gives a spear into his hand.*

LONGIUS	I'll gladly go with 'ee all, to be helpful in this brawl. For service I am fit.
4TH TORTURER	'Tis nothun' much what you have to do:

Take hold of this spear, and on my cue,
thrust it strongly upward so.

LONGIUS 'Es. I will thrust 'un the best I can,
but it may not go 'zactly to plan,
for I can't see His torso.

Here LONGIUS *pierces the heart of* JESUS.

1ST TORTURER Spot on blessèd Sir Longius!
May sweet Saint Jove love 'ee long!
You thrust 'un perfect with no fuss.
He's done in now, after that prong.

Then let the blood flow over the spear as far as the hands of LONGIUS THE SOLDIER, *and then he shall wipe his eyes and he shall see, and he says:*

LONGIUS Lord forgive me. Now I can see.
Right down on my knees I do pray.
I knew not what was here my lot,
for only now I see His way.
If I'd have seen, I wun' be mean,
and have here slayed my dear Lord Christ.
For now I know. A debt I owe.
The Son of God you are unpriced.
Born of virgin. I bring ruin.
Son of God the Father I know.
Forgive trespass. Lord bounteous.
To me, Your mercy please do show.

The TORTURERS *shall go home.*

LUCIFER Oh, I've been too full of myself here,
and have made some moves proper queer.
A lash-up – the 'Pilate-killing-Christ' ploy,
and Christ will take Adam from us,
and take Eve too, with little fuss,
and for sure, many a stout Cornish boy.
Therefore, Satan and Beelzebub,
let's head back to our exclusive club,
and there, bar and bolt all the gates,
for if He comes to our stores,

He'll break down our lovely doors
and'll set free all of his mates.

BEELZEBUB
Lord Lucifer, from what I view,
He is showing His colours true,
crucified there on the cross.
It is so terrible to see,
the wicked'll shudder n' flee
when they see Christ as a loss!

SATAN
The barring of the gateway I've begun.
He won't be able to fetch anyone
however robust He thinks He is:
Yet I fear if He comes inside,
then He will take them from our side,
every one of them, from all ages.

LUCIFER
Beelzebub, give your horn a loud blow,
and call home from every pit and hole
all my pure and wonderful devils.
They'll be useful, I have no doubt,
to stop entry and keep Him out
of my subterranean levels.

BEELZEBUB
Right, I will give my huge horn some stick.
Every devil'll hear the lick,
from St Mary's up to Bude.
I'm sure if He can enter our gates,
He will overturn our fates,
and do some ill-turn to our brood.

BEELZEBUB *blows his horn.*

SATAN
Boys, shore up yourselves against the gate.
Put your shoulder in, to give 'un weight.
Push up against it proper hard.
For if we do not, I tell 'ee,
the rascals in here, He'll set free.
We have got to be on our guard.

LUCIFER
Get on y'rogues, push 'un hard!
Push now and keep vengeance at guard,
or else... there'll be hell to pay!

For certain, He will be coming to us.
All our strength won't be worth a single cuss.
Our power'll be in array.

CENTURION

Truthfully He indeed
is the Son of God upon high.
It was a wicked deed
to cause the Son of God to die!
The sun would not blacken
if the son of a man had died.
The graves would not open,
nor would the ground crack apart wide.
For certain, He is God's son,
since the temple's fabric was torn.
It's terrible what's been done
and that this day I have to morn!
Those who executed Jesus
are now accursed where they do dwell.
They should pay for deeds s'monstrous,
be condemned to the fires of hell!
His slaying has in me struck a chord.
He constantly did much that was good.
His kindness now goes without reward
since they killed Him, in falsehood.

Then comes JOSEPH OF ARIMATHEA *and he shall beg for the body of* JESUS.

NICODEMUS

Joseph of Arimathea,
please now act as our conveyor,
and seek Christ's body from Pilate.
As He is now dead on the cross,
we'd do well to bury our loss,
sent here by God for our comfort.

JOSEPH OF ARIMATHEA

If dear Jesus is truly dead,
all joy and cheer from me is fled.
In this world, many a kindness
He has done for the poor people,
healing the sick, His principle,
who were living in sacredness.

And let him go to PILATE.

Hail! I've not come to argue.
Please allow me, I pray you,
to take down the body of Jesus,
Who upon the cross hangs dead,
so He may be laid out, and his rites read,
then sealed in a tomb, without fuss.

PILATE — Without a question, I believe
Jesus is not dead.
Centurion, do not deceive;
spout the truth instead.

CENTURION — By the ninth hour, He was dead
but His body His spirit did yield,
since the sun's light had fled
when He went from the world's field.

PILATE — I wanted to preserve Him,
but I could not stop the deed;
I followed everyone's whim.
Kill Him at all costs, their creed.
Please take His poor body away.
You, I cannot refuse.
Bury Him in the tomb this day.
You will end this abuse.

JOSEPH OF ARIMATHEA — May mercy fall on you, your Grace;
He will be buried in a place
where no one has ever been.
He will be placed in alabaster:
milk-white, made by a carving master.
It has a wonderful sheen.

A sepulchre is made ready and a stone is laid over it.

NICODEMUS — Joseph, have you the permission
to make Christ's burial our mission?
Let's go and take Him off the cross,
if you've been given consent.
I have money on myrrh spent,
as fitting for the world's loss.

Here let NICODEMUS *have pincers.*

JOSEPH OF ARIMATHEA — Friend, following our petition,
we have been given permission
to bury Him in the tomb.
Let us head over to Him right now.
Have you the pliers and know-how
to rip out the black nails of doom.

NICODEMUS — The pliers I have for definite.
I'll draw the nails out this minute.
Firstly, the two from each poor wrist,
and then the others from His feet.
Then, Joseph, take His body sweet
and in linen Him wrap and twist.

JOSEPH *shall receive* JESUS *in his arms, and he carries a linen cloth.*

JOSEPH OF ARIMATHEA — Gladly, of course, I will do what you ask.
Though I wish Him alive, I'll do the task.
That is it, place Him upon each arm.
I have linen clean and trim,
ready for the burying of Him.
They were so sinful, doing Him harm.

MARY — Kind men, thanks for all you've done.
Lead me to my darling son,
and... oh... let me hold Him tight.
I wish for His suffering and dread,
I instead could be the one dead.
If only this were the sight.
Son, once a king of us all;
Your heart fills me with such gall.
I'd have gone in Your place.
It's criminal – Your feet all ripped;
your disjointed bones all racked,
Your hands bloody and base.
But when I see You lying there,
my utter yearning fills the air.
It is no wonder
seeing His body like it is, all torn
as beneath mine stamps,
his bones crushed and worn.
God's son gone under.
For You son, no tomorrow.

How great can be my sorrow?
That You were given such a wound
by those wicked and evil folk.
Sure enough, my heart is near broke,
leaving us wrecked and marooned.
I can only express my grief;
my son picked off like a rose leaf
and treated so... detrimental.
He who's the Lord, and full of grace.
Let woe and sorrow fill this place
for You Jesus, You so gentle.
But still, I am happy and will be bold,
as Your body I can forever hold.
I know that You are the Son of God!

MARY *shall receive* JESUS.

NICODEMUS

Let us anoint Him with a myrrh broth,
before wrapping Him in the clean cloth.
This myrrh and aloes water I presume
will preserve His body beyond this day,
so that it shall nevermore decay,
if for a thousand years stands His tomb.

Here they anoint the body: MARY *anoints the head,* MARY MAGDALENE *anoints the feet, and the rest anoint his body.*

His skin will not shrivel or peel.
Enough anointment now I feel.
Next, the cloth must Him consume.

JOSEPH OF ARIMATHEA

I will wrap Him tightly with little room.
Now, let us put Him into the tomb:
Then let us haul the stone over it.

JESUS *is buried.*

Now 'tis only fit for us to worship Him.
Our once great Lord, now the victim.
May the angels find Him fit.

Here MARY, JOHN *and the others kneel at the sepulchre and give thanks to the Father, and retire.*

NICODEMUS

This heavy coverstone's route I'll retrace.
See how it slides neatly into its space.
Let's go home. Remove the tears from your face.
Father, God, who made all the things and more,
allow us all, when from this world we soar,
to end our life's play in such a state of grace.

Nicodemus

But listen, hush your bal, all of you,
for Jesus's blessing, good and true
goes to you watching us out there.
Now you have seen in our short play,
how Christ was martyred on this day,
for the sake of us, and all we bear.

You'll be thinking about the Passion now.
And in the depths of your heart, make a vow,
to keep it steadfast, the truth there install.
As Mary knew, though grieving in her loss
it wun' for Himself Christ went on the cross,
but for the total love of one and all.

See if you can show your love to Him.
Worship Him. He is a synonym
for the truth, day or night.
When you leave this land of tin,
Christ will welcome you in.
Jesus will treat you right.

The blessing of Jesus on you again.
I think I will keep on praying for that.
So let's leave this playing place, this Gwary Plen
– homewards to kin and kindred, wound our chat.
But come again tomorrow mind...
You'll see how it's not all doom...
Christ's resurrection you will find;
how gently He rose from His tomb.

Detail from the Callaway Window at St Neot's Church, Cornwall, 16th Century.
The Resurrection.

Resurrexio Domini

The Resurrection

Cast in order of Appearance

** before the character indicates a role in Origo Mundi*
+ before the character indicates a role in Passio Christi

+ PILATE
COUNSELLOR
+ JOSEPH OF ARIMATHEA
+ NICODEMUS
+ GAOLER
+ JESUS CHRIST (SPIRIT)
* + LUCIFER
* + BEELZEBUB
TULFRYK
* ADAM
* EVE
1ST ANGEL
2ND ANGEL
3RD ANGEL
4TH ANGEL
5TH ANGEL
6TH ANGEL
7TH ANGEL
8TH ANGEL
9TH ANGEL
ENOCH
ELIJAH
+ DISMAS
* + SATAN
* + GOD THE FATHER
+ MICHAEL
+ GABRIEL
1ST SOLDIER
2ND SOLDIER
3RD SOLDIER
4TH SOLDIER
+ MARY
+ GAOLER'S BOY
+ MARY MAGDALENE
+ MARY MOTHER OF JAMES
+ MARY SALOME
+ THOMAS
+ PETER
+ JAMES THE GREATER
+ JOHN
+ BARTHOLOMEW
+ MATTHEW
+ PHILIP
+ SIMON
+ JUDE
+ ANDREW
+ JAMES THE LESSER
CLEOPHAS
CLEOPHAS' COMPANION
EMPEROR TIBERIUS CAESAR
CAESAR'S COUNSELLOR
LIGHTFOOT – MESSENGER
VERONICA
1ST TORTURER
2ND TORTURER
3RD TORTURER
4TH TORTURER
TRAVELLER

Here begins the Script of the Resurrection of Our Lord Jesus Christ.

PILATE	The buried Jesus, I assume has now been placed in a stone tomb by Joseph and the others He knew: Of course, this Jesus himself did say that without fail, on the third day, He would rise again into view. If He happens to rise again many people will believe then that He is a God of Heaven; Judea's end will have begun and all of our Law undone, such reasoning makes it certain. Counsellor – quick, tell me I pray, what is best to be done today about this weighty matter in hand: I've been so worried about it: I don't know what answer does fit. My soul's anxious you'll understand!
COUNSELLOR	Of all the worry, that this brings I'm most anxious over two things – about today's body in the ground – that Joseph o'Arimathea will steal the Son of Mary, and then say it's real that a risen Jesus has been found.
PILATE	Then, what would you advise to deal with Christ's rise? Say now, your idea put, and you'll be rewarded, for what you will have said, before the week is out.
COUNSELLOR	Lock tightly, under nine keys thus both Joseph and Nicodemus. Make sure they are kept quite secure, so they can't secretly steal Christ's body from the tomb's seal, and against their sly tricks assure.

Here JOSEPH OF ARIMATHEA *and* NICODEMUS *shall come to* PILATE.

JOSEPH OF ARIMATHEA
Greetings Sir Pilate, to you and your reign!
Christ's body, which I was allowed to obtain
is now in the tomb at last.

NICODEMUS
Oh – how you transgressed I contend!
Our grief at seeing His end
almost blinded our eyes fast.

PILATE
The body you put in the tomb's dolmen
made a boast about rising again
right at the end of the third day.
Tell me where the body may be found.
Unless you give me an answer sound,
you'll be in prison, on my say.

JOSEPH OF ARIMATHEA
Through the body we laid in the tomb –
joy without end shall surely resume
in His Kingdom, when it does rise –
on the third day, it shall walk again
and we will be able to see it then
before us, with our own eyes.

PILATE
You liar! You rapscallion!
You will surely go to prison
so you won't ever see the light of day.
In there, no stealing will you implement,
nor a single word, at any moment,
that He is to rise again, will you say.

NICODEMUS
Again, Jesus Christ will surely rise.
He redeemed this world in my eyes
with His flesh and His blood red.
This is the truth I tell you.
It has been written as true
by many a prophet I've read.

PILATE
Ah! You can go with him as well then
under my gaoler's nine keys again.
Certainly, you should be in fear.
You'll be imprisoned by nightfall,

so you will see no light at all
for the whole of the coming year.

JOSEPH OF ARIMATHEA

Throw us into prison if you desire!
While we still live, we'll keep our fire.
A cell won't bother us, never;
for Jesus, full of mercy
will bring us, you will soon see
to unfailing joy forever.

PILATE

Yew! Gaoler, you poor, unlucky wretch!
In the devil's name, open the latch
of your fast doors to the gaol!
Put these two in your cold prison.
When to a cell they've been driven,
give me the keys without fail.

The GAOLER *takes them to prison.*

GAOLER

Ah! Now traitors, start to despair,
and get in there y'foolish pair.
God, how stupid you two beauties be!

He says to PILATE*:*

Sir Justice, here, without fail,
are the nine keys of the gaol,
so you won't have to fear treachery.

Here the GAOLER *shall deliver to* PILATE *the keys.*

PILATE

Gaoler, as you're trusty and bright,
right now, I will give to you
the fiefdom of Kennel outright,
Merthen, and Carmynow too.

GAOLER

Many thanks for this, Sir Justice,
I'm forever in your service.

Here the SPIRIT OF CHRIST *comes to the gates of Hell.*

SPIRIT OF CHRIST

Devilish princes, your black faces show.
Do it at once, and open your gates so,

for if you do not, there'll be much woe,
before I pass on from this place;
for Hell's gates, lasting and timeless
shall be thrown open regardless,
so that the glorious King of Bliss
may go in, and enter this space.

LUCIFER

Who are You to fool with me?
This King of Bliss – who is he?
Immediately, what's his name? Come, tell.

SPIRIT OF CHRIST

He's a mighty Lord, most miraculous,
who in battle is truly marvellous.
Therefore, open up ye princes of Hell!

LUCIFER

Who are You to mess with me?
Who's the King of Bliss I plea?
Tell me Who He is today!
Don't think You'n come inside the gate,
so turn around, and start walking straight,
and then You can stay away.

SPIRIT OF CHRIST

Against such a mighty Lord's advance;
the weak gates of Hell won't stand a chance,
before I pass on from this evil space,
because my grace is so great.
In battle, He is first-rate,
this King of Bliss, ye princes of this place!

The gates of Hell are broken. And so the third time. Then the SPIRIT OF CHRIST *shall go into Hell, and* LUCIFER *says:*

LUCIFER

Ah! Help! We've had it! Watch out – robbers!
The gates have been reduced to splinters!
Surely, we are done for.
Beelzebub, stop his revolt:
Let forth a beauty lightning bolt
that'll burn Him for sure!

BEELZEBUB

Lightning will not stop this rascal:
a million devils are feeble
against His mighty power!
Dive down any of Hell's holes

until all of Heaven's souls
depart from here this hour.

TULFRYK — Go Leviathan, my changeling,
or we shall die here, firing
flames beneath this bubbling brew.
I had there, in many bowls
more than a million souls
in a most lovely stew.

Here the SPIRIT OF CHRIST *holds forth His hand.*

ADAM — I see the hand that created me,
its odour sweeter than honey,
and now coming my way.
Through my own sin You did lose me,
but by Your blood, You set me free.
For Your mercy I pray.

EVE — Great glory on Jesus Christ I afford,
for worship is due to You mighty Lord,
for delivering us out of Hell.
When to a woman Jesus was born,
upon that time, may blessings adorn –
the task to the Virgin Mary fell.

Here comes the SPIRIT OF CHRIST, *with all, into the plain.*

SPIRIT OF CHRIST — O souls, together, make the right choice.
Come with me and you shall rejoice,
as those do, who follow my Father's will.
And for those who will not repent,
let them remain there in torment,
misery forever following still.
O Adam, peace to you then,
and to all of my children
who have always been faithful.
Come to sanctuary in Paradise:
to redeem all of you, my sacrifice
was giving my heart's blood full.

Here the SPIRIT OF CHRIST *leads them.*

ADAM

O Lord, much thanks to You this day,
for there was no joy where we lay.
In the devil's dark domain,
there's been nothing but fumes and burning,
then horrible scorching and stinking.
Like dogs, we howled in pain.

EVE

O dear Jesus, Heaven's King.
You heard our voices crying
up from the fiery depths of Hell.
Woe to those who do not believe!
They shall stay in Hell and there grieve,
'til the end of the World's knell.

SPIRIT OF CHRIST

Because I redeemed you with my pain,
my hurt, being your wondrous gain,
go now into Paradise above.
When in Heaven, wait for Me there,
so we will be able to share
your redemption and all of God's love.

Michael, straight-away, lead them to the light,
in great joy, and in marvellous delight,
which because of sin, were lost before;
for when to Heaven, I ascend,
my coming time, I wish to spend
with angels and saints, whom I adore.

The SPIRIT OF CHRIST *goes to the sepulchre with a company of* ANGELS. *And then* ADAM, *when he sees there* ENOCH *and* ELIJAH, *wondering asks:*

ADAM

You creatures born of a woman's womb,
but were not with us in Hell's gloom,
how did you come to be here?
The truth of it, I'd love to know.
How you came to be here, please show.
Who are you both? Tell me clear.

ENOCH

Enoch is my true and given name,
and transported to this place I came
in flesh, as a prophet most eminent.
I'm destined to return to the earth,

whereby I might have to suffer death
before the ultimate Day of Judgement.

ADAM

Alas! How will you fare in the world –
with sadness and misery unfurled
at every turn you make.
After your time spent here in complete bliss,
I'd hate you to find the world loveless,
or think you've made a mistake.

I will tell you the truth for it's worth:
I lived a very long time on earth,
and in misery did dwell.
I broke dearest God's commandment,
and through that, was condemned and sent
to be forever in Hell.

My Lord Christ, by His mercy,
did completely redeem me,
letting me out of Hell flee,
through His flesh and His suffering for us.
The poor souls he took out of such pains,
bringing them, to where the light still reigns.
Listen to what my advice contains –
don't seek to go into the world thus.

ENOCH

It is the Antichrist whom I must fight.
In Lord Jesus's lists, which I've had sight,
the Antichrist will slay me and win;
though after three and a half days,
I'll be walking Heaven's pathways
with Lord Christ, a King most genuine.

ADAM *speaks to* ELIJAH.

ADAM

I find it hard to understand
that you too, are amongst this band,
arriving here, as a mortal man.
I pray, please proclaim
and tell me your name,
for Judgement Day, has not crossed its span.

ELIJAH My name – Elijah – is what you desire.
I was carried in a chariot of fire
to this place where we now stand.
In this place, I shall patiently wait
until the Antichrist meets his fate.
On earth, Him I'll countermand.

ADAM Why do you go against the Antichrist?
Christ the redeemer, Who was sacrificed,
brought you here, through His pain and might.
You've come from a hard world I've met,
where there is trouble, toil and sweat,
during the day, and in the night.

ELIJAH People will be turned from God's good wishes
by the Antichrist of all parishes,
and wherever he walks on earth's sod.
To the world we shall go against him.
His talk and power, we shall always dim
by the grace of the dear Son of God.

He will order us to be slain
because our wills he cannot gain
by his words alone.
You know that before reaching peace,
we must needs suffer death's release –
our own death sown.

And then let ADAM *turn to the* THIEF DISMAS *and he says to him:*

ADAM O You, you blessèd creature,
how is it here, you feature
but weren't with us in Hell?
I'm not bothered that you're here,
but now that you are this near,
who are you? Come, please tell.

THE THIEF DISMAS I'm a thief, sentenced and sacrificed,
put on a cross beside Jesus Christ,
left there like him, for dead.
I cried out to Him such a lot,
when in His torment, He had not
a place to rest his head.

I called Him the Son of God see,
so that He might remember me
when He came to His Kingdom's land.
To me, a message of hope, He did say:
'That within the evening of the day
in this Paradise I would stand.'

ADAM

Well thief! How fortunate you have been!
Because crucifixion you have seen,
you have experienced none of the grief
we had, of being burnt in Hell's grate.
Smouldering in fire was our fate
in misery and pain, with no relief.

THE THIEF DISMAS

Christ is the Lord of Mercy.
Believe, and this, you will see.
Pray to Him, and always be devout –
the Lord will know your soul's worth.
When you pass on from this earth,
you'll enter Heaven, I have no doubt.

TULFRYK *speaks in Hell.*

TULFRYK

In faith, if I had boy Adam now,
I would fling 'un by the wing, I vow
into the middle of our cosy pyre!
A pity I didn' let out of me rear
a lightning flash to burn the little dear,
followed by a thunderous back-fire!

BEELZEBUB

You'm right there about how we did fail
to let out lightning or a thunder trail
to burn Adam to a crispy cinder!
It's a proper lash-up, you'm right,
to see many souls leave our sight.
Souls goin' to Heaven, I'd like to hinder!

SATAN

Oh woe! 'Tis a whisht job being a devil!
In truth, Christ did Hell completely dishevel.
He almost blinded us with His light.
Away from darkness and pain
the many souls have made gain.
Alas, that we've no power to fight!

Then says JOSEPH OF ARIMATHEA *in prison:*

JOSEPH OF ARIMATHEA — Jesus, Son of Grace and Saviour,
come and aid us. Please give help if you can.
Please help us, Trinity Father,
maker of each land, creator of man.

NICODEMUS — Amen to that, for we have laid you thus
within a tomb made out of stone.
Chief of Kings, give succour and help to us.
Let your angels to us be shown.

GOD THE FATHER — Go my two angels, to these servants who call
from inside their prison cell.
Without opening or breaking any wall
release them from where they dwell.

MICHAEL — Dearest Lord, readily we will do what you will,
without any hesitation at all.
Anywhere, at any time, we'll use our skill,
to serve you truly, whatever your call.

Here let the ANGELS *go down, and they shall go over to* JOSEPH OF ARIMATHEA *and* NICODEMUS *in prison.*

GABRIEL — Come out of prison, with no need of a key,
nor is there need to break out from your cell.
Truthfully, from now on, chief lords you will be,
as both of you honoured Christ's tomb so well.

JOSEPH OF ARIMATHEA — Thanks to dear Christ, for He is full of grace.
Jesus is full of mercy I am sure.
Not a wall has been broken in this place,
nor had He come to us through any door.

NICODEMUS — I knew He was a God of power bold.
I never doubted His mercy on us.
He shed His blood for both the young and old,
who, if they keep faith, will be saved thus.

Here FOUR SOLDIERS *shall come to* PILATE.

1ST SOLDIER — Sire, you would like, I presume

to appoint men t'guard the tomb
where the dead traitor Christ is lain;
for 'Ee did very often boast and say
He'd come back to life again on the third day,
however cruelly 'Ee were slain.

2ND SOLDIER

And if 'Ee wudn well-guarded I feel
His disciples, in secret, would steal
Him out of the tomb there.
They would tell a tale then
that He'd come t'life again
an' gone to live elsewhere.

3RD SOLDIER

If any o'that was to become true,
'twould be a thousand times worse to undue.
I swear it by Saint Jove.
You'd have more trouble than you've already met.
Therefore good Sire, now is the time to set
armed men in the tomb's grove.

4TH SOLDIER

If 'Ee idn' guarded, without doubt,
'Ee'll be stolen by those devout.
The body will be taken out
and carried to another district.
His people will all say, with words vain,
that from the tomb He's risen again,
joining up with His angels, to reign
in full truth, in a Heaven bright and perfect.

PILATE

Quick then men, your soldiering resume!
Go now, and guard well Jesus Christ's tomb.
And, as you are soldiers strong and grim,
the penalty of death I will use
if you can't guard the King of the Jews,
stopping Christians from stealing him.

1ST SOLDIER

Peerless Sir Pilate, on me own head
we will guard the body that is dead.
This Jesus Christ won't slip by us.
If anyone seeks the body to steal,
I'll make sure they won't get past the seal.
They'll pay for it with their life, thus.

PILATE

Well, in faith, be on the look out,
for He has boasted, with no doubt
that after three days, He would rise again.
Grugith and Dansotha Down will be yours
if you can prevent the Christians' cause.
If He escapes, each of you will be slain.

2ND SOLDIER

I'll guard 'Un, even if He comes alive.
I won't fear 'Un, if this Christ does revive,
and thieves passing us, I very much doubt!
Though, if the body does start to walk,
His escape I shall easily balk,
by giving 'Un a good old clout.

3RD SOLDIER

Neither do I have any fear of that.
He can rise up from being laid our flat,
but I would soon give 'Un such a scat
that 'Ee would tumble onto the ground.
The sepulchre is shut fast they say.
I will guard 'Un surely night and day,
in spite of where His disciples stray;
however sneaky they come to the mound.

4TH SOLDIER

Let's head over there then boys!
I'd like to see all His ploys
and foolish attempts to rise!
If He even thought of coming back,
I would break His head with a deep crack!
I wudn' listen to His lies.

And then the SOLDIERS *shall go to the sepulchre.*

1ST SOLDIER

Boys, I have given the tomb a glance:
there's a great stone over the entrance.
I tell 'ee – He wun't escape from that,
so let us get in a good bit of kip.
If He rises, from there He'll never slip;
that stone won't budge any for the brat.

2ND SOLDIER

Here! Hold your horses a minute boy!
That idn' goin' t'bring us any joy.
Dun't be s'silly me beauty!
One of us should keep a watch out,

each taking turns to walk about.
Who's goin' to start sentry-duty?

3RD SOLDIER — I dun't care who does the first part!
I need some sleep for a start.
By Saint Jove, I am knackered out!
I'm sure dead men won't rise
'till Doomsday greets our eyes.
This view I've no reason to doubt.

4TH SOLDIER — Keep watch on either side of He Who's dead,
and then I will sleep right beside His head.
That way He'll be properly guarded.

1ST SOLDIER — Good idea boy, for thas' smart advice.
I cudn' think of a better device
than that which you have just said.

Here the SOLDIERS *sleep. Then* JESUS *rises from the dead, and He shall go wherever He likes, and the* ANGELS *sing 'Christus resurgens'. And afterwards* MARY *says:*

MARY — O dear Father whom I face,
You created Heaven and Earth;
for You are full of grace
and power of much worth.
You know in every respect my loss,
how my Son, His death met:
Between two thieves upon a wooden cross
His sweet body was set.
When I saw the lance
pierce Him straight through His kind heart,
I fainted at the glance.
My son was being torn apart.
Oh, I long to see Him again,
and speak to Jesus, my dear son.
If He doesn't come to comfort my pain,
my mourning will never be done.
I buried Him after He'd been killed
and put His body in the tomb.
Certainly, if it was what You willed,
and He rose, my love could resume.
O Father, help me with this.
I ask of You not to delay.

Allow me, my son to kiss,
for the reasons you've heard me say.
I ask of you, my son dear,
from the very bottom of my heart
to quickly come to me here,
as You promised me before you did part,
that on the wondrous third day still,
You would rise again, my son.
Yet remember my love, Your will
not my wishes, must be done.

JESUS

O Hail to you, my holy parent!
Delight fills me to see you as before,
and my heart can once again be content.
Of your own goodness, I have reason sure,
so Mother, I should not have to tell you
that when your own sweet life comes to an end
my throne in Heaven, you will come to view.
Above all angels and saints, you'll ascend.

MARY

Are You really Jesus, my Son,
coming back here as He did foresee?
The third day is now nearly done
since He was taken away from me,
yet I could not, in any way,
know His fate, or how He fared.
I'd love to see Him, as you say,
and if for His mother, He still cared.

MARY *kneels.*

JESUS

My sweet mother and love most true,
I am Jesus, your dear Son!
I have come here to comfort you
to show how joy can be won.
Don't doubt that I have risen again,
for mother, I am truly from death.
But try to understand, that though slain,
I speak the truth with every breath.

MARY *embraces and kisses* JESUS.

MARY

O dear Son, You've ended my pain!

The world's heartache you'll relieve!
That You have now risen again,
I do wholeheartedly believe!
I am comforted at what You said,
now You have risen from the tomb.
The nine months were truly blessèd
when I bore You here in my womb.
Is Your body still racked with pain?
Do Your afflictions still torment?
Are all Your wounds healed again
where the spear and the nails went?
I saw how these objects gashed You
and ravaged at Your precious skin.
Tell me beloved, my Son true,
now what condition, are You in?

JESUS *kneels.*

JESUS

May reverence come to you this day,
and with it honour and happiness!
No pain afflicts Me in any way,
nor will I ever be harmed I stress:
Yes, you should know that I overcame
death, sorrow and anguish – these three,
so My well-being I can proclaim.
Now, nothing at all troubles me.

MARY

My heart is comforted, gone is the dread,
because now I've just heard You maintain
that the pain of Your Passion has ended.
You suffered so much torture and pain.
To the Supreme Father at His throne,
I give thanks dear Lord, for Your loving deeds,
to have sent to me, as You have known,
Your beloved Son to comfort my needs.

They kiss and separate.

1ST SOLDIER

Deary me! Of some deep sleep I was glad,
but what terrible nightmares I have had.
Honestly, in my sleep I dreamed
that He Who was lying in the tomb,

rose up, and walking did resume,
with angel's song, or so it seemed.

2ND SOLDIER

Thas' funny boy! I dreamt the same.
On my back, the risen Christ came.
In truth, I felt 'Un walk over me.
It looks t'me like He has got away,
for the tomb now stands in disarray.
The sealing stone is at the edge, see!

3RD SOLDIER

Boys, both of 'ee are right for goodness sake,
for I saw Him rise while I was awake.
He crossed right over me as well,
carrying both a cross for this world,
and a banner which He unfurled.
This idn' no dream what you d'tell!

4TH SOLDIER

He's right there – for with my own eyes
I saw the dead Jesus Christ rise:
He looked awesome in such a guise.
Then boys, out of the tomb he went.
I was blinded in fear from the light.
His radiance was so very bright,
and I near fell over from the sight.
We've no time to be complacent!

1ST SOLDIER

Look sharp then – and get looking,
in case He's gone into hiding.
Into both vurze and bracken he may stray.
If we'n find 'Un, make 'Un into mincemeat,
and so food he won't be able to eat,
bind 'Un strong like a good bale of hay.

2ND SOLDIER

By God's blood, I'll find 'Un you'll see,
however mazed the rogue may be,
or how exalted His newly risen reign;
for I am not scared, by my brood
of His red banner, nor His Rood.
We will bring Him before Pilate once again.

3RD SOLDIER

Nope! We can't find 'Un, on my soul,
though we've gaked in every hole,
and ran around all over the place.

I believe I saw 'Un flying off,
with His many companions aloft.
Pure white was each one's clothes n'face.

4TH SOLDIER

And I too, saw Him fly across the land,
taking with Him His great and wondrous band,
attendants following every command.
I couldn't count them as past they flew.
Gaa – 'tis a useless task, I am sure,
t' even search for 'Un any more.
As our confidence was premature,
let's talk about the best thing we'n do.

1ST SOLDIER

Now boys, carefully think this one through.
What are the four of us goin' t'do,
when we all return to Pilate's hall?
That Christ rose from the tomb
bodes bad for our doom.
It idn' goin' t'profit us at all.

2ND SOLDIER

I've had a think – my advice is thus:
we'll say that soldiers come upon us,
an' carried the body away.
Then we'll make it look good for Pilate,
that we'm wounded an' are in some state.
I reckon thas' what we should say.

3RD SOLDIER

That wudn' work at all – no way!
I believe that we should say
that out of the tomb He's risen again,
because He's truly the God of Grace.
We'll say how a battle he did face,
an' won against the cross' pain.

4TH SOLDIER

I believe what you say.
That's surely the best way.
From the truth we shudn' stray.
A tale'll catch us in a snare.
In telling a lie, there's nothun' t'gain,
in spite of all my fear o' being slain.
He has surely gone to Heaven's bright reign,
with all the saints and the angels fair.

1st Soldier	But boys, who is goin' to say that He rose to life this day, out of the earthen tomb so? Who'll go to the Justice with this news, for 'tis very likely it won't amuse? For fear of death, I won't go.
2nd Soldier	No fear! Our view I will argue and in case I need to support you, I will say how it happened, and turned out.
3rd Soldier	But if he starts to rant and rave our lives I hope we can save. Keep out of his way if he starts to shout!

And then let them go to Pilate*; and the* 4th Soldier *says:*

4th Soldier	Sir Pilate, to you a thousand joys! In spite o' us being four stout boys, I'm afraid we could not guard the tomb. We expected t'give 'Un good whacks, but 'Ee tricked us behind our backs, and fled from us, or so we assume.
Pilate	You call yourself soldiers and stout men! Are the rumours and gossip true then, that I have heard all over the place? By Mahomet, prepare to meet your doom, if Jesus Christ is stolen from the tomb. For this, a fitting death you shall face.
1st Soldier	Sir Pilate, it does not matter what you say: Whoever fails to follow the Saviour's way will, by God, meet a woeful end! I saw 'Un with my own two eyes, lift the seal of the tomb and rise; then from the grave t'Heaven ascend.
Pilate	Be quiet you fool! Get out of my sight! If you don't find him before the fall of night you will pay for guarding so shoddy! When I sent you to the tomb,

you promised, on your own doom,
that no one would steal the body.

2ND SOLDIER — I put this challenge to you.
Let us Nicodemus view,
and Joseph of Arimathea see,
and we will show you, on our doom,
the body that you put in the tomb,
who was called Jesus Christ, Son of Mary.

PILATE — Gaoler, you unlucky wretch,
open up the prison's latch
and fetch out those from inside.
Here are the nine keys for the task.
Now – if you don't do what I ask,
on your death I will decide!

GAOLER — Sir Pilate, if you have the nine keys,
I will open the nine doors with ease.
Behind them are the two men.
But in case you think there's any foul play,
you'd best see the cell where the follows stay.
No blame'll fall on me then!

PILATE *goes down. And then let him go to the prison, and he shall not find them; and* PILATE *says:*

PILATE — That's not an unreasonable request.
Where are these two, who are under arrest?
Wretched Joseph and his friend Nicodemus!
The prisoners have escaped! They've got out!
Find them quickly! Search all about,
or your death's requiem we'll have to discuss.

BOY — Hang about Sir! Don't blame we!
To make the gaol secure,
the nine keys were kept with thee.
We bolted every door!

PILATE — You're right! I had the keys I know.
This is a marvel, and no mistake.
The heavy doors no damage show!
In the wall, there's no crack or a break!

Soldiers, you are not guilty of neglect.
Your story about Christ I now respect.
That Jesus left you, I have no doubt.
Though tightly locked under nine keys,
the prisoners here, have gone with ease,
and they, like Jesus, did not break out.

3RD SOLDIER

Well then, we will make known this wonder
wherever we happen to plunder,
for the truth is that Christ has again risen.
Even as He rose from the tomb,
we four saw 'Un, we did assume,
ascending with many angels to Heaven.

PILATE

Silence now, for Lucifer's sake!
No noise may your tongues make.
Don't say a word about all of this,
and you shall have a great reward:
Penryn as well as Helston ward
will be gifts you will not want to miss.

4TH SOLDIER

Well, when you put it that way Sir,
of course we'll do anything you say.
Each of us here, we all concur
are at your disposal night and day.

And then shall come MARY MAGDALENE *and* MARY, MOTHER OF JAMES, MARY SALOME *and* MARY MAGDALENE *says:*

MARY MAGDALENE

Alas, it is hard to still be brave,
now My Lord has gone to the grave.
Now's the third day to see
if an end has come to my pain,
and if Christ has risen again,
just as He once told me.

MARY, MOTHER OF JAMES

I too, will see if the body
which so painfully redeemed me
has from the dead risen again.
Much comfort He gave to us:
alas, that His death I saw thus.
Alas! That Christ suffered such pain.

MARY SALOME — It is the third day I ascertain,
to see if Christ has risen again.
He had such torture on his body.
There is always sorrow in my heart,
a grieving that never seems to part,
a sadness that won't ever leave me.

Here, she meets the other MARYS.

MARY MAGDALENE — Joy to you, women who here gather:
to you dear Mary, James' mother,
and you, Salome as well.
The sorrow inside leaves me broken hearted!
If the body of God Himself has departed,
where shall it be found? Please tell.

MARY, MOTHER OF JAMES — I feel exactly the same inside.
Here, in my heart, such torment does reside.
I offer a prayer:
If He does not help more speedily,
my heart will surely break within me!
It's so full of care!

MARY SALOME — My torment is also great;
may the Lord relieve my state
of longing for Him in such gloom!
I'm sure today that He will rise.
To me, it will come as no surprise
when the King of Kings leaves the tomb.

MARY MAGDALENE — You're right! Look how the stone's been moved.
That Christ's risen, 'tis surely proved!
Where did He go, after He got out?
Lord, how shall we find the King of Kings?
From the tomb, the risen Christ now wings
his way over the land hereabout.

MARY, MOTHER OF JAMES — We delayed too long – thas' what I say,
for our Lord has now gone away,
gone forever out of the tomb, I'm sure!
I won't be able to see Him again,
not put an end to all my hurt and pain.
At He Who is of God, my heart is sore!

MARY SALOME	I know it's for real that He's risen, and that He's left the tomb's prison on this very day. But what will be our reward if we cannot find our Lord? Our torment will stay!

They sing.

THREE MARYS	Mourning we sing, Mourning we call, Our Lord is dead, Who bought us all!

MARY MAGDALENE *weeps at the tomb.*

MARY MAGDALENE	Sorrow will forever spread; for my sweet, dear Lord is dead! His awful crucifixion occurred, but His suffering was of much worth, for all the people upon the earth, and the pain He bore without a word!
MARY, MOTHER OF JAMES	I can see no sight of my Lord fair in this direction or over there. At this, I am filled with woe! With my Lord, I should love to speak, but unless Us, he chooses to seek, it seems we will not meet though!
MARY SALOME	This longing for Him won't halt. He may have left the tomb's vault, but sorrow fills my heart! Alas, almighty Lord, Jesus and dear God's word from us should never part!

They sing.

THREE MARYS	Mourning we sing, Mourning we call, Our Lord is dead, Who bought us all!
MARY MAGDALENE	Lord, Your power we justify! But now, please hear our joint cry! You Lord, whom some still defy,

will show them how they will not be saved!
When I think of Your Passion, how it did smart,
at such pain, no joy enters into my heart.
O alas! Alas – that I cannot depart,
and speak with you, for 'tis truly craved!

MARY, MOTHER OF JAMES Jesus has gone to another land,
joined by His glorious angel band.
Sorrow still fills me though, where I stand,
for I am worried about how You are!
I pray to you, Graceful King,
some message to us three wing,
so we may have an inkling
of how, since rising, You're faring so far.

MARY SALOME Jesus, full of mercy and wisdom,
hear us and please remember us some!
We pray that we'll come to Your Kingdom.
Hear our song of love!
In longing for You Lord, I languish;
I can barely stand with such anguish.
Tell me now what I must accomplish
Lord of Heaven above?

Cantant.

THREE MARYS Mourning we sing, Mourning we call,
Our Lord is dead, Who bought us all!

1ST ANGEL Whom you all seek is clear:
But Jesus is not here,
for it is certain now
that He has risen up again.
His rising is the world's gain,
for He is worthy I vow.

MARY MAGDALENE Then O Angel, tell us more of this miracle.
Where is the body of He who has no equal?
Where has the body gone now?
As He was full of grace, and was wise,
grant me to see Him with my own eyes.
Will He allow it somehow?

2nd Angel — O Mary, with this message from Heaven,
go and tell His disciples eleven,
and give the news to Peter as well,
that just as Christ said, they'd one day see,
He will soon return to Galilee.
This message, all of them quickly tell.

Mary, Mother of James — Then the Lord has truly risen again!
Saviour Jesus, the angel did explain,
has departed straight from the tomb!
Glory to Him and all His worth,
for He's Lord of Heaven and Earth.
The King of Kings ends our gloom.

Mary Salome — Let us three hurry back home,
and tell all, as there we come
about the joyous sight we have seen.
The risen Christ ends our gloom,
and has gone away from the tomb,
into Heaven, from what we d'glean.

Mary Magdalene — No, I will not go back home yet,
for on seeing the Lord I'm set,
my Lord Who went upon the Cross!
O Jesus, dear King of Grace,
let me again see Your face.
Amen! Amen, to our loss!

Mary, Mother of James — Sweet Mary, may you have then,
the blessing of all women
as you seek for the Lord.
We wish you well in your desired quest,
and grant us the grace to do our best,
and act in God's accord.

Mary Magdalene — My blessings on you in return!
Christ's death caused us all much concern,
so allow us to do what is right!
Dear Lord, if it is your will,
grant us an appearance still,
for I long to have you in my sight!

Mary Salome — Amen to that which you said,

for though Jesus Christ is dead,
His flesh and blood redeemed us all:
He endured much torment and pain
for the sake of the world's gain.
He's the King of Might I recall.

MARY SALOME *and* MARY, MOTHER OF JAMES *retire from the tomb, and seat themselves a little way off.*

MARY MAGDALENE

In the tomb, He Who made Heaven, does lay,
but I long for Him greatly every day.
O dear Jesus Christ, hear my voice, I pray.
Be with me at my end; the sooth to say.

Sweet Lord Jesus Christ, please grant me the grace
to make me worthy, and my love embrace;
so with You today, surely in some place,
I may have a view and sight of Your face.

You are Creator of Heaven and Earth,
Redeemer to us always, full of worth.
Of Your care for us, show there is no dearth.
Speak with those waiting at your tomb's dark berth.

MARY MAGDALENE *goes to the garden.*

In yearning, my tiredness starts to show;
my body and limbs ache from head to toe.
Where is He tonight? Does anyone know?
So much, to this worthy Lord, we all owe.

CHRIST (GARDENER)

Now, where are you going, woman so fair?
Why do you cry, why such wailing despair?
He Whom you seek, I truthfully declare,
you dried His feet with your own plaited hair.

MARY MAGDALENE

Kind sir, if just now, you happened to see
sweet Christ my Saviour, tell me where is He?
All that I own, I'd give to you for free,
if a glimpse of Him, you can get for me.

CHRIST (GARDENER)

Mary, I know how your faith in Him grew;
that you were one of His worldly crew.

But if you saw Him standing before you,
could you then recognise Him, as Christ true?

MARY MAGDALENE — Well, I am sure I would know Him anywhere.
One glance would be enough to know Jesus fair.
But as I can't find my Lord without compare,
your joy, I'm afraid, I'm unable to share.

And then CHRIST *shall show His side to* MARY MAGDALENE, *and He says:*

CHRIST (GARDENER) — Mary, behold the five wounds on my body!
Believe that I have risen, and can walk free.
Because such waiting and patience you bore,
in my Kingdom, you'll have joy evermore.

MARY MAGDALENE — Dearest Lord, Who upon the cross was spread,
it would be wrong for me to kiss Your head.
But, I ask You to let me kiss Your feet,
for that would make my new found joy complete.

CHRIST (GARDENER) — O sweet woman, do not touch me!
Please o woman, don't touch me at all,
since from it, no advantage will fall.
There will come a time, you will see,
when having ascended to my Father,
in this country, we will again gather
and I will return to speak to thee.

MARY MAGDALENE — Hear me dear Lord, when shall You return?
The hour of it, I'd love to learn,
when from Heaven you'll speak with us again,
for surely you know the news,
that all the powerful Jews
cause Your disciples much trouble and pain.

CHRIST (GARDENER) — O sweet Mary, tell them from me
that I shall go to Galilee,
as I once promised them I would:
Give comforting words to them all,
but especially on Peter call,
for he's much loved, and a man good.

Here MARY *comes to the* APOSTLES *and says to them in Galilee:*

MARY MAGDALENE

Apostles, I've some news to end your gloom.
Gather round, I'll tell you what I know:
Jesus has risen up from his tomb!
I just saw Him a short while ago!
I spoke to Him, I tell all o'ye:
I saw His wounds: they were real,
and though they were pitiful to see,
the world they will help to heal.

THOMAS

Woman, be quiet with your tales.
Such fables only add to our pain.
On a cross Christ was pinned with nails.
I can't believe He's alive again.
I'll listen to no more from your head,
for I do not like this kind of lie.
Everyone knows the Lord is dead.
The truth no one has tried to deny.

MARY MAGDALENE

Thomas, it is the truth that I speak,
and I will prove it before we part.
Just now, at the risen Christ I did peek –
the Lord with redemption in His heart –
and by me, says that He'll soon return,
when you are least expecting Him to.
He won't break His promise, as you'll learn.
Peter, by name He did mention you.

THOMAS

Hold your tongue woman! Stop this fuss!
I pray you – do not fool with us.
Please woman, keep your mouth in check:
I don't care how strong your fine castle is,
Magdala, if you don't stop this treatise,
I will personally break your neck.

MARY MAGDALENE

You won't be able to silence me:
I will prove it as the truth to 'ee
before we all leave this place.
Even now, as we here gather,
He is with God the Father
at His right hand, and in grace.

PETER

Well, I for one, am happy again
that Christ has risen from being slain

and is now out of the grave;
for I know that He's Mary's one,
but He is also God's dear son.
More news of Him's what I crave!

THOMAS
Peter, you bufflehead! Be silent!
All this tale she's had to invent.
Only a fool would think Christ arose!
Up the garden path you have been led,
for no one can rise after they're dead.
It's a truth that everyone knows!

JAMES THE GREATER
Oh yes they can, dear Thomas:
The Son of God clearly has.
He said He would rise as I recall,
for Jesus, Mary and God's son,
Who made Earth and Heaven as one –
it was clearly no problem at all.

THOMAS
James, can't I get through to your thick head?
It is the truth that a man who's dead
will not live again anymore.
That shudn' come as a surprise.
You're mad to think otherwise,
but what I say, you just ignore.

JOHN
O Thomas, on my ears, your words jar.
I can't believe how crazy you are.
Our beliefs you betray!
Christ was to be placed into a tomb.
Afterwards, He'd rise and life resume
at the end of the third day.

THOMAS
O John, now please don't be so silly.
Do you accept this so readily?
I'm surprised you see this as fit.
So great was all of our loss
when Christ suffered upon the cross,
that I still curse those who did it!

BARTHOLOMEW
Tom, believe me, before my hair turns grey!
Nobody has the power or the say
to order that Jesus Christ should be slain.

He was willing to die for all of us,
be buried in the tomb, then arise thus,
to bring each Christian into Heaven's reign.

THOMAS

You're a complete fool Bartholomew!
Could anyone be as blind as you?
It's like you have gone insane!
Surely God could have saved everyone,
His best for world He would have done
without all that death and pain.

MATTHEW

You're right there. Since for His own gain,
God could have destroyed things again:
Devastation would be rife.
Nevertheless for our own sake
willingly did Lord Christ death take,
than later, came back to life.

THOMAS

Matthew, what foolishness is in your head!
I'd advise you to take back what you said,
and withdraw that comment!
No matter how much you talk about it,
on the cross was where Christ took death's exit.
We all saw how He went.

PHILIP

Thomas, you're the one who needs to be slurred,
as you're adamant in doubting the word
of Jesus Christ, the King of Kings,
when He said to all of us,
that He'd rise from the tomb thus.
Only you, seem to doubt these things.

THOMAS

I'd advise you to hold your tongue Philip.
On these matters, you need to get a grip,
for you're wrong about all of it.
Jesus Christ, Who had every limb broken –
I assure you – won't be rising again.
A thousand times His skin was split!

JAMES THE GREATER

How can you say such a thing!?
That Christ our sublime King
cannot leave his dark tomb distant,
for I am sure He has risen again!

O yes – everything's becoming plain.
You're not fit to be His servant!

THOMAS

Well James, if He were alive,
to be His servant I'd strive.
Gladly, I'd follow His train.
But He 'idn alive! He's dead!
Sharp thorns were put on His head,
and pushed right through to his brain.

SIMON

Tom, although sharp thorns were put on His head,
and a spear, in an instant, made Him dead
by piercing His loving heart,
now surely, you must believe inside,
that in the tomb He doesn't reside,
for of God, He is a part.

THOMAS

Hush Simon, for your words offer no sooth.
We all know that this is the grim truth!
He's never risen and never will boy.
But imagine... if He did rise from the tomb.
O then what wondrous comfort would resume!?
All of us would be overwhelmed with joy.

JUDE

But Thomas, there is joy and an end to pain:
for today, He has really risen again.
Listen – He has walked out of His tomb;
Mary saw it with her own eyes.
For if Jesus were not to rise,
unending joy could never resume.

THOMAS

You're living in a dream world Jude!
I always thought that you were more shrewd.
I saw how his heart was torn apart.
Whatever anyone may say,
on this, or any other day,
from the tomb, we won't see Christ depart.

ANDREW

O silence Thomas! We will hear no more!
Your arguments are beginning to bore!
'Tis right that Christ has risen again.
Your disbelief has gone way too far,

for 'tis true that Mary, whom you mar,
spoke with Him, even though He was slain.

THOMAS — It doesn't matter how much I try.
This wicked wench only spouts a lie.
Please don't even think of believing her!
As long as I live, I won't believe
that the Lord Jesus will the tomb leave.
No resurrection will ever occur.

MARY MAGDALENE — I swear I haven't told a single lie.
The joyous sight of Christ near made me cry.
He revealed to me each wound,
and for the sight of those,
the truth of it I chose –
that the risen Lord I had found.

Here let THOMAS *and* MARY MAGDALENE *go down.*

THOMAS — You can talk all you want to maid.
I won't believe you I'm afraid.
You'n talk on, 'til your face is blue!
However persistent you are,
it will not get you very far,
for you can't make me believe you.

MARY MAGDALENE — It's the truth I tell you:
As the tomb we did view,
an angel came to us,
and said that Christ was risen,
and had gone up in Heaven
with all his angels thus.

THOMAS — O shut up – and end your essay:
I don't believe you when you say
that the body's in Heaven now.
I'm still upset that Christ is dead –
my mind still full o'fear and dread,
with deep furrows across my brow!

MARY MAGDALENE — But surely, Mary Salome you'd believe,
and Mary, mother of James, I conceive,
you would trust as a witness?

They saw it the same as I,
and so have no reason why,
to tell the truth any less.

THOMAS

That the dead body once before us
has now risen up from the tomb thus,
well, I just never can see it as so.
Whenever I think of His Passion,
truly my grief I cannot fashion
into anything more, than utter woe.

MARY MAGDALENE

I am astounded, for my part,
that you should be so hard of heart
not to believe all that I have said.
You'll never feel Heaven's joy
unless some belief you deploy.
Yours seems another future instead.

THOMAS

Well, that's rich coming from someone like you!
That you're in Christ's confidence isn't true.
You're a fallen woman – a whore!
You were quite a sinner in your day.
Yes, that's what I have heard people say.
Round here, your antics are folklore!

MARY MAGDALENE

That I was a sinner is true.
To the great heights of sin I flew:
but I cried upon Christ anew
to forgive any errors of mine,
and the Lord said directly to me:
'Your unending faith has been the key,
and your sin shall be forgiven thee:
Go – be sure new sin you decline!'
Only yourself, you deceive,
in that you still don't believe
that the Lord Christ did achieve
His rising on the morn of Easter day.
Those who refuse to believe anew
God above will not save or rescue,
and therefore Thomas, I pray to you
to believe everything that I say.

THOMAS

Stop your yap – and your tale review,

because I will never believe you.
The body, which I myself did view,
was high upon a wooden cross nailed.
On Him then, soldiers advanced.
His still beating heart they lanced,
and Jesus' blood I glanced,
as it ran down where he was impaled.
Surely that body can't live,
nor a rising ever give?
Don't you know that dead men can't walk?
There is no one on the earth,
who'd view your tale with worth.
I can't believe a word you talk.

MARY MAGDALENE

Well, you're madder than I thought.
In a one-track mind you're caught.
I'm sorry, but I give up on you.
I have advised you to believe,
but for certain, before I leave,
remorse'll come like you never knew.

THOMAS

Since I'll get no peace if I stay here,
off out of all your ways I will clear.
This country is full of fools and lies!
O help me dear God, to remain true:
I can't get through to any of you.
Falsehood and dishonesty I despise!

Then comes JESUS *to the* APOSTLES *and says (in Galilee, the doors being closed He kisses them):*

JESUS

Peace unto you! Now hear my call!
Believe fully, apostles all
that I, Christ, have risen from the grave.
Those who believe their eyes,
I shall truly baptise,
and eventually those I'll save.

PETER

O dear Lord, gone is my pain
now You are risen again.
Jesus, although 'tis true I did deny You,
Your full mercy we could all use,
as these days, there are always Jews

trying to capture us, and Your work undo.
Jesus, Lord illustrious,
on my saving, don't hesitate.
Please forgive me my trespass,
for my remorse is deep and great:
Lord, I am now full of much repentance
for once denying You.
In Your heart, can You end my life sentence
and offer mercy true?

JESUS

My full forgiveness may you meet,
for you repentance is complete
through the power of the Holy Ghost.
Now, as I have fully redeemed you,
go install in the others I view,
the true faith again, amongst their host.

JOHN

Lord, You won't know the gladness I feel
to have You back here with us, for real,
for You have cheered us up, no end.
That O Lord, I have to say
for we were pining away.
Now such longing, we may amend.

JESUS

John, from here I will go to My Kingdom,
and God the Father's right hand man become.
In Heaven, beside Him, I shall sit.
But to strengthen your faith in Me,
I will send to you – you will see –
the comfort of the Holy Spirit.

Here JESUS *goes away from the* APOSTLES.

JAMES THE GREATER

O God, wasn't that marvellous news
that Lord Jesus, the King of the Jews
came here to see us, at last!
And wished 'Peace!' to us,
even though the door thus
which was locked tight and shut fast!
The Lord has a mighty reign
Who with His own blood and pain
redeemed all of the people on this earth.
That He's risen we must admit.

Woe to those who don't believe it,
for on doomsday the Lord'll know their worth!

MATTHEW

Well, He did tell us all this before –
about everything he foresaw –
while He was still alive.
He said He'd die to redeem us,
and that afterwards, He'd rise thus.
To save we, He'd always strive.

JOHN

He spoke the truth as far as I can see!
He, Who created both the land and the sea
and everything for our benefit,
was born of Mary, the Virgin.
On His birth, much love we should pin,
or else all joy we would have to forfeit.

JAMES THE LESSER

Let us rejoice anew
now we know it is true
that Jesus, who with no fuss,
redeemed us high on the cross,
still understood our loss,
and came back to speak to us.

SIMON

Now let Thomas say for his gain
that the Lord's not risen again:
Together, we'll all give evidence.
The complete proof will him enthral,
that Mary's son spoke to us all
and stood in our very presence.

JUDE

In my view, he still won't believe
that from the tomb Christ can now leave
by the Lord's great grace alone.
I don't think he will believe it
unless Christ pays him a visit,
for that's the concern he's shown.

ANDREW

Belief will come to Thomas' heart,
because the Lord loved him from the start.
He thought much of him before He died.
In the end, Christ will draw in everyone

with His benevolence, for through God's son,
comes Heaven, wherein joy does abide.

PHILIP — I reckon we need to join together,
find where he's gone walking in the heather,
and tell Him Christ has risen from the tomb.
He must not have any doubt
that the Lord Jesus is out,
and with us, his conversation resume.

CLEOPHAS *and his* COMPANION *walk in the plain.*

CLEOPHAS — Here, listen boy. So I d'hear
a miracle happened round here,
just now, on this very day.
Christ, Whom they did crucify
– so my sources verify –
has risen from where He lay.

COMPANION — Well, if what you have heard is true boy,
a bit o'speed we ought t'employ,
and go and see 'Un right away.
An offering we should make,
and then to the tomb it take,
for He's God and man, so they say.

CLEOPHAS — You'm right! Let's do it this instant!
O how I hated His treatment:
the way the lance pushed through His heart,
the crown of thorns placed on His head.
He suffered such pain and such dread,
and yet of God, He was a part.

COMPANION — My burning heart still aches with grief,
since Christ was given no relief.
With sympathy for him, I am filled.
Nothing could justify the death of Christ,
and how the Son of God was sacrificed:
There wudn' no need for Him to be killed.

JESUS — What has happened to make you so sad?
Why are your faces in mourning clad?
Dejection is all you seem to shout.

Troubled voices is what I've heard.
Has some sort of disaster occurred
that somehow I have not heard about?
Are you strangers around here?

CLEOPHAS — Well, I reckon You must be a stranger round here,
or You wudn' have t'ask anything s'queer.
You'd knaw what disaster there has been
concerning the death of a holy prophet.
On a cross, limbs all torn, they felt it fit
t'crucify 'Un and treat 'Un mean.

COMPANION — And after suffering all o'that,
people laid the body out flat
an' buried 'Un in the tomb then.
Thas' where we'm heading to now,
as we was told that somehow
He has risen right up again.

JESUS — O what a right pair you two are!
Your want of faith has gone too far!
You see 'twas a necessary thing
for Jesus Christ to enter the tomb.
Then, only after three days of gloom
of His resurrection, you could sing.

CLEOPHAS — Well, I'm sure He has risen again,
but think of how He suffered such pain.
They tore His body t'shreds!
We saw 'Un martyred on the cross,
such lacerations, such a loss.
Thas' why sadness fills our heads.

JESUS — Well, I wish you deep peace and joy!
May you some rest and bliss enjoy.
Now, where do you aim to reach tonight?
In my view, in the same Glory as He
the two of you both shall be.
That He's close to you is surely right.

COMPANION — Because both of us felt such a loss
over Christ's grim death upon the cross –
and how His body they did maim –

we hadn't planned to go for miles today,
just to a small village not too far away:
I have heard Emmaus is its name.

JESUS

Then in truth, I believe it is right
that I will go farther than you tonight.
I have a longer journey ahead:
But nevertheless, believe it plain
that the body has risen again.
It is a marvel, so it's said.

CLEOPHAS

Oh no, we won't hear of it my friend.
It's late, so make this day's journey's end.
Please stay and spend the night with us here.
T'tell 'ee the truth, You're a good old boy
and have given the two of us much joy.
What You said, made a lot of things clear.

Here bread is got ready.

JESUS

Well, your kind offer I'll enjoy.
Remember, to unfailing joy
you will be led.
Sit, the weight off your feet take.
In your presence I will break
a loaf of bread.

JESUS *shows them His wounds.*

COMPANION

O Lord, chief of salvation,
I see each laceration,
and every wound on You.

Here JESUS *shall pass away from* CLEOPHAS *and his* COMPANION.

As soon as You broke the bread,
I knew that to Christ we'd been led.
See, it was Him we did view!

CLEOPHAS

Were we not just thinking,
and our hearts burning
about Jesus, Mary's son,
the moment He broke bread?

Then, the scripture He said –
a message for everyone.

COMPANION
What a marvellous thing eh!?
For He brightened our day
the very moment He met us.
Yet the smile was wiped off my face
as He stood before us in this place,
and we saw His hands and feet thus.

CLEOPHAS
Even so, we should be full o' joy,
as we've seen this mighty Jesus boy.
They d'call 'Un the Lord of Grace.
He is head t'toe full a' mercy.
and I think they who d'pray t'ee
are sure that salvation they'll face.

COMPANION
We'll tell everybody in the land!
We will make everybody understand
how we two spoke with Jesus,
how we met the Lord today,
on our journey this way.
'Tis certain He spoke with us.

CLEOPHAS *and his* COMPANION *go over towards the* APOSTLES. *Then* THOMAS *shall come to the* APOSTLES, *and* PETER *says:*

PETER
Thomas, now please try to believe me.
In truth, the risen Christ you can see
since He has been right here with us.
News of this, I wish you would receive,
for woe comes those who don't believe.
We tell the truth about Jesus.

THOMAS
Peter, you're the one who to denial leant,
in spite of Jesus' cruel punishment,
so I certainly won't believe you.
So I say, don't listen to gossips!
Don't let such tales pass from your lips
and pray brother, don't continue.

JOHN
I'm telling you Thomas, he isn't lying.
God's dear son, Jesus Christ, full of loving

came right up into our house,
even though all the doors were shut tight.
'Peace to you all!' did Christ then recite,
and I stood quiet as a mouse.

THOMAS

John, please stop being so childish!
Your delusions are truly selfish,
and they d'break my heart to hear.
On no account may Christ rise again.
Can't you recall now how He was slain?
Surely the truth of this is clear.

JAMES THE GREATER

Thomas, believe on your part,
and pray with a zealous heart
to Christ of Heaven above.
He has surely risen from the tomb,
for His speaking ended our gloom
and assured us of His love.

THOMAS

Don't cause me any more distress,
for my heart has grief in excess!
I am consumed with the pain of it.
See James, my sorrow is still great
that my Lord was taken of late.
His love we've had to forfeit.

MATTHEW

If away from your home, you didn't drive,
then you would've seen Jesus Christ alive,
in good health, standing right before you.
'Tis amazing – though you hear it,
on no account will you see fit
to believe what is certainly true.

THOMAS

O dear Matthew! Saint Mary be blessèd!
If you only listened to what I said
you would stop this ridiculous tale.
Go on, carry on making fun of me!
You seem to have no shame from what I'n see.
Any old story you'll buy wholesale.

PHILIP

Thomas, he wasn't being uncouth!
In fact, Matthew told the complete truth,
just as it happened today:

Christ, King of men and women thus
has most certainly been with us
in this very house I say.

THOMAS — Now the Lord has not been in your presence!
If you don't put a stop to this nonsense
amongst all of you here,
I'll hit someone square on the chin!
End the anguish you put me in,
else you'll have me to fear.

JAMES THE LESSER — Thomas, it's no use being angry.
Jesus Christ has risen, can't you see?
The merciful Lord has returned.
How can you be so naïve?
If you don't start to believe,
your foolish soul will be spurned.

THOMAS — 'Tis no wonder I am angry
when you are all ganged up on me,
intent on teasing me beyond belief.
My discontentment over your talk,
and how you said Jesus Christ did walk
makes me taissy, and gives no relief.

BARTHOLOMEW — But if you are sad at losing Christ,
and lamenting what's been sacrificed,
think again, you should be full of joy:
Believe that He's risen from the tomb,
and everlasting joy will resume.
No grieving will you need to employ.

THOMAS — See my belief is put under such strain
to say Christ's body has risen again.
I myself saw that He was dead.
The evil torturers wreaked terror on Him.
They hit Him around, then tore Him limb from limb,
and I saw how thorns pierced His head.

SIMON — I give up offering you advice.
In Hell's dread fire you'll pay the price
for not believing all that we have said:
Thomas, you're making a huge mistake

in rejecting the joy you could take.
May such renouncement fall on your own head.

THOMAS O Simon, of that I have no fear.
Although what you've said is very clear
I'm sure nothing'll happen to me.
The greater misfortune
is that Christ died too soon.
It is that which breaks my heart you see.

JUDE Believe us who saw Him stand here bold,
for He has risen from the tomb's hold.
He was alive when He was with us.
Though no one unlocked the door,
we know exactly what we saw:
then 'Peace to all of us' wished Jesus.

THOMAS Anything but the truth isn't it?
Jude, if you give me any credit
pray, please leave my sight.
Ghosts like that can come to anyone,
and through their closed doors easily run
when folk sleep by night.

ANDREW You are, Thomas, for what it's worth,
the silliest man on the earth.
This bodes badly for your future.
If you won't believe Christ's risen again,
you will find yourself burning in Hell's pain,
in fire, and endless torture.

THOMAS Andrew, I can hardly conceive
how much you want me to believe
that which is your foolish and false ploy:
that from the tomb He rose up clear,
and again returned to us here!
Ha – You'm the one who is the fool boy!

Here THOMAS *goes down.*

CLEOPHAS 'Ee isn't the one whom reason has escaped.
You'm the one who's daft as a carrot half-scraped,
and properly mazed as a curly.

You wudn' believe your Apostle friends!
With such doubt, you'll never make amends.
Complete stubbornness is what I see.

COMPANION

We were traipsing along t'Emmaus,
so at the village we might pause.
We were going along proper thus,
when we met – not a yard before my face
Jesus Christ – honest – Who is Lord of Grace.
Now do you believe the two of us!?

THOMAS

O everyone knows that pilgrims of your sort
are of a few fantastic stories never short.
I know you tell yarns like there's no tomorrow!
Take not a bit of notice of these two.
Saw Christ did you? I know your sort of crew.
You didn' speak with Him, for all of my sorrow.

CLEOPHAS

'Ee opened up the Scripture for us,
from the Creation to Moses thus,
then down to the wise prophets of old.
I know His glory and His worth;
that He's Lord of Heaven and Earth.
On what 'Ee said, I was quickly sold.

COMPANION

'Twas dear Lord Jesus as I said.
In our presence a loaf of bread
with His hands He slowly broke,
and before our wide eyes
His wounds we could recognise.
Of the cross they did evoke.

THOMAS

Shame on each of you rogues for your lies!
He wouldn't come to you in that guise,
for you are only a common pair.
O by the true Lord God of Grace,
a right pair of tricksters I face!
I don't trust you two in this affair.

CLEOPHAS

I wish you weren't so cynical,
and of our words less critical,
for the Lord spoke to us in broad daylight.
T'us your situation is proper plain;

you should believe that He has risen again,
or else not being saved, will be your plight.

THOMAS

Sorry, but beggars I can't believe!
Even your clothes, from what I'n perceive
have on them odd patches of cloth sewed.
You're impostors with some fairy tales,
travelling along the many trails.
You're both just droll-tellers on the road!

COMPANION

You're insane! Against it you argue
because you don't want to believe us two.
Well, Thomas the foolish, that's as may,
but in your disbelief you're too far gone.
I can't understand why you carry on!
I've no wish t'hear what you d'say.

CLEOPHAS

Thomas, please give yourself some relief,
and give up this act of unbelief,
since it brings only sorrow and grief
– as you don't believe He's risen again.
Thomas, you are so hard-hearted.
End this heresy you've started,
and from your pride now be parted,
otherwise unending joy you'll not gain.

THOMAS

I don't know what to do!
As Christ I can't right now view,
I just can't believe He's risen again.
Though 'tis true I wouldn't feel such grief,
if I might touch His heart for some relief.
My hand on Him once more would end the pain.

Here THOMAS *moves towards the* APOSTLES, *then* JESUS *shall come to the* APOSTLES, *the doors being closed, He kisses them and says:*

JESUS

Apostles, I wish you peace tonight!
And even though the door was shut tight,
with you all locked inside,
I have still managed to see you.
Let everyone's faith remain true,
wherever you reside.
As you wished Thomas, hold out your hand.

Place it into my heart I command,
through the wound in my chest.
Press it also upon my hands and feet:
redemption for Christians is what you meet.
Touch the wounds which are blest.

THOMAS

O Lord, please have pity on me!
God of mercy in charity,
I know exactly who You are now!
Until then – and it's clear You're not dead,
I still didn't believe what they said.
I pray You may forgive me somehow.

JESUS

Thomas, in the tomb I once dwelt,
but now that my cuts you have felt,
you believe again that I live.
Many more will never see me,
yet their believing I foresee.
On them, my true blessing I give.

THOMAS

Lord, blessèd You will always be!
In as much as You are full of grace,
Your mercy is always ready
to Your servants in every place.
They won't suffer from lack of joy
if they can continue to see You.
And when death sends me his envoy,
save me from the devil and his crew.

O God, I was so foolish, so naïve,
when despite it all, I would not believe
that Christ had risen from the grave.
So great has been my sin,
I must have had ears of tin,
yet my forgiveness the Lord gave.

JESUS

Apostles, recall the teaching I gave.
In your belief, stay faithful and steadfast,
for I have risen again from the grave.
Your final salvation I have forecast.
To all Christians will come the same,
so long as they pray for forgiveness.

By my angels they will be reclaimed,
with the Holy Ghost as their witness.

My blessings on you, my brave band!
I must now travel on to my own country,
to sit in Heaven's wondrous land:
at the right-hand of My father I must be.
And so, to the Christians all around,
I leave to them the gift of My grace.
May they live forever, may joy abound,
in Heaven's Kingdom, their future place.

And so endeth 'The Resurrection of Our Lord'. And 'The Death of Pilate' begins. Here EMPEROR TIBERIUS CAESAR *plays and says:*

EMPEROR

In case you don't know, I'm Tiberius Caesar
and I am truly, the world's greatest leader.
Pity is, I have got leprosy.
At what to do, I'm unsure!
If I can't find a quick cure,
I don't know what will happen to me.

COUNSELLOR

Lord, my advice for your comfort
is to send word to good Pilate,
via the swiftest messenger from here.
Hearing of your sickness, he should choose
to send you Christ, the King of the Jews.
To the needy, I know He's brought much cheer.

I've heard He can make people sound
from every sickness they've found,
as He is of God Himself.
He is the Lord of Heaven and Earth
and I am certain that through His worth
you will return to full health.

EMPEROR

A marvellous plan counsellor!
O Lightfoot, my good messenger,
come over here a while.
I've an errand for you to run.
You need to go and see someone.
I hope you feel agile.

MESSENGER — By my hood, I'm here Tiberius sir,
and fit as a fiddle, as you prefer:
'Lightfoot messages – quicker than a flash!'
What can I do you for today?
Tell me what you want me to say.
Whatever it is, I will make a splash!

EMPEROR — Go to Pilate's straightway,
and this is what you should say:
ask him to send me the King of the Jews,
the one who says He's God without peer.
To Pilate, make my needs very clear.
Then thank him. That's it. No other news.

MESSENGER — All is sweet. Your wishes I'll complete.
Sir, I know what I must say.
I won't be long. Just try to be strong.
I'm already on my way.

To PILATE *he says:*

Sir Pilate, joy to you great Lord.
I come here on Caesar's accord.
The Emperor sends his greetings to ye.
From him, my simple message is this:
Send Christ to the door of his palace;
amazing doctor that He's said to be.

PILATE — O really? Is this what Caesar wants now?
Messenger, some time for yourself allow.
Take a stroll 'round the countryside here,
while I myself will go and see,
if I can find Jesus, and quickly –
I am sure He will be somewhere near.

And then the MESSENGER *shall go and walk about in the plain a while, and* VERONICA *shall meet him.*

VERONICA — Young man, why do you stroll about?
Tell me, who has sent you as their scout,
and what are you looking for?

MESSENGER

Well, what is that to you?
There's nothing you can do.
I'm fine, and need nothing more.
The Emperor has sent me
to seek help in this country:
You see, he has leprosy:
And can find no doctor to give him a cure.
If you can help, tell me where Jesus is?
The Emperor would give Him such riches
if Christ healed him at his premises.
The end of disease I've heard He can secure.

VERONICA

Then of a cure, Caesar will have a dearth,
for Jesus Christ has gone into the earth.
He is dead – gone is our Lord of Worth.
Pilate executed Jesus you see.
In Christ's death He did connive,
but if Christ were still alive,
to cure Caesar, He would strive,
no matter how bad was his leprosy.

MESSENGER

Alas! That I ever went on my way,
because if He were still alive today,
dear Caesar, Jesus Christ could heal!
But now, the dreaded leprosy will start to grow,
and my face back there, I hardly dare to show.
From the shock of this, I still reel!

VERONICA

I'll go to the Emperor with you
because I am a Christian true.
You should know that I was one of Christ's women.
In His name, a remedy I'n prepare,
so the dreaded leprosy may him spare,
if Caesar believes Christ is God of Heaven.

MESSENGER

Lady, you have saved the day!
Let us be on our way.
If the disease you can turnabout,
your freedom Caesar will guarantee,
and you'll have lots of money for free!
Your true wishes will be carried out.

To the EMPEROR:

Sir, no longer be distraught!
The same prophet that you sought
has been put to death, so I'm told;
though I have a woman here with me
who will be able to heal thee.
She'll loosen the leprosy's hold.

EMPEROR

Messenger, I can barely eat for dread.
And now I learn that the Prophet is dead
– the very one who could have healed me.
So woman, what have you to say?
Please tell me, if in any way
you can help cure me in some degree.

VERONICA

Believe in Christ, the Lord of Grace.
I'll show you a print of His face,
He gave to me upon a handkerchief.
As soon as this kerchief you view,
on its own, it will heal you
of your dreaded leprosy and its grief.

EMPEROR

Woman, what was your name again?
Great admiration you will gain
if what you have to say is true.
I will put a reward into your hand
and you'll be a lady over much land.
You'll have riches you never knew.

VERONICA

Lord, Veronica is the name that I bear.
I have the image of the face of Jesus here
left on the kerchief by his sweat.
Whoever sees the stain,
and believes in Christ plain,
on a course to full health is set.

In dear Christ, you must believe thus,
that He is Lord to all of us;
to the world, our one salvation.
Healed you shall surely be
of your dreaded leprosy,
if you pray with complete affirmation.

EMPEROR With a full heart, your advice I'll do.
I pray, please send health to me anew.
Even now, I know You as a God true,
and do believe that You are full of grace.
On the earth, dear Lord most pure,
know that my belief is sure.
With speed, please send me a cure.
O, let me see the sweet Saviour's face.

Show the image to me I insist.
That such a thing should ever exist
seems marvellous indeed.
If you can, please being it over here,
so to Christ's image I may be near.
Don't leave me yet I plead.

VERONICA Look at it; to its power yield,
and soon enough, you shall be healed.
That the disease will leave, I'm resolute.
Then I say again to you,
believe He is of God true,
and of all souls the Saviour absolute.

Then VERONICA *shall show him the kerchief and the* EMPEROR *shall kneel, saying:*

EMPEROR O Jesus, Lord of bliss,
Your dear face I will kiss.
Please heal me of this,
and give my poor heart some ease.

The EMPEROR *kisses the kerchief.*

O Lord Jesus Christ of Heaven and Earth,
now I really understand your worth.
The leprosy's gone; 'tis like a rebirth.
I'm healed of the disease.

The EMPEROR *is healed of his leprosy.*

Lord, You are truly blessèd.
Woman, it's just as you said.
What a shame that He is dead now,
for there is no lord of comparable worth,

either in Heaven, or here on the earth.
We will remember Him I vow!

VERONICA

Now that you're healed of leprosy,
you'll know how it is easy to see
that there is no other God but He.
It is Pilate you should be talking to
for Christ's death, and the pain He put Him through.
Avenge Pilate for his killing spree.

EMPEROR

Sweet Veronica, I'll do this task.
You helped rid me of my leper's mask,
and I have been freed from disease.
So before Pilate takes another breath,
I will have him instantly put to death.
His followers I'll also seize.

Torturers! Come here this instant!
Hear the fury that I can rant!
My anger'll explode before summer's here!
I'm so worked up over this
that I am almost speechless.
O Pilate, from me you will have much to fear.

1ST TORTURER

My Lord, we've come to you right away!
You were terrifying by the way.
I've never heard 'ee shout s'loud.
You did summon us with such might,
tell 'ee truth, I near died of fright.
I quaked like the rest of our crowd.

EMPEROR

See if Pilate you can find.
Don't be slack about this mind:
You've always been valuable men to me.
Bring him to me as soon as you can.
When I get hold of him in my plan
I'll make sure he dies immediately.

2ND TORTURER

With speed Caesar, off we go.
We'll make sure we find the fellow;
that detestable piece of scum.
'Es, boy Pilate was always a bad lot.

Doin' evil didn' worry 'ee a jot.
He followed the beat o' that drum.

3RD TORTURER

On Pilate, we will pay a little call,
n' bring him to 'ee in no time at all,
no matter how strong he thinks he is.
He won't get away on any account.
Our combined strength, he'll never surmount.
He won't get past big muscles like this.

4TH TORTURER

Pilate, you're coming with us to Rome:
Caesar says tha's t'be your new home.
I know that you won't want to go,
but be sure that you'm coming with us.
The advice is not t'make a fuss,
an' 'tis best t' move along so.

PILATE

I'll go with no hesitation at all.
Upon Tiberius I'll gladly call.
To Rome you say? Well, it's been a while.
Caesar is courteous to everyone.
O, this journey should be excellent fun.
Perhaps promotion may on me smile.

1ST TORTURER

Caesar, here's the fellow, brought by us,
who executed the prophet thus.
He is the one who condemned Jesus,
and put Him upon the cross.
On that is where Jesus died
with His poor wounds gapin' wide.
But over pain he could ride
t'save people from their loss.

The EMPEROR *comes down.*

EMPEROR

Dearest Pilate, welcome to Rome!
Make sure you make the place your home!
You know you are well-thought of here;
your good health always a concern of mine.
O let me look at you! Don't you look fine?
I'll always protect you from fear.

PILATE

O Lord Caesar, many thanks are due.

I always like to report to you.
It is such a pleasure to come to Rome though.
On earth, it is true you have no peer,
and your speech is always good to hear.
There's none to equal you wherever I go.

2ND TORTURER

Do 'ee hear of our Lord there?
I tell 'ee, that just idn' fair.
Is this why we brought him to you so quick,
so Pilate is welcomed like an old friend?
We'll put that kind of thing to an end.
Come with us you – Pilate, y'make me sick!

The TORTURERS *try to hold him.*

3RD TORTURER

We'll have no more of that sort of thing!
So Pilate, some sorcery you bring.
Then are you a magician or a peller,
so whatever the day,
you will force us away?
Don't worry boys! We'll have the little heller!

The 3RD TORTURER *shall let* PILATE *go, and he retires to no great distance.*

4TH TORTURER

Just let me get my bare hands on him.
His magic powers'll soon look grim.
By the clothes I stand in, I'll kill the sod.
I dare 'un t'more magic transmit.
He destroyed the glorious prophet;
he is the one who killed the Son of God.

Here the TORTURERS *withdraw for a short time.*

EMPEROR

Stop this! What on earth was I thinking of then!?
Pilate wields magic on me and my men.
Indeed, I have to do something quick.
He'll pay for his magic this fellow,
for my heart is filled with such sorrow.
Indeed, my soul has become quite sick.

When Pilate came to see me,
the villain spoke cheerfully.
He put a spell upon me to give way,

and in him I found no fault at all.
Into his dark power I did fall,
then I couldn't even kill him today.

I think that Pilate's become a wizard.
The magician's art he's uncovered.
He will make everything awkward.
There's none to match him in the land.
What do you think is the best course to take?
Some difficult decisions we must make.
Veronica, how can we make him quake?
Pray, how do we take him in hand?

VERONICA

I know how much he causes you alarm.
I believe you can't do him any harm,
as long as he wears about him
the garments of Lord Jesus.
Until they are removed thus
his power won't begin to dim.

He's wearing them 'neath his clothes I swear
He stole them from Jesus I declare
You need to get him here again,
and strip them off Pilate somehow;
else he'll do you more harm I vow.
On you, he'll continue to gain.

EMPEROR

Veronica, you're right in what you say!
Since this is the way he wishes to play,
I will remove the garments from him.
Torturers, your strength I wish to employ,
so my heart may again feel some joy.
This time, let's make Pilate the victim.

1ST TORTURER

Lord, we're with you on this all the way.
We've always followed what you d'say,
'un boy Pilate could do with a few knocks,
so tell us your mind's desire.
What is it that you require?
We'll be on it faster than a fox.

EMPEROR

Please bring Pilate to me once more.
I was careless with Him before.

Be sure, I won't be deceived again.
Watch him though, for he's made of evil
and the chancer is full of dark skill.
How I hate him and his stinking reign.

2ND TORTURER

We'll fetch him here without delay.
To Pilate I've a few things t'say.
I'm ready t'bash the bastard t'hell;
but we have got to be careful son,
because if you see 'un, you love 'un.
'Tis like 'ee places 'ee under a spell.

3RD TORTURER

He'n make me full of love or desire,
yet I'll soon cause his life to expire.
He won't be singing in any choir
time I'd finished smacking 'un in the gob.
See boys, there 'ee is, right now look!
Our Lord'll have you soon y'crook.
'Tis time for you to be brought to book,
then cruel torment will finish the job.

PILATE

I've no problem going to see Caesar,
for in truth, he is a mighty leader.
I see him as a noble Roman Lord,
straight as a die, and a man for great things.
Of all lands, he is the noblest of kings,
and far and wide is his law heard.

4TH TORTURER

Lord Caesar, the fellow is now in your view.
I believe that when he stands before you –
despite your imperial might –
you'll be unable to do him any harm.
He will continue to give you much alarm
as long as he is in your sight.

EMPEROR

Torturers, from chasing Pilate step down.
Go and see if anywhere in the town
whether there are people who speak against me.
Now then Pilate, I do declare,
I'll have that seamless coat you wear.
I will have it eventually you'll see.

PILATE

But Caesar, you are a lord of this land,

used to costly clothes and dressing grand.
his ancient coat is just not fit for you.
Someone of your imperial status
should hope to wear something much more gracious.
This here coat is soiled and dirty too.

In truth, it's not been washed for a while.
I'm really sure it's just not your style,
not for an emperor like you.
So I hope that you will see fit
not to even ask me for it.
Sir, the garment I shan't undo.

EMPEROR

But Pilate, I would feel no shame
wearing that garment about my frame,
for surely it came from Jesus?
I would like to try it on today.
I pray, hand it over straight-away
with no more debate between us.

PILATE

Lord, if I were to take it off right now,
I'd be completely naked before thou.
It just wouldn't be respectful surely.
Tiberius, you know it's just not the done thing
to stand stripped before an emperor or king.
Sir, it wouldn't be decent to see me.

VERONICA

Lord, you should command him I vow
to strip off the garment right now
without saying another word,
or else, he will continue to flatter you,
and never remove it as we want him to.
Speak, for Pilate must be deterred.

EMPEROR

Take off the garment right now!
Not on my account, I vow
will you get away with this anymore!
And don't even think you can try it on.
I'll have the coat before you're gone,
even though on it, you keep a grudging paw.

PILATE

O well, I suppose I can remove this shawl,
or I'll never have any peace at all.

Alas, I know what fate has for me in store.
I just can't see how I can save myself now,
unless I'm paid a little gold somehow
for handing the garment to the emperor.

EMPEROR

Pilate, you rascal, you think you're so righteous,
but you're the one who executed Jesus,
our Lord beyond all compare!
Quick, hand me my broadsword there!
His life I'll no longer spare.
I'll slay him where he stands, I swear!

VERONICA

No Lord, think of something else in the interim,
so we may find a more hideous death for him.
That's what his ending should be worth.
He is the villain who made death fall
on the very same son who made us all,
then Heaven, the sea and the earth.

The best thing to do for the moment
is into prison throw the tyrant.
Shut the man into a cell.
Then later, he may be tried,
and learn lessons about pride.
The law'll condemn the rebel.

EMPEROR

Then straight to prison he will go:
Into a cell, Pilate we'll throw,
and a hideous death he'll have therein.
I'll ensure he's tortured good and proper.
In such torments, he will come a cropper,
and no one will be there to save his skin.

Gaoler, come here immediately,
or your guts for garters soon will be!
Be quick about it as well,
and bring your apprentice too!
I've a job for both of you –
someone I know needs a cell!

GAOLER

Lord, we'm here in an instant!
Tell us your requirement
and what you Caesar wants done?

Y'knaw we'll do it right away,
and from the task we'll never sway.
We finish what we've begun.

EMPEROR

Gaoler, put this Pilate, with no delay
to the darkest dungeon to rot away
so he'll never more see the light of day,
for he is an evil wizard we've found.
Then later on, I will decree
that a hideous death he'll see.
Our Saviour he wouldn't set free,
and the order for His death he did sound.

BOY

No problem Lord, we'll do our bit.
I'll put him in the vilest pit
with huge rats and fleas as his friends!
They don't call me Arsewhip for anything.
To him some beauty tortures I will bring.
He'll suffer all the latest trends!

GAOLER

Right Arsewhip, into prison 'eave 'un.
His tortures have only just begun.
Don't spare the bugger any pain at all,
and what'll happen if he tries to escape:
The length of his body we will reshape!
If he is smart, he'll stay behind this wall.

BOY

Now, here's the lovely room where you'n stay
until all of your flesh rots away.
Then you will be on trial you idiot.
Your death'll be harder than hell:
it seems that you deserve it well.
You're the lowest form of life Pilate.

PILATE

Gaoler, in faith, tell me truthfully,
what kind of death is lined up for me?
What do you think the decree will say?
I know that I am going to die,
but the 'how of it' please don't deny.
Truly, I'm anxious over which way.

GAOLER

Look Pilate, the way I'm told your death is,
'Twill be the most hideous in ages.

That is what is decreed for you
You've not long now upon the earth.
Of days left alive, you've a dearth.
Anything else just isn't true.

PILATE

Well then, against that I'll still stand guard.
No one'll force me to die that hard.
No hideous death am I going to face.
With this sheath-knife, my own heart I'll stab.
Suicide is the best chance to grab.
O alas and woe that I've sunk to this base!

EMPEROR

As you have helped me in this task,
Veronica, to you I ask,
what's the very best death for Pilate?
How may we give him the most pain
so that full despair he may gain?
His death, he shouldn't suffer quiet.

VERONICA

Give the Gaoler a call
to find out first of all
what state this Pilate is in right now.
Lord, the way I feel, I believe
I can't even begin to conceive
enough torments for him anyhow.

EMPEROR

Gaoler, come away from the dungeon's din,
and tell me in what state is Pilate in?
Where is he right now,
and what does he look like in gaol?
We both need to know the whole tale.
Tell the truth I vow.

GAOLER

Lord, thc truth is that He is dead.
Pilate killed himself instead,
to put an end to his grief and pain.
He suddenly drew a knife on his heart,
stabbing it there, until his life did part.
A more frightful death you couldn't gain.

EMPEROR

Jesus, thou art truly God's son!
Pilate the prisoner has gone
to meet the most terrifying fate.

There is no end worse in all the land
than for a man to die by his own hand.
This suicide was appropriate.

Gaoler and boy, by the body meet,
and carry him by his head and feet
to bury him deep in the ground.
I believe people will be full of fear
if to Pilate's corpse they ever come near.
It's dreadful and mustn't be found.

GAOLER

Arsewhip, grab hold of his head
an' drop 'un as the Lord said
backwards inta the grave.

BOY

A'right master, heave, by my anus!
May a bad ending come t' the tuss!
Stamp down hard on the slave!

And then PILATE *shall be thrown out of the earth.*

Look master, Pilate's back in our sight!
On my faith, he's a devil alright.
The body is accursèd!
His leap from the grave gave me a start!
For fear of it, I let forth a fart!
'Tis cursed Master, as I said.

GAOLER

When Pilate's body leapt up like that
on a few farts o' me own I sat.
I near soiled me pants with fright.
How could a shift his body.
'Tis a strange thing I tell 'ee.
We both packed 'un in the earth tight.

BOY

Let's carefully go over to 'un
an' try to finish what we've begun.
See his ghastly colour, an' gory locks.
I reckon he'll stay buried alright,
long as he's with God, in Heaven's light.
If not, he'll pop up like a jack-in-a-box.

GAOLER

You'm right there, for if he idn' on God's side,

’twould need everyone from the Parish wide
t’stay here an’ guard the body,
and make sure that it stays in the grave.
Arsewhip, for our own skins to save
let us cover ’un over quickly.

And then the GAOLER *and the* BOY *shall put him in the ground, and* PILATE *shall be thrown up again.*

BOY

In faith, for Hell this devil must be meant!
He won’t stay underground for a moment.
That ’ee’s proper wicked ’tis clear.
Even God an’ the Saints have no time fur’n.
Pilate’s burial we’d better adjourn
and tell Caesar what’s happened here.

GAOLER

Caesar, I’ve some bad news t’say.
We can’t get the body t’stay
’neath the ground.

EMPEROR

I knew that Pilate was evil.
I had him down as a devil.
O, the hellhound.

BOY

No sooner had we laid ’un in the grave
than bedevilment comes upon the slave.
Lord, the ground itself ’eaves him out clear,
as if he’d fallen upon a spring.
In faith, ’tis a frightening thing.
The breakin’ ground is terrible t’hear.

EMPEROR

O what am I to do with this man?
Against this one I need to plan.
The devil’s power I must quench.
Unless dear Christ helps me some,
he’ll destroy all my kingdom
with his diabolical stench.

VERONICA

Lord, you need to find an iron chest.
In the Tiber’s waters he should rest,
sealed tightly inside of it.
He will stay there, locked away

until the start of Doomsday.
To the riverbed, he'll plummet.

EMPEROR

Veronica, you've answered my question!
That really is the perfect suggestion.
You've given me wise advice again.
My torturers! I need you once more.
I won't rest 'til you settle this score.
Report to me quickly, all four men.

1ST TORTURER

Lord, in me mind, I was off t'Spain.
'Tis siesta all the time, an' no rain.
Else in France, tuckin' inta' a gateau.
But when you called for we four
you knew we'd be at your door.
In your service Tiberius, we'm never slow.

2ND TORTURER

What 'ave 'ee got fur us to do,
because we'll sort it out for you?
We dun't loaf around either.
Lord, whatever is on your mind,
we'll stop it from being a bind.
We 'ent slow at ut neither.

EMPEROR

Take the body of the evil wizard
which now stinks like a decaying pilchard,
and place it into an iron chest.
Cast it in the Tiber's flow
in a river creek you know,
so that in the depths it comes to rest.

3RD TORTURER

Emperor sir, you'n sleep safe at last.
Into deep water, the chest we'll cast.
In the Tiber, he'n lie in comfort!
Then, there will be no need for we,
or indeed anyone you see,
to have any more fear of Pilate.

4TH TORTURER

I tell 'ee, I d'reckon 'tis so cursed
that even when the body is submersed,
it'll still bring us fear an' dread.
Its bedevilment has just begun.

The fires of Hell need t'burn 'un,
else back here, the curse of 'un will spread!

1st Torturer

Well, I've got hold of an iron chest!
To get it in the creek I suggest
we lift it together, as a team of four.
Then we'll all run to the water with it
an' sling 'un out in one big crazy fit.
It'll sink like a stone to the river floor!

2nd Torturer

Thas' the body laid out straight!
Now boys, start t'take the weight,
and carry 'un over to the river.
'Ee was born wicked, an' the way I see
a million in gold wouldn't stop me
from 'eaving this one into the Tiber.

3rd Torturer

May the devil have 'un when he's immersed,
for this vile body is truly cursed!
The River Tiber can have this treasure.
Let's get on, an' do what we oughta,
an' sling this scum into the water.
To see 'un sink down'll be a pleasure.

4th Torturer

There, that's accursed Pilate launched away!
Down in the deep he won't have much to say.
I hope that you will remain down there,
with the curse of every Parish,
for dear Pilate, you were so foolish
to kill the Son of Mary fair.

And let the Torturers *throw the body into the water.*

Traveller

Travelling can make you feel dirty.
So I might look a little more pretty,
I think I'll wash me hands and face.
The river water here looks cool and clear.
No defilement do I have to fear.
For cleansing, this is quite the place!

And the Traveller *shall wash his hands and die immediately.*

Alas, this water's cursed, I can tell!
Suddenly, I've come over unwell.
I'm dying, from what I can see.
I no longer have the will to live.
That feeling the waters here did give.
In faith, death creeps upon me!

MESSENGER

Lord, to some better advice you should refer!
Anyone who tries crossing the Tiber
is by the waters, killed outright.
One was even killed just by washing there.
To prevent repetition of this scare
move Pilate from his present site.

EMPEROR

O will this problem never end?
Help me Veronica, my friend,
Nothing I do will solve anything!
I pray, please advise me now for the best.
I'll never have peace of mind with this pest,
learning of Pilate's endless haunting.

VERONICA

As long as in the water it lays,
it seems the body's vile curse stays.
Both beasts and men it kills with ease.
It was full of evil when it was alive,
and though dead, the defilement does thrive.
Lord, this moment you have to seize.

Whatever the cost, I plea,
you must dredge up the body.
Send it in a cheap boat, out to sea,
and that boat, so far as I can tell
will carry the body straight to Hell.
And this time Lord, I'll answer for thee.

EMPEROR

Veronica, my blessing you have won,
and the blessings also, of Mary's son,
Jesus Christ, our dear Lord.
O torturers, your ways to me weave!
You can raise my spirits I believe,
and I'll give you good reward.

O where are the scoundrels when you want them?
They're usually up for some mayhem.
Good, I hope that I scared you calling you then.
Massive is the grief in your emperor's heart,
so listen carefully before you depart.
Saving the Empire is up to you men.

1ST TORTURER

Sir Lord, we dun't hang around long,
whatever the occasion or day.
All we ask Caesar is be strong,
for you know we will do what you say.

EMPEROR

Here is your full mission then.
To the river return men
and there, dredge up Pilate from the deep.
Then place him on a boat sailing out to sea.
The completion of this will guarantee
three million in gold for you to keep.

2ND TORTURER

Sir, we'll dredge 'un up right away.
He deserves all 'ee gets I say,
for Pilate sought this kind o' treatment,
when he did Christ a great injustice.
Pilate was completely prejudice
when t' the cross, he had Jesus sent.

3RD TORTURER

Let's get on then, and heave 'un up from the deep.
I like the sound o' that gold we get to keep.
Boys, the best thing is t'thraw down a grapnel:
That'll help us to grab the chest,
and assist with this body quest.
We'll get 'un up, despite the terrible smell!

4TH TORTURER

Two of the grapnels are on tight:
All we need is a bit of might
to raise the body from below.
'Tis coming, though 'tis heavy as a rock.
Now each of 'ee, pull hard an' use the block.
Heave 'un steady mind, nice an' slow.

1ST TORTURER

The devils ought to give a hand here!
Look, the stinking mess has risen clear.

There he is on the surface now.
As he's risen boys, I reckon
we should get the spawn of Satan
up on the riverbank somehow.

2ND TORTURER — Then as quickly as we can,
we should place this vile man
into the boat just over there.
Bring Pilate's putrid body aboard.
With it comes the curse of the dear Lord,
His Saints, and all His angels fair.

3RD TORTURER — This'll end Pilate's grisly tale!
Now splice the mizzen, hoist the sail!
Be sure the vessel's well-trimmed and her line true.
May the westerlies drive it far from here,
and along with it, the dread and the fear.
The curse of God and the Saints blow on it too.

4TH TORTURER — Now shove the boat off from its mooring!
Do you start to hear the sea roaring?
At his coming, fierce tempests begin to grow.
Hideous waves will crack against the rocks;
and rolling seas'll give the boat some knocks.
They sense him sailing; the devils always know.

1ST TORTURER — Boys, 'tis time we headed home for a spell.
I sense the devils coming out of Hell.
Their gleeful laughter is something t'fear.
I'n hear their diabolical cries,
so before they catch us by surprise,
in faith, let us four hurry out of here!

LUCIFER — My devils, come with me and riot!
I pray, in harrowing excel
and quickly fetch the soul of Pilate
into the burning pits of Hell.
There, he'll stay in the roaring fire,
roasting in endless agony,
and there, on the sulphurous pyre
his song'll be 'O woe is me'!

BEELZEBUB A more accursed body I've never found,
and so consequently, it falls down to we.
It surely idn' fit to be in the ground,
nor in fresh water, nor in the salty sea.

SATAN It couldn't be buried in a thousand holes,
so in the Tiber they placed an iron chest,
and there, it put an end to a thousand souls;
its pure waters were defiled and possessed.

BEELZEBUB Every vessel that passed over the chest
struck fast, foundered, and sank without a trace.
The truth is that he deserves not to be blest,
but to be consumed with fire in this place.

LUCIFER From the River Tiber, they dredged Pilate up
and brought him once more onto the mainland thus;
then placed him in this lovely lugger lash-up,
so that he'd end up down here with all of us.

SATAN The lugger had a strong sail of its own,
so it would sail clean away from the land,
but onto a set of sharp rocks it was thrown,
and then Pilate was tossed right into my hand.

BEELZEBUB And that set of rocks then opened wide,
just as his destiny had said.
for this Pilate, far too full of pride,
had renounced heaven instead.
And that's where we lovely devils came in.
'Tis horrible to hear his voice.
In the flames, he makes a right old din,
that rock a symbol of his choice.

LUCIFER He can have scorching heat, then shivering cold,
and the monstrous devils can grin at his face!
We'll offer him every torment of our fold,
all the horrible pleasures of our place.

SATAN So it's off to Hell, with your pathetic soul!
I don't mind dragging your accursèd body
thro' the smouldering mouth, to your new hellhole.
There, your song shall be 'O woe, O woe is me'!

BEELZEBUB — So, come on then you devils all, lay a claw
upon this boat, so we'n reach the bowels of Hell.
And you Tulfryk, sing a melodious score,
suitable for Pilate as he says farewell.

TULFRYK — You, my devilish pal, can suck my ass!
It's not difficult to miss, as you pass,
for in truth, my tale sticks out a long way!
I'll only do it if you two boys o'Hell
serenade Pilate too, and sing the bass well,
then my lovely treble I'll add to the fray!

And so ends the Death of PILATE, *and there begins the Ascension of* CHRIST *into Heaven, and* PETER *says:*

PETER — Dear Lord, it will be hard to be strong
as You have to leave us before long.
Then how will it be for all of us?
We will be downcast for sure:
Until we see You once more,
we can never be truly joyous!

JESUS — Peter, try to put on a brave face!
The true faith, the brothers'll embrace
with you guiding all of them through.
I shall be at my Father's right hand.
Remember, that wherever you stand
the Holy ghost'll comfort you.

PHILIP — Lord, since You are great of grace,
please show us the Father's face,
so at last, all of us may be content.
For Lord, You are a mighty God indeed;
of a sight of God, many are in need.
Have mercy Lord, and to this, please consent.

JESUS — Philip, how long have you been with me?
And you so lax, from what I can see!
I wish your disbelief wouldn't gather;
so this is what I shall say to you:
Whoever sees Me and what I do,
shall surely then, also see My Father.

Remember, I am God and man equally.
The Father is in me additionally,
and I likewise, am in Him just the same.
From your faith, have no deviation,
and then you will attain salvation.
Now I can go to Heaven, in God's name.

JAMES THE GREATER

Lord, tell us where should we go from here?
Where can we live without fret or fear,
so no one'll punish us for our belief?
We need a place we may worship God in peace,
where eleven can stay and their faith increase.
A habitation would give us such relief.

JESUS

Brothers, to avoid being captives,
go at once, to the Mount of Olives.
There, the Father will listen to your prayer.
I'll go with all of you,
and from the Mount you'll view
Me ascending into Heaven's full care.

The DISCIPLES *pass over to the Mount of Olives.*

ANDREW

Lord, we will go there straight-away.
In the town, there's nowhere to stay,
for no one'll have us overnight.
The Jews continue to harass us
with threats of death and grim hangings thus.
They spit at us when we'm in their sight.

JOHN

Good reasons to go to the Mount of Olives,
and there, we may avoid becoming captives.
It is like the scriptures said:
we will wait for Christ's ascent.
From dear Mary He was sent;
a light to put an end to dread.

BARTHOLOMEW

Then brothers, let's get on with this!
May Jesus Christ, the King of Bliss
be with us for ever more!
To those who doubt He's our Saviour,
may thy have woe and fall from favour.
Their lack of faith I deplore.

SIMON — Jesus, You are King beyond compare.
Dear Lord of Heaven, hear our prayer
that we will not be tempted into sin.
For I reckon if we carry Your grace,
the most cunning temptations we can face.
Over them, I've no doubt that we can win.

JUDE — As I see it, we all need never doubt
that the Son of Mary is here about.
His grace is with us all the time.
He created us first of all,
then redeemed us from our fall.
His blood we should treat as sublime.

JESUS *kisses them all.*

JESUS — May full peace be on all of you,
as upon this Mount we accrue.
I see you patiently waiting for me.
Tonight, forty days you may mark
since I rose from the tomb's dark.
Brothers, my resurrection you did see.

JAMES THE LESSER — Lord, we respect your endeavour,
but wish You could stay forever.
If only You could still remain here,
then we could be at ease.
Our fears please appease,
for on our future, I'm not clear.

JESUS — Of fears, you are to have none:
I am with everyone
who lives their life in a state of grace.
People may talk as much as they care,
but 'tis my blood that answers their prayer.
Otherwise, they'd not reach Heaven's space.

THOMAS — Lord, what new seeds must I sow
when towards Heaven You go,
to God the Father above?
You'll be with God himself up there.
Our grief will be hard to bear.
I hope I'll still know Your love.

JESUS

Thomas, to India you shall go,
and in my name, you must preach there so.
Spread the gospel far and wide!
Only a few believers live there now,
but you must try to convert more somehow.
I'll be with you as your guide.
And likewise, I say to the rest of you,
go preach the Gospel you know to be true.
Take it to the four corners of the sphere,
to lands as far away as Cornwall.
There, fish for believers, such lands trawl,
and tell them death, the baptised, need not fear.
But non-believers cannot serve me,
yet they shan't be saved, and won't be free,
not even for the whole of the earth.
And those who do not follow my bidding,
will be condemned to eternal burning.
Believe this, for my words are of worth.

MATTHEW

Lord, we'll preach and answer your call,
and show that You created all,
and that there's no other God but You.
Anyone who doesn't believe that
will in Hell's fire soon be sat,
and soon, all will know Your faith as true.

Here JESUS *kisses them all.*

JESUS

On all of you, my blessings I extend!
In your very sight, I will now ascend
up to Heaven's bliss straight-away.
By My Lord Father, I will fit,
and at His right hand I will sit,
the Saviour of all, at doomsday.

Here JESUS *ascends.*

1ST ANGEL

Who is that – every inch a man
– who's so soon part of the Kingdom's plan?
And tell me, why is He clad in red?
There is great joy at His coming though,
and in Heaven, He seems cherished so.
Behind this valued man, let us tread.

2ND ANGEL — I don't know who He is at all:
His features I can't quite recall.
Someone could travel seven thousand years,
and might walk forty miles a day,
though they'd never come along this way.
It would drive the toughest person to tears.

3RD ANGEL — Who's He then, that has come from below,
blood covering His whole body so,
His head, shoulders, legs and feet?
That He was of human kind, I'm aghast:
not even an angel comes here that fast.
Yet, He seems one we should greet.

4TH ANGEL — I think He must have come from Eden.
I 'spect the devils He did weaken.
I'd be astonished if He hadn't.
I'm sure He's the one Who went there.
He is the King of Bliss I'd swear,
the same Son, Who beat the old serpent.

5TH ANGEL — How come here You have been led,
when Your clothing is so red?
To me, it's all still unclear!
Though to Heaven, You have flown,
unless You are of God's own,
there is no place for You here.

JESUS — I'm a King Who's been battling
to bring Adam and Eve's offspring
out of their evil plight.
It is the King of Bliss that you see,
and the victory was gained by me,
in a most bloody fight.

1ST ANGEL — Dearest King of Heaven! Now we know Your worth!
As You are creator of Heaven and Earth,
I give much honour to the Lord!
Great worship and joy are filling my breast.
We'll sing glory to God in the highest,
and never cease, please be assured!

Then let all the ANGELS *sing Glory to God in the Highest.*

6TH ANGEL

So, in appearance, why are you red?
Why, for the supreme realm, do you head
when people have never been there before?
The Angels are clad in white,
like the sun when it shines bright:
no other colours have they ever wore.

JESUS

Red was the colour I wore
when they were beating me sore.
There's no difference between the cloth and me.
It matches the length of my scourged skin.
The thousand holes you must imagine
that were cruelly pierced into my body.

6TH ANGEL

Lord, I wouldn't have been so frivolous
had I known You were so courageous,
and suffered such torment so.
I knew not of Your destruction,
nor about Your resurrection
until a moment ago.

7TH ANGEL

Who are You and why such gear?
Red clothes are unheard of here.
Why do You wear them I pray?
Here, clothes like that I can't ever recall,
and that colour isn't in vogue at all.
See, no one dresses that way.

JESUS

To bring Adam and Eve up from Hell
I had to wear for a lengthy spell
a crown of thorns upon my head.
You cannot conceive what pain was borne,
since into my head poked each sharp thorn.
Each prick caused me such fear and dread.

7TH ANGEL

Apologies Lord, I didn't know
that out of Heaven You went so,
that You were recently down below:
No doubt, when You redeemed Adam and Eve
much torture and pain, you did receive.
For sinners, Your own life You let go.

8TH ANGEL — O Lord, of marvels, You are boundless,
and in truth, You are the King of Bliss.
This explains why all Your clothes are red,
and how You came to be back up here.
Your power's great for You have no fear,
even though You faced such evil dread.

JESUS — See, I am a just and mighty King.
From the start, human sin offended me,
but nothing ever left me reeling.
The enormous gates of Hell, I broke free,
and out of trouble, I did gather,
souls who'd spent time in harm and turmoil.
This was the will of my Lord Father
that they should reach joy, far from Hell's soil.

My castle was just a cross of wood,
and even though I was God, King and man,
instead of a helmet, where I stood,
sharp thorns upon my head, were part of their plan.
All my limbs were stretched to breaking point,
though several Parishes watched the sight.
Each socket was ripped out from each joint,
then a spear through the heart ended my plight.

A rascal banged nails through my feet
so upon the cross, they'd be set in place.
The only gauntlets that I did meet
were the nails used for my hands to brace.
My bright tabard and my strong breastplate
were a royal purple to disgrace me.
Death on the cross, Pilate did dictate,
and blood clung to the purple that you see.

When the purple robe was snatched away,
stuck fast to it, was my redeeming blood.
And as the men all laughed at their play,
my flesh stuck to the robe tossed in the mud.

To rub salt in the wound, after this
I asked if they might offer me a drink,
but they gave gall to the King of Bliss.
I didn't want to swallow it I think.

And so, I was crucified in this way.
There was I, stabbed through the heart I assume,
but assuredly, on the third day,
I rose again once more, out of the tomb.

8TH ANGEL

Lord, you are truly blessèd!
What joy there shall be ahead,
to know that to Heaven, a human did fly!
Through the Holy Ghost, God of great worth,
has sent sweet salvation to the earth,
while the Son of God shall stay here on high.

9TH ANGEL

O dear Jesus Christ, Lord full of grace,
I never knew you'd joined the human race,
and gone forth into the world below.
To hear You again makes me full of joy:
I'll be happy to act as Your envoy,
but what blissful news that you're here though!

JESUS

Blessèd Father, on Your throne,
unto You, I have now flown
in human form from the earth:
With my life, I paid the ultimate cost,
so none of those we created would be lost.
Those we made, all have their worth.

GOD THE FATHER

Welcome, My Son, you art in Heaven.
Of lasting bliss, you may be certain.
Come, sit at My right-hand, where You are meant!
You have come through tremendous toil
by triumphing over turmoil,
and then delivered the souls from torment.

EMPEROR

Good people around, all your friends tell
how you saw Christ's resurrection from the tomb,
and how He broke down the gates of Hell
to save Adam and Eve from the firey gloom.
All of those who followed what God willed
were brought through Him unto everlasting bliss.
The world's redemption, He instilled,
and He truly showed much love and forgiveness.

And as the ending of our play did show,

Christ did ascend to eternal bliss.
May He preserve you everywhere you go
and from the devil and his darkness.
The Lord's blessing will be upon all of you,
as homewards from this place, you advance.
Now my joyous minstrels, pipe up loud and true,
so one and all, may join our dance.

Further reading

This is a select bibliography only, but it is still fairly full, intended as a guide to the most accessible studies of the Ordinalia, Cornish literature and medieval theatre in general. It does not list, however, articles that are especially hard to track down because of age or the relative obscurity of the journal in which they appeared. Brian Murdoch gives editions of some of the works referred to (such as the interestingly spelt Mistére du vieil Testament); as useful as it may be for scholars to know where to find the fascinating play by Arnold Immessen, it is not easy to obtain outside the major research libraries, and besides, it is still, alas, un-translated.

Anderson, M.D., *Drama and Imagery in English Medieval Churches*, Cambridge: Cambridge University Press, 1963

Chamber, E.K., *The Medieval Stage*, Oxford: Clarendon, 1903

Chubb, Ray, Jenkin, Richard and Sandercock, Graham (eds.), R. Morton Nance and A.S.D. Smith: *The Cornish Ordinalia, first play: Origo Mundi*, Redruth: Agan Tavas, 2001

Combellack, Myrna, *The Camborne Play: A verse translation of Beunans Meriask*, Redruth: Dyllanow Truran, 1988

Crawford, T.D., 'The Composition of the Cornish Ordinalia' in *Old Cornwall*, 9, 1979

Cross, Sally Joyce, 'Torturers and Tricksters in the Cornish Ordinalia' in *Neuphilogische Mitteilungen*, 84, 1983

Deane, Tony and Shaw, Tony, *Folklore of Cornwall*, Stroud: Tempus, 2003

Bakere, Jane A., *The Cornish Ordinalia: A Critical Study*, Cardiff: University of Wales Press, 1980

Beadle, Richard (ed.), *The Cambridge Companion to Medieval English Theatre*, Cambridge: University of Cambridge Press, 1994

Denny, Neville, *Medieval Drama*, London: Edward Arnold, 1973

Dubruck, Edelgard (ed.), *New Images of Medieval Women*, Lampeter: Mellen, 1989

Edward, Ray (ed.), *Pascon Agan Arluth: The Passion Poem*, Sutton Coldfield: Kernewek dre Lyther, 1993

Ellis, Peter Berresford, *The Cornish Language and its Literature*, London and Boston: Routledge and Kegan Paul, 1974

Fudge, Crystan, *The Life of Cornish*, Redruth: Dyllansow Truran, 1982

Gardiner, Harold C., *Mysteries' End*, New Haven: Yale University Press, 1946

Hall, Jim, 'Maximilla, the Cornish

Montanist: The Final Scenes of Origo Mundi' in Payton, Philip (ed.), 1999
Halliday, F.E., *The Legend of the Rood*, London: Gerald Duckworth, 1955
Harris, Markham (tr.), *The Cornish Ordinalia: A Medieval Dramatic Trilogy*, Washington D.C.: The Catholic University of America Press, 1969
– *The Life of Meriasek: A Medieval Cornish Miracle Play*, Washington D.C.: The Catholic University of America Press, 1977
Hays, Rosalind Conklin, McGee, C.E., Joyce, Sally L., and Newlyn, Evelyn S. (eds.), *Records of Early English Drama: Dorset and Cornwall*, Toronto: University of Toronto Press and Brepols, 1999
Higgins, Sydney, *Medieval Theatre in the Round: The Multiple Staging of Medieval Drama in England*, Camerion: Laboratorio degli studi linguistici, 1994
Holman, Treve, 'Cornish Plays and Playing-Places' in *Theatre Notebook*, 4, 1949-50
Jenner, Henry, *A Handbook of the Cornish Language*, London: Nutt, 1904
Kent, Alan M., *Out of the Ordinalia*, St Austell: Lyonesse, 1995
– *The Literature of Cornwall: Continuity, Identity, Difference 1000-2000*, Bristol: Redcliffe, 2000
– '"In Some State...": A Decade of the Literature and Literary Studies of Cornwall' in Payton, Philip (ed.), 2002
– and Saunders, Tim (eds. and trs.), *Looking at the Mermaid: A Reader in Cornish Literature 900–1900*, London: Francis Boutle, 2000
Kolve, J.V.A., *The Play Called Corpus Christi*, London: Arnold, 1966
Longsworth, Robert, *The Cornish Ordinalia: Religion and Dramaturgy*, Cambridge, Massachusetts, Harvard University Press, 1967
Lyon, Rod T., *Cornwall's Playing Places*, Cornwall: Tavas an Weryn, n.d.
Meyer, R.T., 'The Liturgical Background of Medieval Cornish Drama' in *Trivium*, 3, 1968
Murdoch, Brian, 'The Place-Names in the Cornish Passio Christi' in *Bulletin of the Board of Celtic Studies*, 37, 1990
– *Cornish Literature*, Cambridge, Brewer, 1993
– 'The Cornish Medieval Drama' in Beadle, Richard (ed.), 1994
– 'Various Gospels: Die Erlösung, Pascon Agan Arluth, and the Sermone of Petro de Barsegape' in *Studi Medievali*, 26, 1995
– 'Legends of the Holy Rood in Cornish Drama' in *Studia Celtic Japonica*, 9, 1997
– 'The Mors Pilati of the Cornish Resurrexio Domini' in *Celtica*, 23, 1999
– *Adam's Grace: Fall and Redemption in Medieval Literature*, Cambridge: Brewer, 2000
– *The Medieval Popular Bible: Expansions of Genesis*, Cambridge: Brewer, 2003
– 'Rex David, Bersabe, and Syr Urry: A Comparative Approach to a Scene in the Cornish Origo Mundi' in Payton, Philip (ed.) 2004
Nance, Robert Morton, 'The Plen an Gwary or Cornish Playing-Place' in *Journal of the Royal Institution of Cornwall*, 24, 1935
Neuss, Paula, 'Memorial Reconstruction in a Cornish Miracle Play' in *Comparative Drama*, 5, 1971
'The Staging of The Creacion of the World' in *Theatre Notebook*, 33, 1979
The Creacion of the World: A Critical Edition and Translation, New York and London: Garland, 1983
– (ed.), *Aspects of Early English Drama*, Cambridge: Brewer, 1983

Newlyn, Evelyn S., *Cornish Drama of the Middle Ages: A Bibliography*, Redruth: Institute of Cornish Studies, 1987
– 'Between the Pit and the Pedestal: Images of Eve and Mary in Medieval Cornish Drama' in Dubruck, Edelgard (ed.), 1989
Norris, Edwin (ed. and tr.), *The Ancient Cornish Drama*, Oxford: Oxford University Press, 1859; repr. London and New York: Bloom, 1968
Olson, Lynette, 'Tyranny in Beunans Meriasek' in Payton, Philip (ed.), 1997
Payton, Philip (ed.), *Cornish Studies: Five*, Exeter: University of Exeter Press, 1997
– (ed.), *Cornish Studies: Seven*, Exeter: University of Exeter Press, 1999
– (ed.), *Cornish Studies: Ten*, Exeter: University of Exeter Press, 2002
– (ed.), *Cornish Studies: Twelve*, Exeter: University of Exeter Press, 2004
Peter, Thurstan C., *The Old Cornish Drama*, London: Elliot Stock, 1906
Rastall, Richard, *The Heaven Singing: Music in Early English Religious Drama* Volume 1, Cambridge: Brewer, 1996
–*Minstrel's Playing: Music in Early English Religious* Drama Volume 2, Cambridge, Brewer, 2001
Sandercock, Graham (ed.), R. Morton Nance and A.S.D. Smith: *The Cornish Ordinalia, second play: Christ's Passion*, Cornwall: Cornish Language Board, 1982
(ed.), R. Morton Nance and A.S.D. Smith: *The Cornish Ordinalia, third play: Resurrection*, Cornwall: Cornish Language Board, 1984
Shafer, Ingrid (ed. and tr.), Othmar Weis, Joseph Alois Daiseberger, Otto Hubner and Christian Stückl, *Oberammergua Passion Play 2000: Textbook English*, Oberammergua: Gemeinde Oberammergua
Southern, Richard, *The Medieval Theatre in the Round*, London: Faber, 1957
Sticca, Sandro (ed.), *The Medieval Drama*, Albany, New York: SUNY, 1972
Stokes, Whitley (ed. and tr.), T*he Life of Meriasek, Bishop and Confessor, A Cornish Drama*, London: Trübner, 1872
Thomas, Graham C.G., 'The Middle Cornish Plays: A Note' in *National Library of Wales Journal*, 32, 2002
Tickner, F.J. (ed. and tr.), *Earlier English Drama: From Robin Hood to Everyman*, London and Edinburgh, n.d.
Toorians, Lauran, *The Middle Cornish Charter Endorsement: The Making of a Marriage in Medieval Cornwall*, Innsbruck: Institut für Sprachwissenschaft, 1991
Wakelin, Martyn, *Language and History in Cornwall*, Leicester, Leicester University Press, 1975
Wellwarth, George F., 'Methods of Production in the Medieval Cornish Drama' in *Speech Monographs*, 24, 1957
Whetter, James, *The History of Glasney College*, Padstow: Tabb House, 1988
Wickham, Glynne, *Early English Stages 1300-1600*, London: Routledge and Kegan Paul, 1959-81
– *The Medieval Theatre*, London: Weidenfeld and Nicolson, 1974
Williams, Nicholas (ed. and tr.), *Testament Noweth agan Arluth ha Savyour Jesu Cryst*, Redruth: Spyrys a Gernow, 2002
Woolf, Rosemary, *The English Mystery Plays*, London: Routledge and Kegan Paul, 1972
Young, Karl, *The Drama of the Medieval Church*, Oxford: Clarendon, 1933